DIY Watercolor Cards

Simple and Sweet Projects to Create and Share All Year Long

Mary Wu

Dedicated to my husband, Alex, and to Annabelle, Annaliese, and Aaron, who fill my life with color and joy. And to Annaliese, thank you for always believing this book would be real.

DIY Watercolor Cards:

Simple and Sweet Projects to Create and Share All Year Long

Mary Wu

Editor: Kelly Reed
Project manager: Lisa Brazieal
Marketing manager: Koryn Olage
Interior layout: Anthony Paular Design
Cover design: Aren Straiger
Cover images: Mary Wu

ISBN: 979-8-88814-483-1
1st Edition (1st printing, 2026)

Rocky Nook Inc.
1010 B Street, Suite 350
San Rafael, CA 94901
USA
www.rockynook.com
info@rockynook.com
(415) 747-8756

Distributed in the UK and Europe by Publishers Group UK

Distributed in the US and all other territories by Publishers Group West

Library of Congress Control Number: 2025947811

Represented in the E.U. by: Rheinwerk Verlag GmbH, Rheinwerkallee 4, 53227 Bonn, Germany
service@rheinwerk-verlag.dev

This book is printed on acid-free paper.

Printed in China.

Contents

CHAPTER FOUR:

Seasonal and Holiday Cards 94

Bonus Content 150

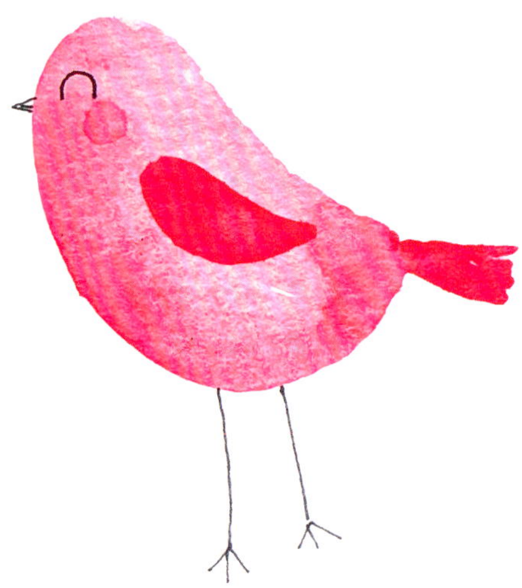

Introduction

I still remember the first handmade card I got, and how my heart fluttered just holding it. Someone had taken the time to make something just for me. I kept turning it in my hands, looking at the colors and the tiny details. That kind of quiet thoughtfulness stayed with me.

A few years ago, when I was bedridden and struggling with illness, painting big pieces felt like too much. I barely had the energy to get through the day. But small paintings, little bursts of color and play, I could manage those. Making cards became something I looked forward to. It was calming. Healing. Each one reminded me that I was still here, still creating, still connected.

I started sending them to friends and family, simple notes to say thank you, I am thinking of you, or you mean so much to me. And what I got back meant more than I expected. I felt less alone. I felt joy. I felt like myself again.

The best part is, handmade cards do not have to be packed away. You can frame them, hang them, or tuck them in little corners. A wall of tiny paintings tells a beautiful story. A single card can brighten a room. These are not just cards. They are little pieces of love, made by hand.

Inside this book, you will find fifteen guided card projects, along with bonus cards you can explore through simple follow-along videos. Each project is just a starting point. Feel free to change the colors, switch the words, and turn any card into something that fits whatever moment is in your heart.

Let go of perfection. It is the happy little oopsies that make handmade cards so special.

With love,
Mary

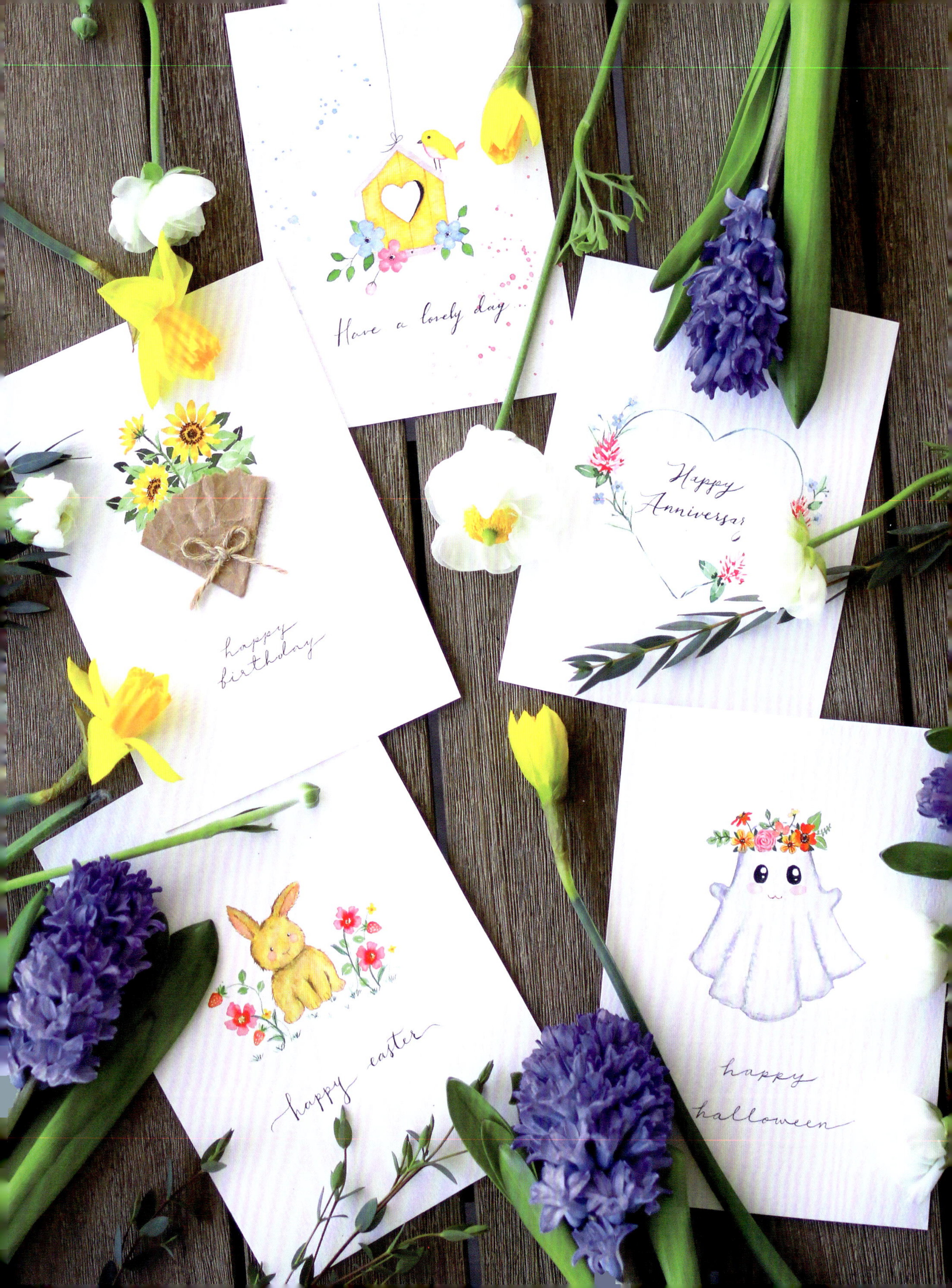
Have a lovely day...
happy birthday
Happy Anniversary
happy easter
happy halloween

CHAPTER 1

Getting Started the Easy Way

If you have ever thought, *"I can't paint,"* you are in the right place. Watercolor is not about being perfect. It is about learning as you go. There is no single right style or outcome, but with a little practice, you will start to see how the paint moves and what feels natural to you.

Let's talk about what you need to get started. A lot of people think they need fancy paints or every brush before they can begin, but that is not true. Start with what you already have or what is easy to find. The most important thing is simply to begin.

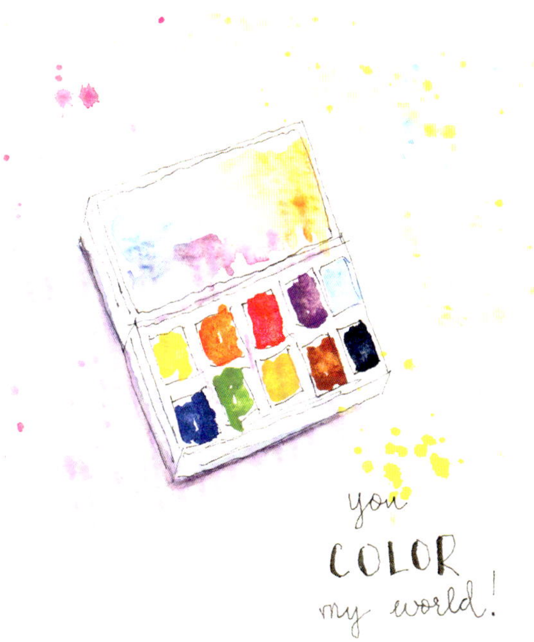

Basic Tools You Will Need

Brushes

Start with a few round brushes and a small flat brush. There are many different types of brushes, but these are enough to begin.

Watercolor Paper

Use any thick paper labeled for watercolor. I like 140 lb cold press because it holds water well and has a soft texture.

Water

A jar of clean water is all you need for painting. Change it when it starts to look cloudy.

Paper Towel and Q-tips

Helpful for blotting extra water, softening edges, or lifting paint. Paper towels and Q-tips are great for small corrections and gentle lifting.

Pencil and Eraser

Use a light pencil and a gentle eraser. A light pencil like HB or 2H works well, and a kneaded eraser is gentle on watercolor paper.

Watercolor Paints

Use whatever paints you already have. Pans, tubes, or travel sets all work. I mostly use watercolor pans because they offer many colors and require little to no mixing.

Mixing Palette

Any clean surface works. It can be ceramic, plastic, or even a plate. Your palette is where you can play with colors and see how they behave with water.

Waterproof Black Fineliner

Helpful for outlines and lettering. I use a black 005 waterproof fineline for outlines and lettering. Any similar fineliner will work.

Masking or Painter's Tape

Keeps your paper in place and edges clean. Remove tape slowly once your painting is dry.

Heat Tool

Helps your painting dry faster, especially when layering colors. You can also use a hair dryer on low.

Watercolor Paint

Watercolor paints come in several forms, including pans, tubes, and small travel sets. I like using pans because they are easy to work with and quick to set up. You just dip your brush in clean water, swirl it in the color, and start painting. They are also great if you don't have much space since everything you need is right there in one set. You can see all your colors at a glance, and if they dry out, simply add a little water and they come back to life.

If you have been painting for a while and want richer colors, tubes are another good choice. They usually have more pigment, so the colors look stronger and more vibrant. You can even squeeze a bit into an empty pan, let it dry, and reuse it later.

As you paint more, you might notice that some colors feel smoother or blend better. That is often because higher quality paints have more pigment and less filler. They can make a noticeable difference, helping your colors look brighter, mix more smoothly, and stay vibrant longer. I have found that they are worth it once you start painting more often, but there is no need to rush. Begin with what you have or a simple student set and slowly upgrade your favorites as you go.

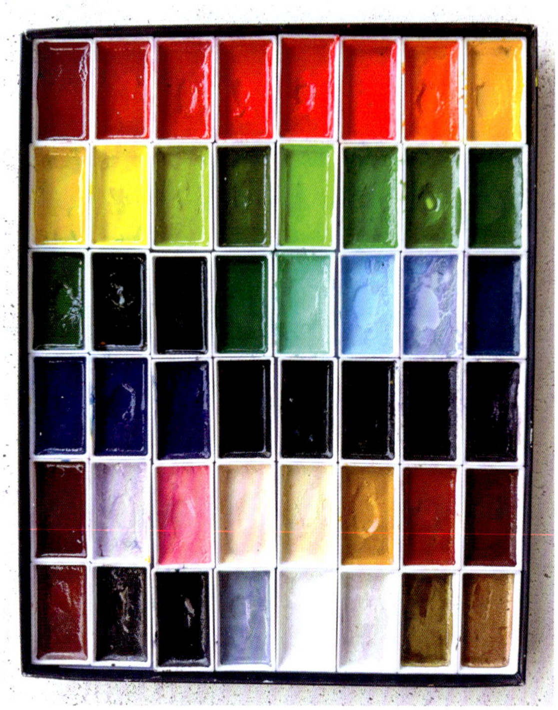

Color Swatch Sheet

Before painting, make a simple swatch sheet to see how your colors look on your paper and how they dry.

Paint a rectangle or a simple brush stroke for each color and label them if needed. Use the same paper you plan to make your cards with.

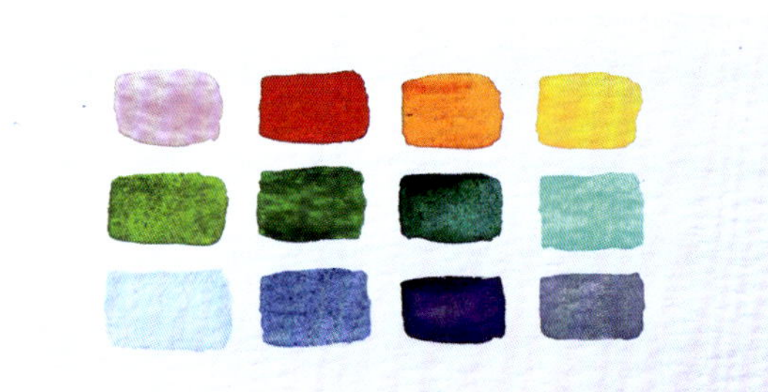

TIP:

Let your swatches dry before judging the color. Watercolor looks darker when wet and dries lighter, and it's easier to darken than lighten. Arrange your swatches in the same order as your palette for easy reference.

Mixing Colors

You will not be mixing many colors in this book, but it helps to understand the basics so you can adjust your paint when needed. It is also helpful to have a mixing palette, so you have space to blend and test your colors before adding them to your card. Start with clean water and a small amount of color.

To Lighten a Color

Add more water.

Test it on scrap watercolor paper.

Remember that watercolor dries lighter than it looks when it is wet.

To Darken a Color

Add more paint or a small touch of a deeper shade such as blue, brown, or another color in the same family.

Add it slowly until you reach the tone you want.

It is easier to darken a mix than to lighten one that has too much pigment.

TIP:

Colors that are close together, like blue and green, mix into bright shades. Colors that contrast strongly, like blue and orange, create softer or more muted tones.

Brushes I Use

These are the only four brushes I use throughout this book.

Medium Round Brush

A round brush (size 6-8) has a pointed tip and a wider belly that holds water. This is the brush I use most often for petals, leaves, shapes, and filling areas.

Small Round Brush

This brush (size 2-4) works like the medium round but is smaller. It gives you more control for smaller shapes and details.

Detail Brush

This is a very tiny round brush (size 0 or smaller). It is used for thin lines, small details, stems, and lettering accents.

Flat Brush

A flat brush (size 2-4) has a straight edge. It is helpful for clean edges, simple shapes, washes, and backgrounds.

How to Hold a Brush

Holding a watercolor brush is simple, and there is no one right way to do it. The most important thing is that your hand feels comfortable. A relaxed hand helps your brush move more gently on the paper and makes painting feel easier.

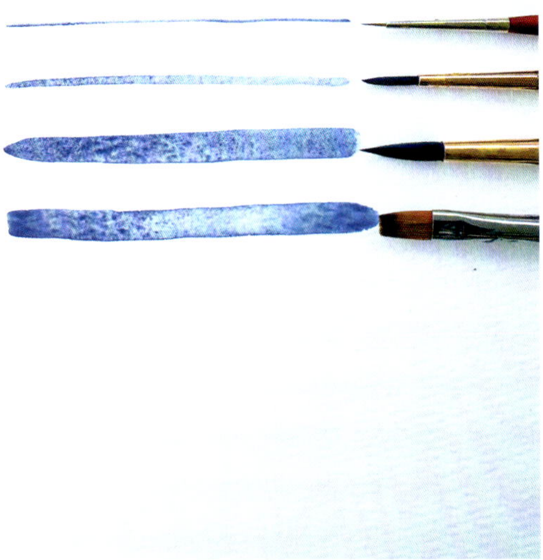

Comfortable Grip (Like a Pencil)

Hold the brush the same way you would hold a pencil. This is the grip you will use most of the time

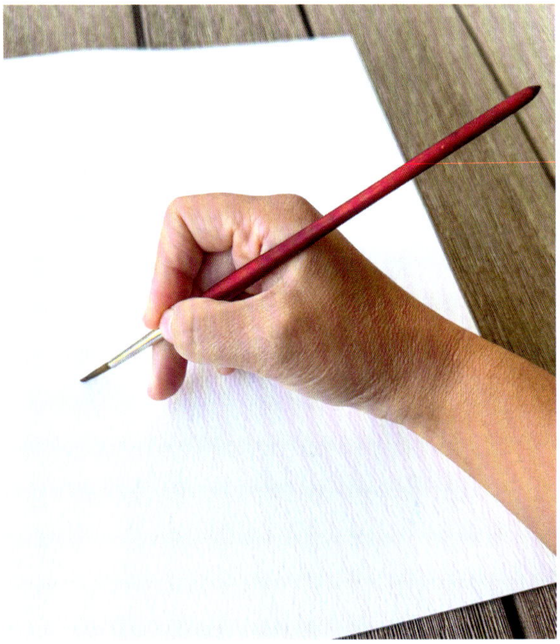

Caring for Your Brushes

Rinse your brushes in clean water after painting, gently reshape the tip, and let them dry flat or with the bristles facing up. Avoid leaving them in water since that can bend the tips and loosen the glue inside the handle. If your brush starts to lose its shape, wash it gently with mild soap and reshape it while wet. With a little care, your brushes can last a long time.

Close Grip (Extra Control)

Move your fingers closer to the ferrule (the metal part of the brush). Rest your hand lightly on the table for added stability. Use this grip for tiny details and careful lines.

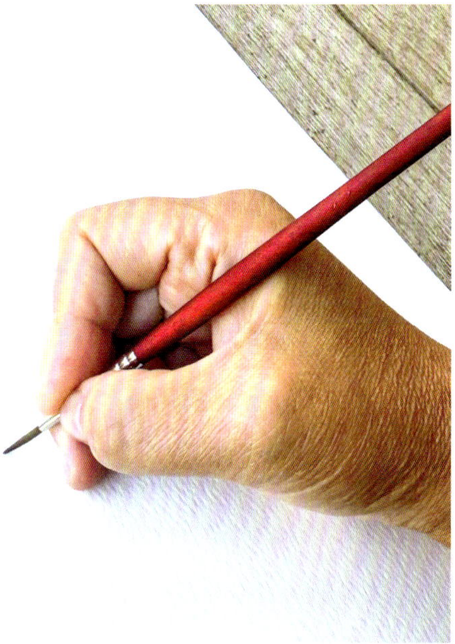

Upright Grip (Thin Lines)

Hold the brush more upright so only the tip touches the paper. This helps create thin lines and small details.

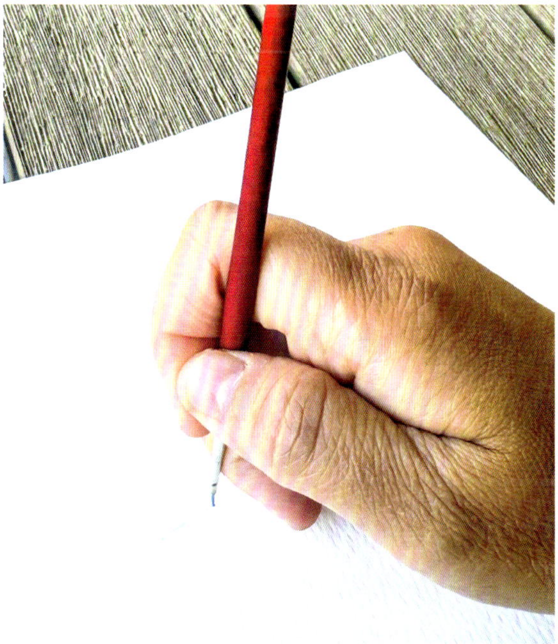

Brush Pressure

When you lower the brush toward the paper, more of the bristles touch the surface. This helps when you want to fill in a shape with soft, even color.

Use a lighter touch for thinner strokes and press down a bit more for wider, fuller strokes. Before starting your card, make a quick test stroke on scrap paper to check your water level and brush pressure.

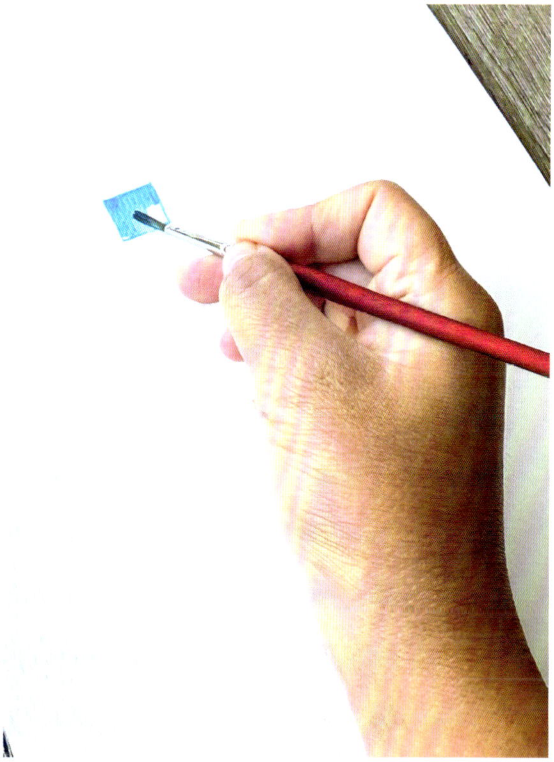

Paper

The paper you paint on makes a big difference because watercolor uses water. Regular paper can wrinkle, tear, or make colors look dull when it gets wet. Watercolor paper is made to handle water, so your colors stay brighter and easier to control.

Use any thick paper labeled for watercolor.

Weight

Watercolor paper comes in different weights, which refers to how thick the paper is. Thicker paper stays flatter when wet, while thinner paper may bend or wrinkle more.

You may also see paper labeled 100 percent cotton. Cotton paper absorbs water beautifully and helps colors blend more smoothly.

Texture

Watercolor paper comes in three main textures:

- **Cold press** — a little bumpy and great for beginners.
- **Hot press** — very smooth and great for clean lines or lettering.
- **Rough** — has more texture for a loose, expressive look.

The best all-around choice is cold-press paper. It is easy to use, gives your brush a nice glide, and works well for all kinds of watercolor cards.

Cold press paper is a versatile choice for most projects. It has enough texture to hold color while still allowing for fine details.

Watercolor paper is sold in pads, blocks, or loose sheets. I often buy loose sheets and cut them down to the size I need for my cards.

TIP:

If your paper bends a little while painting, don't worry. Just tape it down before you start or let it dry flat under a book after you finish.

Water Jars and Palettes

Watercolor uses a lot of water, so keeping clean water nearby makes a big difference. Rinse your brush as you paint, and change the water when it starts to look cloudy. Painting with dirty water can quickly turn your colors muddy.

A palette is where you mix and adjust your colors before painting. You can combine shades, lighten with water, or deepen with more pigment. Any smooth surface, such as ceramic, plastic, or even a plate, will work.

TIP:

Test your color on a scrap piece of watercolor paper before painting on your card. It helps you see how light or dark it will be once it dries.

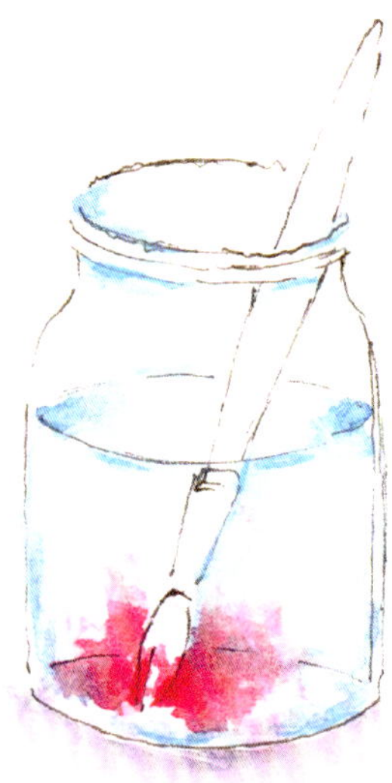

Lettering Tools

A good pen makes a big difference in how your lettering looks. You don't need to know calligraphy to write beautifully, but the right pen helps your lines stay clean and steady. I like to use the Sakura Micron 005 because the tip is fine, which gives smooth, even lines and makes it easier to control your writing. For beginners, thinner pens are often easier to use since thicker pens can be harder to control when you're trying to make small or consistent strokes.

I also sometimes use brush markers for bold or playful lettering, like in the Birthday Balloon project.

When I want to paint lettering instead of using a pen, I use a detail brush. Its small tip makes it easier to create clean lines and curves with better control.

Most of the lettering in this book uses a simple faux calligraphy style. You can find a step-by-step guide in the "Lettering Made Easy" section.

Other Helpful Tools

There are a few extra things that can make painting easier or help you create simple shapes:

White gel pen or opaque white paint
Great for adding tiny highlights or final details once your painting is dry.

Bottle caps, coins, or small round objects
Useful for tracing circles when sketching simple shapes.

Cookie cutters or simple stencils
Great for outlines of stars, hearts, or holiday shapes.

Scrap watercolor paper
Perfect for testing brushstrokes, mixing colors, or checking how a color dries.

Ruler
Helps keep borders straight or center your lettering.

Your Painting Space

You don't need an art room to start painting. All you really need is good light and a flat surface. Keep your main supplies close by so you can reach them easily. If you don't have a permanent art space, store your materials in a small basket or caddy. You can carry it anywhere in the house and having everything in one place makes it easy to paint whenever inspiration strikes. Even a few minutes of painting can calm your mind, ease stress, and bring a quiet sense of joy and focus. The more often you paint, the more natural it will start to feel, and you'll be surprised how much you can grow from just a few peaceful minutes a day.

Color Palette

I chose this palette because the colors work well together and reduce the need for mixing. Some of the color names used in this book reflect the paints I personally use, including brands like Kuretake, Daniel Smith, and Faber-Castell. You do not need these exact brands. If your paints use different names, simply choose a similar shade.

Warm Colors

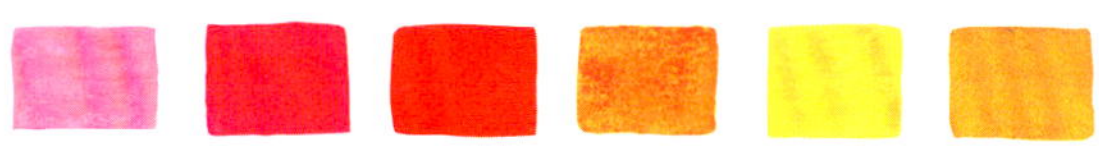

Color names in this row:

- Cherry Blossom Pink
- Quinacridone Rose
- Cadmium Red
- Cadmium Orange
- Cadmium Yellow
- Yellow Ochre

Warm colors make your paintings feel bright and cheerful. I like having a light pink, a medium pink, a deeper red, an orange, and a warm yellow because each one adds a different kind of warmth.

A lighter pink is beautiful for soft petals, cheeks, and gentle highlights. A deeper pink or red adds contrast and stronger shadows. Warm yellows and oranges bring brightness and a cheerful glow.

Mixing your own warm shades takes practice. Having these ready to use makes things simple and keeps your projects consistent. As you keep painting, you will naturally start mixing more, but for now these colors give you everything you need without extra steps.

Green Tones

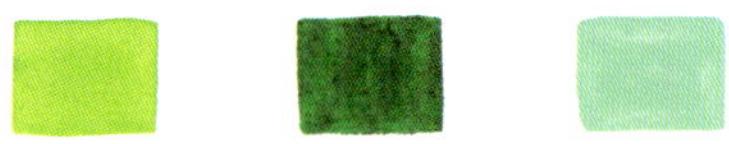

Color names in this row:

- Sap Green
- Forest Green
- Malachite

Green tones help bring your leaves, branches, and plants to life. Greens can be tricky when you are starting out because some look too bright, some too dark, and some do not feel natural. That is why I like keeping a small range of greens ready to use.

A lighter green feels fresh and airy, while a medium green works well for everyday leaves. A deeper green adds contrast and helps shapes sit farther back.

When everything is one green, it can look flat. Using a mix of lighter and deeper greens makes your foliage feel more alive. If you want to adjust them, add a little yellow to brighten, a tiny bit of brown to darken, or a small touch of blue to cool the color down.

As you paint more, you will get comfortable mixing your own greens. For now, these ready to use tones give you natural looking leaves without extra stress.

Cool Colors

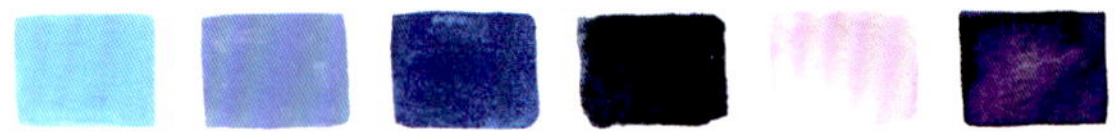

Color names in this row:

- Horizon Blue
- Ultramarine Pale
- Cobalt Blue
- Indigo
- Lilac
- Violet

Cool colors help balance the warmth in your paintings. They are calming and useful for skies, shadows, and backgrounds.

Light cool tones feel soft and airy and are perfect for gentle washes and backgrounds. Medium cool tones add depth without feeling too dark. Deeper blues create stronger contrast and richer shadows. Soft purples can be used for delicate accents and subtle details.

Using a mix of cool colors keeps your painting from looking flat. Lighter blues open up backgrounds, deeper blues add depth, and purple brings in a soft cool touch. These shades help your card feel balanced and finished.

Neutral Tones

Color names in this row:

- Yellow Ochre
- Raw Umber
- Natural Beige
- Gray
- Black

Neutral tones help everything else come together. They add shadows, outlines, and small details that support your brighter colors.

Light neutral tones are helpful for soft shading and subtle backgrounds. Medium browns add natural warmth to everyday elements like branches or baskets. Deeper browns create stronger shadows without needing pure black. Gray and black are useful for gentle outlines and small finishing details.

Neutrals keep your cards from feeling too bright or flat. You do not need to mix other colors to create brown or gray. These ready-to-use shades make it easy to add shadows and small details without extra steps.

TIP: ACTIVATING YOUR PAINT

Lightly spray your watercolor pans with clean water before you start. This softens the paint so your brush can pick up color more easily and helps the paint go on smoothly. A quick spray is all you need.

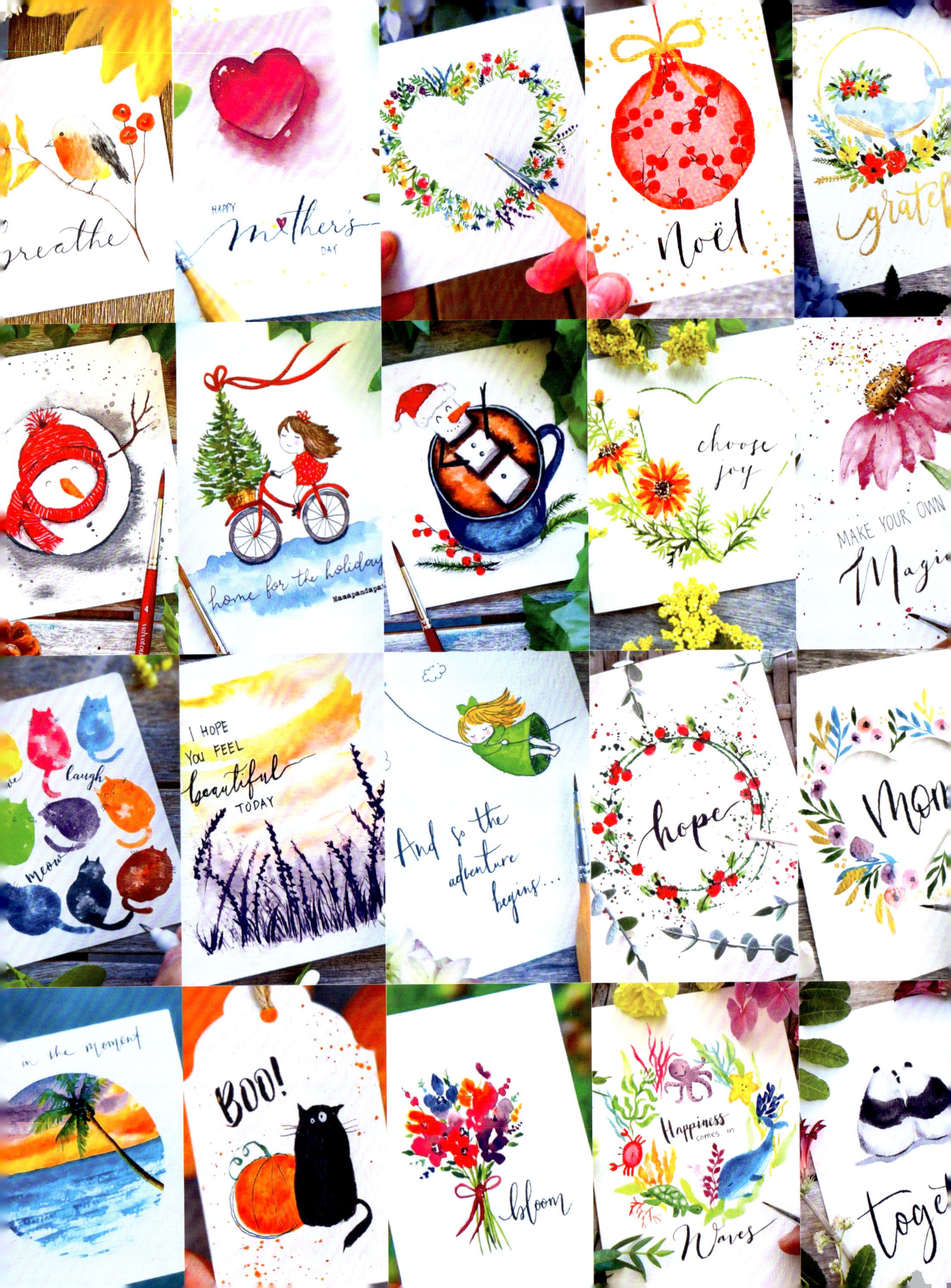
HAPPY
Mother's
DAY
Noël
home for the holiday
choose joy
MAKE YOUR OWN
laugh
meow
I HOPE YOU FEEL
beautiful
TODAY
And so the adventure begins...
hope
in the moment
BOO!
bloom
Happiness comes in
Waves

CHAPTER 2

Watercolor Toolbox

Before starting the projects, take a little time to play with the techniques in this section. There are many watercolor techniques to explore. These are techniques I use often in my own paintings, and once you get the hang of them, they'll help you add texture, color, and interest to your work. So, give them a try and use the ones that work best for you.

Come back to this chapter anytime as you go through the book and think of it like your watercolor toolbox. Each technique is something you can pull out when you want to make your painting feel more fun or expressive.

Technique 1: Water Control

Before you start painting, take a moment to notice how much water is on your brush. Water controls how watercolor moves. It affects how light or dark your color looks, and whether your edges turn out soft or sharp. Understanding this will make every project easier.

How to Control the Water on Your Brush

Wet brush: The brush is fully loaded with water and paint. The bristles look shiny and may drip. A wet brush spreads paint easily and is helpful for wet-on-wet painting or large washes.

Damp brush: The brush still has moisture but does not drip. After loading it with paint, blot (or lightly dab) the brush on a paper towel to remove a little water. A damp brush gives you more control and is great for blending, softening edges, or adding gentle layers.

Dry brush: The brush has little water left. It will still move paint, but lightly. This is useful for lifting, adding texture, or making small adjustments.

Try This!

Paint the same simple shape three times using a wet brush, a damp brush, and a nearly dry brush. Notice how the water level changes the look of the paint.

TIP: WHAT IS BLOTTING?

Blotting means gently touching your brush to a paper towel to take off extra water. Do this after rinsing your brush or loading it with paint. It leaves your brush damp instead of dripping, which gives you more control and helps keep your paint from puddling.

Extra Tips

- Keep a paper towel nearby to blot your brush when needed.
- If your paint puddles or spreads too quickly, your brush is too wet.
- If the paint looks scratchy or skips, the brush is too dry.

Wet   Damp   Nearly Dry

Technique 2: Controlling Values

A value is how light or dark a color looks on the paper. This depends on how much water you mix with your paint. More water makes the color lighter. More pigment (the paint itself) makes it darker. Controlling your values helps your paintings look more balanced and full of depth.

How to Create Different Values

- Start with one paint color and change the amount of water you mix into it.
- To make the color darker, use more pigment and very little water.
- To make it lighter, dip your brush in clean water and mix it into the paint little by little.
- Test your color on scrap paper to see the full range it can make.

Extra Tips

- Some colors are naturally strong, so you may need extra water to lighten them.
- Watercolor dries lighter than it looks when wet, so let it dry before judging the value.
- To check your contrast, take a quick photo and turn it black and white. It makes the light and dark areas easier to see.

Try This!

Pick one paint color and create several value swatches from light to dark by adjusting the water.

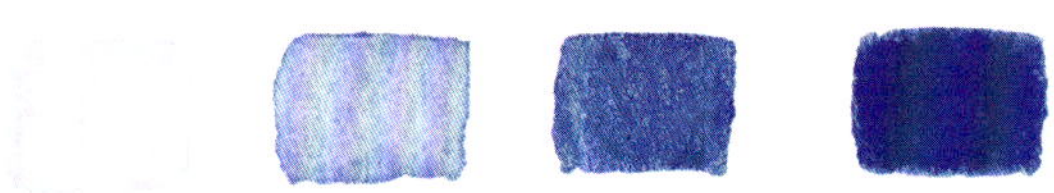

Technique 3: Color Mixing

Mixing colors lets you make new colors from the paints you already have. It gives you more control over getting the color you want. Mixing can feel daunting at first, so it is perfectly fine to start small. Try mixing just two colors and notice how the mix changes when you add a little more of one color.

How to Mix Two Colors

- Start with the lighter color on your palette. This keeps the mix easier to control.
- If you want one color to be the main color in your mix, you can start with that one instead.
- Place the second color next to the first on your palette.
- Add a small amount of the second color into the first color.
- Mix gently until the colors blend.
- Add more of the second color only if you want the value to be deeper or stronger.
- Add more water if you want the mix to look lighter.

Extra Tips

- Add the second color a tiny bit at a time because watercolor shifts quickly.
- Test your mix on scrap paper since colors dry lighter.
- If the mix gets too dark, add more of your main color or a little water.
- When practicing mixing, label your swatches so you remember how you made each color.

Try This!

Pick two colors and mix them on your palette. Make a swatch of your first mix, then add a little more of one color and make another swatch to see how the value changes.

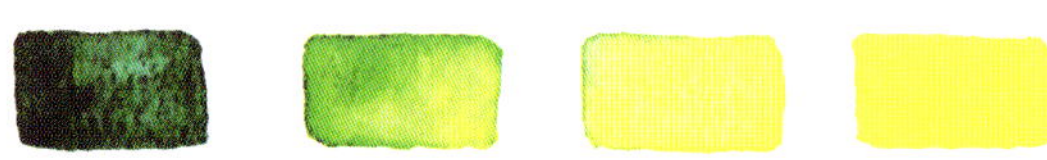

Technique 4: Lifting

Lifting is one of my favorite techniques because it's so simple but incredibly versatile. It can brighten an area, soften a hard line, create gentle texture, and fix small mistakes. Watercolor is transparent, so you cannot erase paint completely, but lifting lets you remove just enough color to adjust or lighten what you need.

How to Lift

- Gently press or dab the area you want to lighten to lift some of the color.
- Use light pressure and repeat as needed to gradually lighten the area. This works best while the paint is still damp.

Extra Tips

- Keep a paper towel nearby to blot or lightly dab your brush when needed.
- If your paint puddles or spreads too quickly, your brush is too wet.
- If the paint looks scratchy or skips, the brush is too dry.

Try This!

Paint a small rectangle and lift a lighter stripe through the center using a Q-tip or damp brush. Try it while the paint is wet and again when it is almost dry to see the difference.

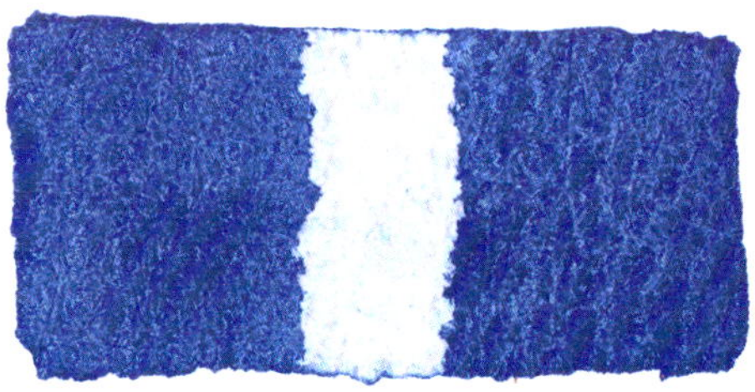

TIP: TOOLS I LIKE FOR LIFTING

Paper towel or napkin: Good for lifting larger areas or brightening backgrounds. A crumpled towel can create soft, textured shapes.

Cotton swab (Q-tip): Helpful for small spots, cleaning edges, or lightening a petal. Rolling the tip gives a smoother lift.

Clean damp brush: Wipe most of the water off so the brush is only slightly damp. This helps you soften a line or remove just a little color with control.

Technique 5: Soft Center Glow

Soft center glow creates a gentle highlight by lifting paint from the center of a shape while keeping the edges darker. I use this often for balloons, windows, petals, and any shape that needs a soft, rounded look.

How to Create a Soft Center Glow

- Paint the shape with an even wash.
- While the paint is still damp, lightly lift color from the center using a clean Q-tip or damp brush.
- Lift just a little so the center is lighter than the edges.
- If needed, softly tap around the lifted area to blend.

Why This Works

The lighter center and darker edges create a natural glow and give the shape a rounded look. This simple contrast makes windows look reflective, balloons look full, and petals look soft and fresh.

Extra Tips

- Practice on scrap paper to see how much paint lifts with different pressure.
- Work slowly until you learn the right dampness stage for lifting.
- This is an easy way to add light without using white paint.

Try This!

Paint a simple circle. While the paint is damp, lift the center with a Q-tip to create a soft glow.

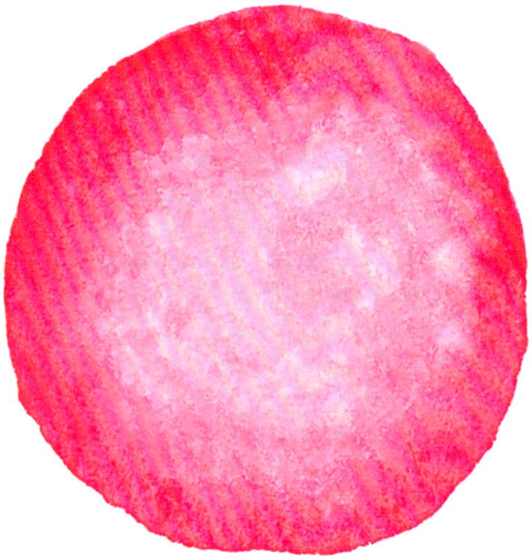

Technique 6: Saving White Highlights

Saving white highlights means leaving a small area of the paper unpainted so it stays bright. This is one of the simplest ways to show shine or light in watercolor. I use it often for tiny details because the natural white of the paper is brighter than anything you can lift later.

How to Save a White Highlight

- Lightly sketch the highlight shape before you start painting. It is usually a small oval, dot, or curved line.
- Paint around the shape and keep that area completely dry.
- Keep the highlight small so it looks natural and does not take over the shape.

Extra Tips

- Soften the paint around the highlight if the edges look too sharp.
- If you paint over the highlight by accident, lift a little color while it is still damp.
- Highlights look best when used sparingly.

Try This!

Paint a small circle and leave two small curved highlight shapes inside it. Notice how bright the untouched paper looks compared to painted areas.

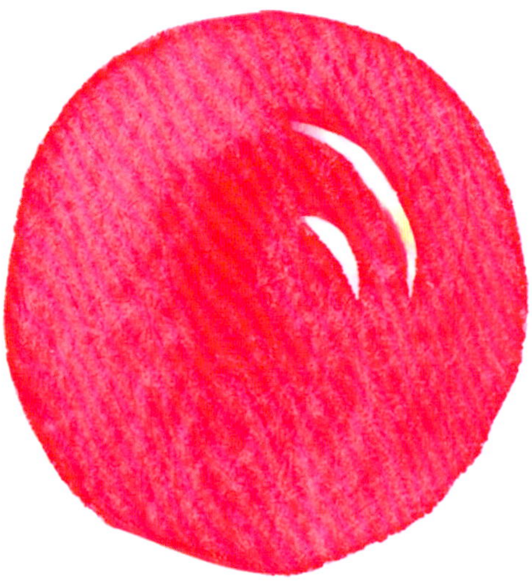

Technique 7: Wet-on-Wet

Wet-on-wet is the magic of watercolor. It's how you get those soft, fuzzy shapes where the color spreads on its own, almost like little clouds or bursts of color. To use this technique, start by wetting your paper. When you touch paint to the damp area, the color moves outward, blends gently, and creates soft edges without much effort. Wet-on-wet is helpful anytime you want that soft, natural watercolor look.

How to Use Wet-on-Wet

- Use a clean brush and water to wet the area where you want to add color. The paper should look shiny but not have puddles.
- The paper should be damp, not soaking wet or dry.
- While it's still damp, load your brush with paint and touch it to the wet area.
- Watch the color bloom and spread.
- Keep your brush light by barely pressing the brush on the paper and let the water do the blending for you.

Extra Tips

- Timing matters. If the paper starts to dry, you may get hard edges. Rewet gently with clean water if needed.
- Use a larger brush to wet the area evenly, especially for big shapes.
- The paper should feel cool and damp, not soaked.

Try This!

Wet a small circle with clean water, then drop in your paint and watch it spread and make soft, fuzzy edges. If you want to try more, add a second color nearby and watch the colors blend on the page.

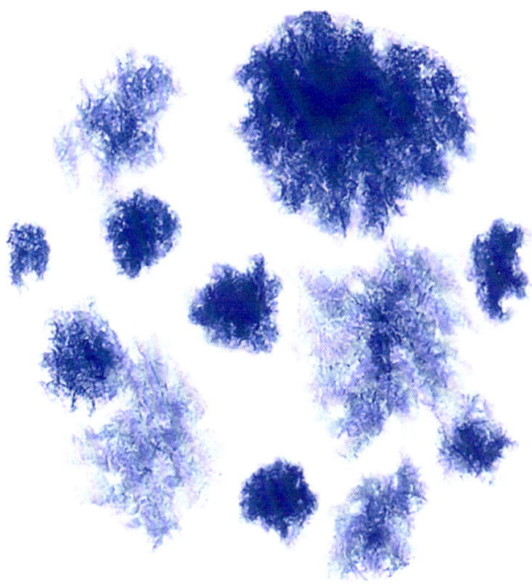

Technique 8: Blending

Blending is a way to make watercolor fade smoothly from one area to another. You can blend a single color from dark to light or blend two colors together. To blend, you use a clean, slightly damp brush while the paint is still wet. This softens the line between the two areas and creates a smooth, gentle transition.

How to Blend One Color (Dark to Light)

- Paint one side of your shape darker.
- Paint the other side with a lighter wash of the same color.
- While the paint is still wet, rinse your brush and blot off extra water.
- Use a clean, slightly damp brush to gently pull the darker color toward the lighter side.
- Use light strokes until the color fades smoothly from dark to light.

How to Blend Two Colors

- Paint either two different colors or different values of the same color next to each other, letting them touch or leaving a small gap.
- While the paint is still wet, rinse your brush and blot off extra water.
- Use a clean, slightly damp brush to gently pull one color toward the other.
- Blend with light strokes until the transition looks soft and even.

Extra Tips

- Blend while the paint is still wet for the smoothest results.
- Always blot your brush so you don't add too much water.
- Light, repeated strokes work better than pressing hard.

Try This!

Paint a rectangle using one color, making one side darker and the other side lighter. While it is still wet, use a clean damp brush to gently blend the two areas so the color fades smoothly from dark to light. If you want to try more, paint two different colors side by side and blend the edges where they meet.

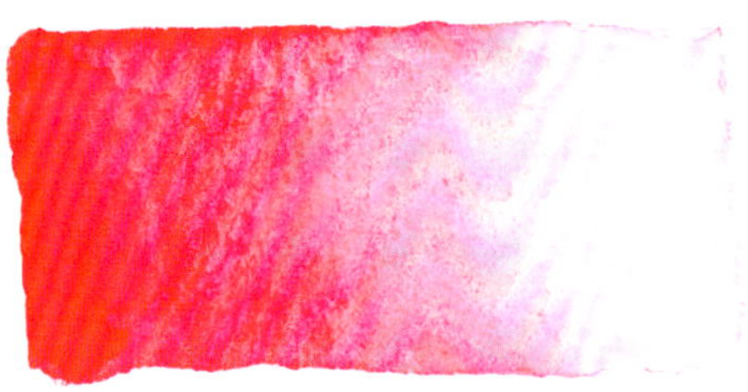

Technique 9: Softening Hard Lines

Sometimes watercolor dries with a sharp line that looks darker or more defined than you want. You may simply want to soften it to give your painting a smoother, gentler look. These lines often happen when one part of a wash dries faster than the rest. With a clean, damp brush, you can loosen the line and blend it into the surrounding color, so everything looks soft and natural.

How to Soften Hard Lines

- Wet your brush with clean water and blot off the excess so it's damp, not dripping.
- Gently brush directly over the sharp line using light, sweeping strokes.
- Let the clean water loosen the edge, then keep brushing softly to blend it into the surrounding area.
- If the line still feels too strong, dab gently with a paper towel to lift a little color.

Extra Tips

- This works best on paint that has recently dried. If the paint is fully dry, rewet the line and let the water sit for a few seconds before softening.
- Use a smaller brush in detailed areas so you don't spread the water too far.
- Be gentle so you don't lift too much color or damage the paper.

Try This!

Paint a rectangle and let it dry. Then use a clean, damp brush to soften one side and blend it into the lighter area.

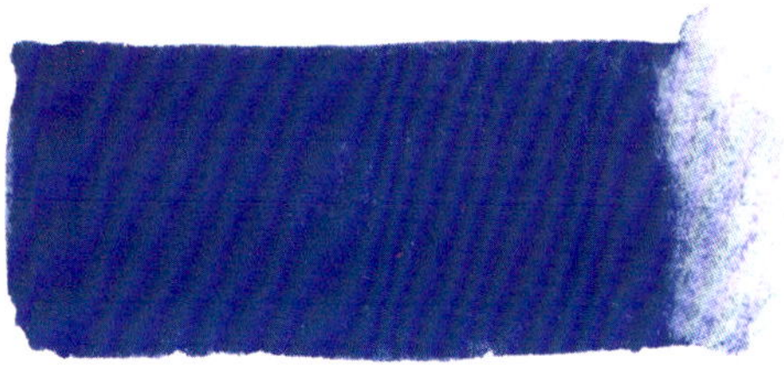

Technique 10: Splattering

Splattering is a fun way to add movement and texture to your painting. It can fill empty space, brighten a background, or give your artwork a loose, playful feel. There are a few easy ways to splatter paint, and each gives slightly different results depending on the brush and technique you use.

How to Splatter

Tapping the Brush with Your Finger (most control)

- Load your brush with watery paint.
- Hold it over your paper and gently tap the tip with your finger so the paint flicks downward.
- This creates smaller, more delicate splatters you can aim more easily.

Tapping with Another Brush or Stick (more random)

- Hold your loaded brush in one hand.
- Tap it lightly near the metal part using the handle of another brush, a stick, or a similar tool.
- This creates a wider, more scattered splatter with less control. It's great for loose backgrounds and fun texture.

Extra Tips

- The size of the brush affects the splatter. A large brush holds more paint and creates bigger, looser splatters. A smaller brush gives finer, more delicate dots.
- The height of the brush changes the spread. Holding your brush higher makes the splatter spread wider. Holding it closer gives tighter, more concentrated marks.
- Always test on scrap paper first and protect any parts of your painting you don't want to splatter.

Try This!

Load a brush with watery paint and try both tapping methods. Use different brush sizes and hold them at different heights. Watch how each one creates different shapes and patterns on the page.

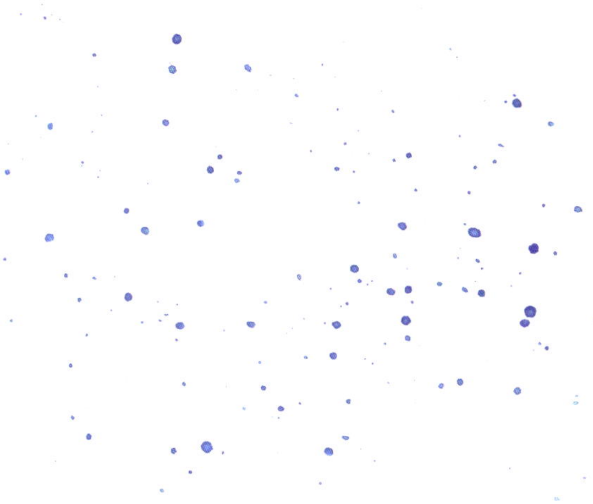

Technique 11: Taping

Taping is an easy way to keep parts of your paper clean and white. I use it when I want to save space for a message, a clean border, or a detail I'll add later. It helps block off areas so you can paint freely without covering them accidentally.

How to Tape Off White Space

- Use a low tack tape, like painter's tape or washi tape, so it removes cleanly without tearing the paper.
- Press the tape down firmly over the area you want to keep white.
- Paint as usual around or over the taped section.
- Let the paint dry completely, then peel the tape off gently to reveal the clean space.

How to Make Shapes with Tape

- To cover a wider area, place two or more strips of tape side by side.
- Overlap tape pieces to make rectangles, banners, or simple shapes.
- Press the edges down well so paint doesn't sneak underneath.

This works great when you want to save space for lettering or keep a design clean.

Extra Tips

- Stick the tape to your clothing once or twice before using it. This makes it less sticky and helps prevent tearing.
- Remove the tape as soon as the paint is completely dry.
- Pull the tape off slowly and at an angle to avoid damaging the paper.
- Heavier watercolor paper (140 lb or more) holds up better with tape.
- Always test your tape on a scrap of the same paper to make sure it lifts cleanly.

Try This!

Place a strip of tape across your paper to block off a section. Paint a wash of color over the top, let it dry, and then remove the tape. You'll see a clean, crisp line underneath.

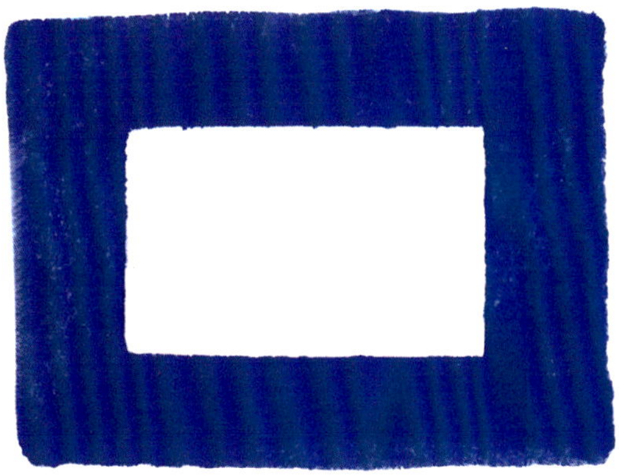

Technique 12: Soft Shadows

A soft shadow is a light, blurry shape of color that sits next to your object. It helps your object look like it is sitting on a surface instead of floating in the air. In watercolor, the easiest way to make a soft shadow is to paint it on damp paper. The water helps the paint spread on its own, so the edges stay soft.

How to Paint a Soft Shadow

- Make sure your object is completely dry first.
- Brush clean water around the edge of the object where you want the shadow to go. Keep the water close to the shape but don't touch the shape itself.
- While the paper is still damp, touch a little light gray or light purple paint into the wet area.
- Add a tiny bit of darker paint right next to the object where the shadow would be strongest.
- Let the paint spread on its own and dry.
- If the shadow spreads too far, gently dab the edge with a paper towel or cotton swab.

Extra Tips

- The shadow will only spread where the paper is damp. Wet a small area for a small shadow.
- Look for a soft shine on the paper. If it looks puddly, it is too wet.
- You can also use a damp brush to gently spread the shadow color if you want it to reach a specific area.

Try This!

Paint a simple shape like a heart. After it dries, wet a small area right underneath it. Add light gray paint to the damp spot and a little darker gray closer to the shape. Watch it spread into a soft shadow.

Technique 13: Radiating Glow

I call this the radiating glow. It looks like a small circle of light that gently fades outward from a dot. The key to this technique is keeping the center dot moist, not too wet, and using a damp brush to pull the glow outward. This helps you avoid blooms and gives you a soft, even halo.

How to Create a Radiating Glow

- Paint a small dot of color on your paper. Let it sit for about five seconds so it settles and isn't a puddle.
- Rinse your brush and blot it on a paper towel so it is damp, not wet.
- Touch the damp brush to the edge of the dot.
- Lightly pull a short stroke outward so the color fades into the paper.
- Repeat these tiny outward strokes all the way around the dot so the glow spreads in a soft circle.
- Keep the strokes light so the glow stays smooth and gentle.

Extra Tips

- If the glow looks too dark or spreads too far, your brush is too wet. Blot again so it is only damp.
- You can use a Q-tip to lightly tap the outer edge of the glow so it fades more softly into the paper.
- You can make the whole glow look brighter by darkening the dot in the center after everything is dry.

Try This!

Paint a small dot in a pink like quinacridone rose. While the paint is still damp, use a damp brush to pull short, soft strokes outward in a circle and watch how the glow gently fades outward.

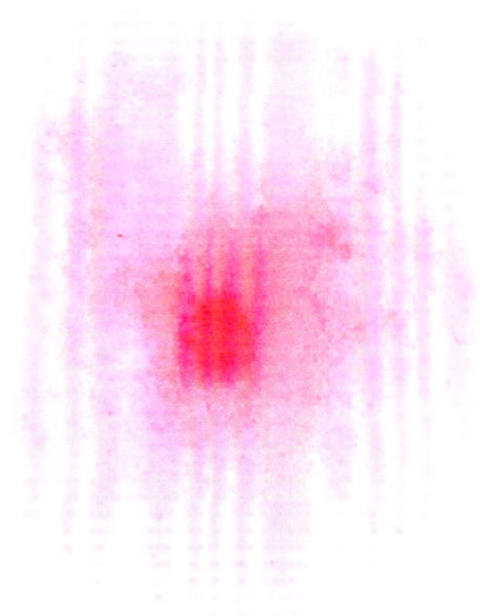

Brush Practice and Play

These brushstroke exercises teach you the basic motions you will use in this book. You will see how your brush reacts when you change pressure, angle, or water. Once you get used to these simple strokes, it becomes much easier to paint clean lines, smooth shapes, and steady details.

You do not need long practice sessions. A few slow strokes on scrap paper can help your brush feel more natural in your hand. Watercolor is a skill, and like riding a bike, it becomes easier once your hand learns the motions.

And remember, a quick test on scrap paper before painting your final card will help everything flow more smoothly.

Brushstroke Exercises

Thin Lines

Use a small round brush and a light touch. Tap off excess water so the tip is not too wet. Hold the brush at a gentle angle and let only the tip touch the paper. Pull the brush in one slow motion, moving your whole arm so the line stays smooth.

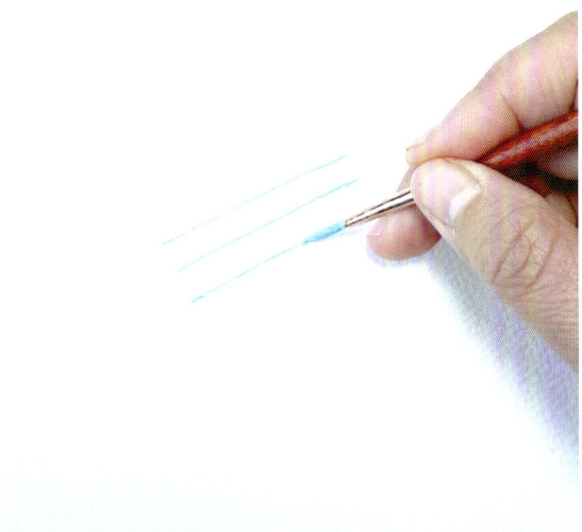

Thick Lines

To make a thicker stroke, press the brush down a little so more of the bristles meet the paper. Keep your movement steady and relaxed. A bit of extra pressure will naturally create a wider and more solid line.

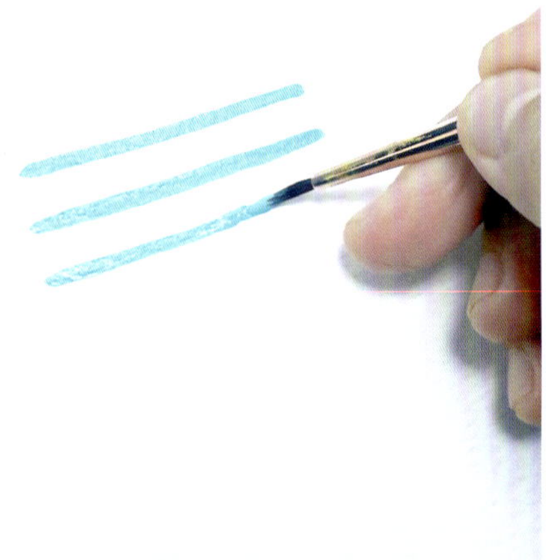

Lines in Different Directions

Turn your paper as you paint so you can work at angles that feel natural. Try a few directions to get familiar with how your brush moves as you change positions.

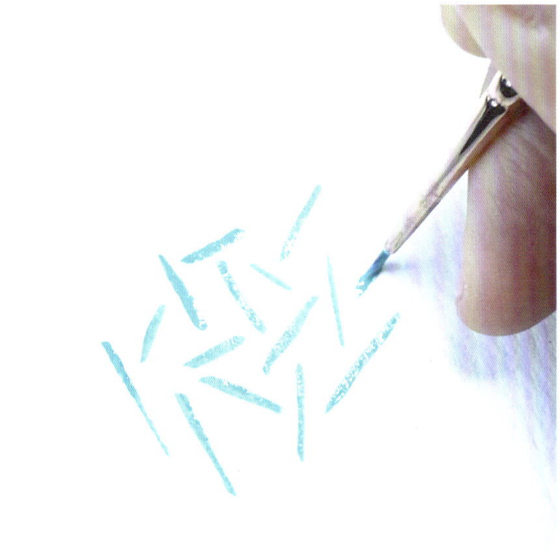

Combining Thin and Thick Lines

Now that you have tried both thin and thick lines, you can combine them by simply changing your pressure as you paint. Light pressure keeps only the tip of the brush on the paper and creates a fine line. Adding a little more pressure widens the stroke and makes it thicker. Try switching between thin and thick in one row to see how quickly the line changes with pressure.

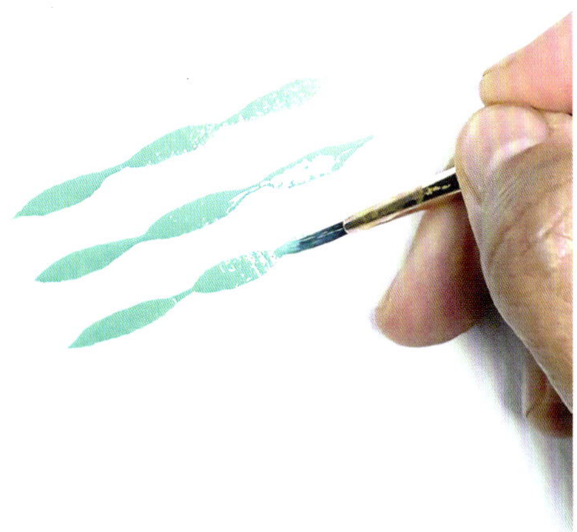

Wavy Lines

Use the tip of your brush to paint a gentle wave that moves up and down in one smooth motion. Try to keep the width of the brushstroke as even as you can from start to finish. Move your whole arm as you paint so the line flows without stopping. A relaxed hand will help your wave look soft and steady.

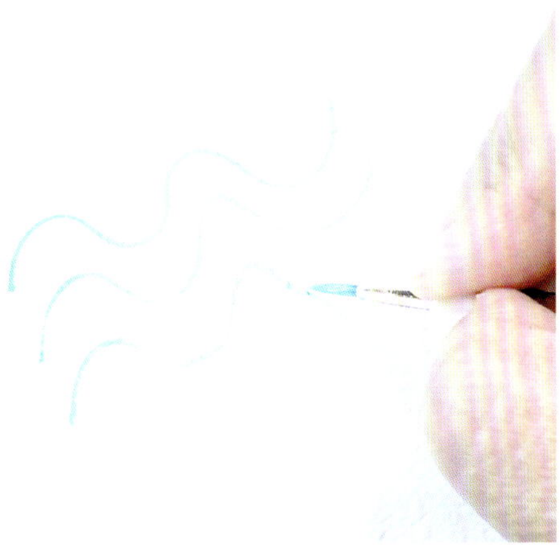

Flicks

Press your brush down to start the stroke. Pull the brush forward in one smooth motion, then lift your hand in a quick motion at the end so the stroke finishes in a sharp point. Repeat a few times until the lifting motion feels natural.

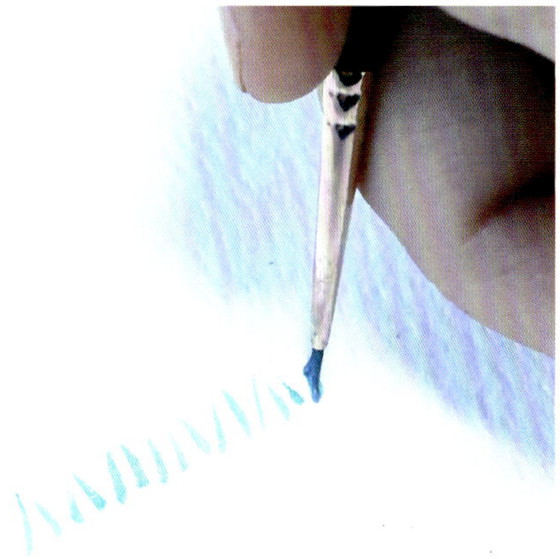

Dotting

Hold your brush upright and tap the tip onto the paper to make dots. Use light pressure for small dots and a little more pressure for bigger ones. Make a few in a row to notice how the size changes. Reload your brush when the color starts to dry so your dots stay smooth and clear.

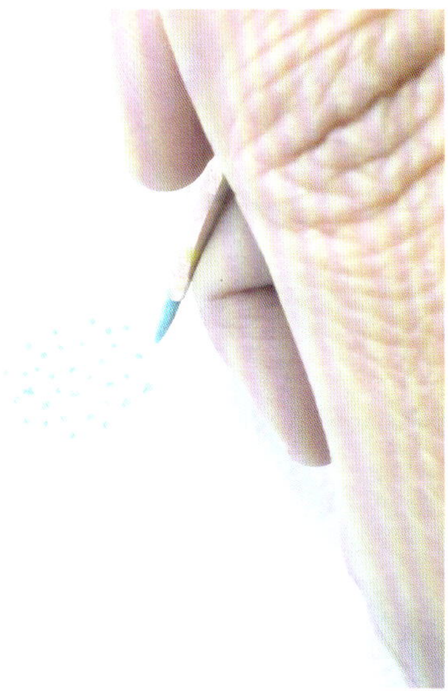

How to Paint and Fill a Shape

You will paint many shapes in this book, either following a pencil sketch or creating the shape directly with your brush. Learning to outline and fill smoothly will help you create clean edges and even color.

How to Paint It

1. **Outline the shape**
   Use the tip of your brush to trace the edge. Turn your paper as needed to keep the line smooth.
2. **Close the shape**
   Take your time around curves and corners so the outline feels even.
3. **Fill it in**
   While the edge is still slightly damp, fill the inside with short, gentle strokes. Keep your brush moving so the color dries smoothly.
4. **Adjust if needed**
   Add more paint to deepen areas, or lift color with a clean, damp brush for a lighter center. Let it dry before adding details.

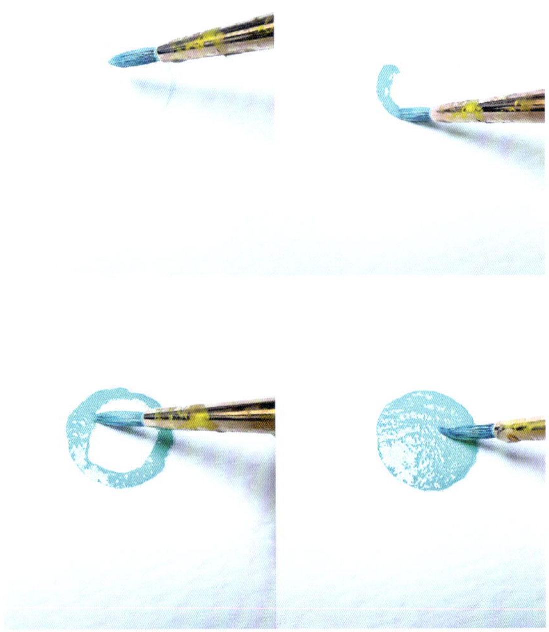

Flat Wash Stroke

A flat wash stroke is a smooth, even brushstroke made in one direction. Repeat the stroke the same way until the shape is filled, keeping your movement steady and consistent.

How to Paint It

1. **Load your brush**
   Dip your brush into plenty of paint and water so it can move smoothly.
2. **Start at the top or side**
   Begin at the top for tall shapes or the side for wide shapes.
3. **Pull one smooth stroke**
   Move your brush in one steady motion all the way down or across.

   Lift your brush at the end.
4. **Repeat in the same direction**
   Reload your brush, place it right next to the first stroke, and pull another stroke in the same direction.

   Continue until the shape is filled.

Why This Works

Keeping all your strokes moving in one direction helps the color go on evenly. It prevents streaks and the back-and-forth marks that can happen when you paint in different directions. Repeating the same stroke also gives you more control and keeps the shape looking clean and smooth.

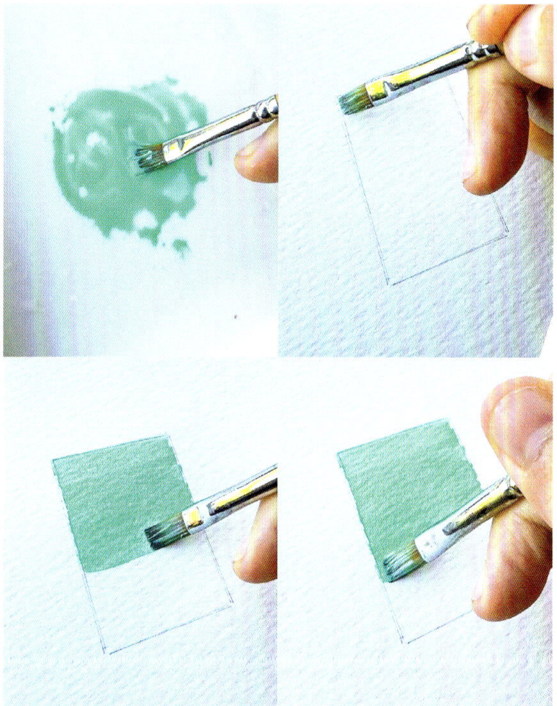

Leaves

Leaves show up in many of the cards in this book, so here are a few easy leaf strokes you can practice before you start.

One-Stroke Leaf

This leaf is made with one smooth motion. It's a great warm up because it teaches you how your brush reacts when you change pressure and angle.

How to Paint It

1. **Start with the tip**
   Touch only the point of your brush to the paper to create a sharp beginning to the leaf.
2. **Press gently**
   As you move forward, let more of the brush touch the paper so the middle of the leaf becomes wider.
3. **Pull the stroke forward**
   Move in a steady, relaxed motion. Keep the pressure even so the leaf looks smooth.
4. **Lift to a point**
   As you reach the end, slowly lift the brush back onto the tip to form a clean point.

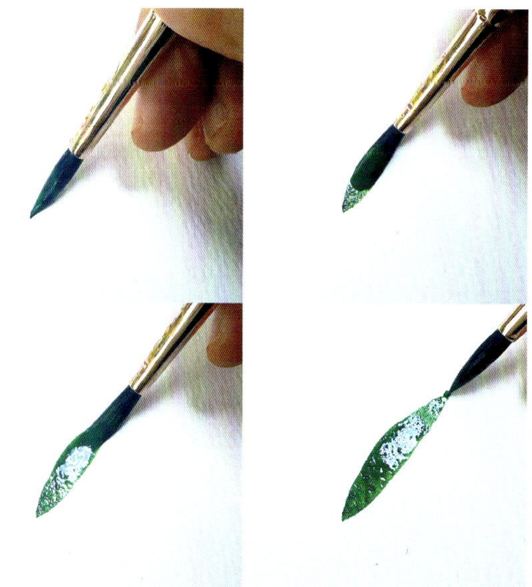

Two-Stroke Leaf

This leaf is made with two smooth strokes that meet in the middle. It creates a thicker leaf, and it is the base for many of the leaf shapes you will use in the projects.

How to Paint It

1. **Paint the first side**
   Start with the tip of your brush on the paper. Without lifting your brush, gradually press the whole brush down and pull the stroke forward to create one curved side.
2. **Lift to a point**
   As you reach the end, slowly lift your brush so the stroke finishes in a clean point.
3. **Paint the second side**
   Repeat the same motion on the other side. Begin at the top point, press the brush down again, and pull the stroke toward the first one so they meet.
4. **Connect the ends**
   Let both strokes touch at the tip and at the base so the leaf looks full and smooth.

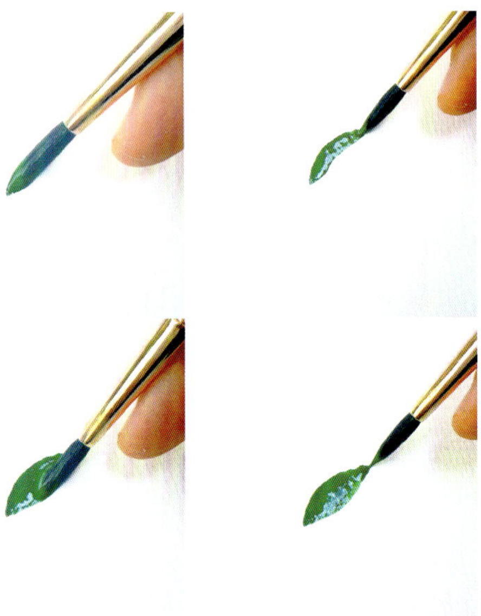

Two-Stroke Vein Leaf

This leaf is painted like the two-stroke leaf, except you leave a thin white space in the middle for the vein. This little space creates an easy vein and makes the leaf look livelier and full of character.

How to Paint It

1. **Place your brush**
   Start with the tip of your brush touching the paper at the base of the leaf.
2. **Paint the first side**
   Press down and pull the stroke upward to make one side of the leaf. Lift on the tip of your brush at the end to make a pointy end.
3. **Paint the second side**
   Go back to the starting point and paint the other side the same way. Leave a thin white space in the middle for the vein.
4. **Fix the top if needed**
   If the two sides do not meet at the tip, use the tip of your brush to connect them. If the white line is too wide or uneven, lightly adjust the edges.

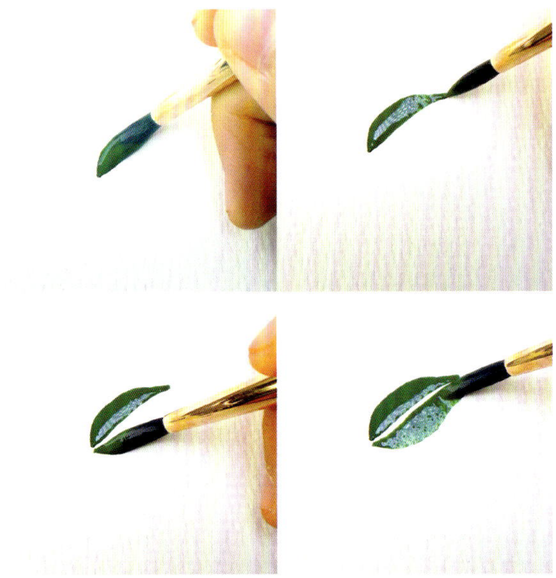

Rounded-Base Leaf

This is one of the quickest leaves to paint once you get used to it. The shape comes from one press and a gentle lift back toward the starting point.

How to Paint It

1. **Start with the tip**
   Touch only the tip of your brush to the paper to make the point of the leaf.
2. **Press to make the rounded base**
   Keep your brush in place and press it down until about half of the bristles touch the paper. This creates the round base.
3. **Lift back toward the start**
   Gently pull the brush back toward the starting point without lifting it off the paper. This keeps the base soft and rounded.
4. **Lift straight up to finish**
   Once the brush tip is back at the starting point, simply lift the brush straight up to make a clean finish.

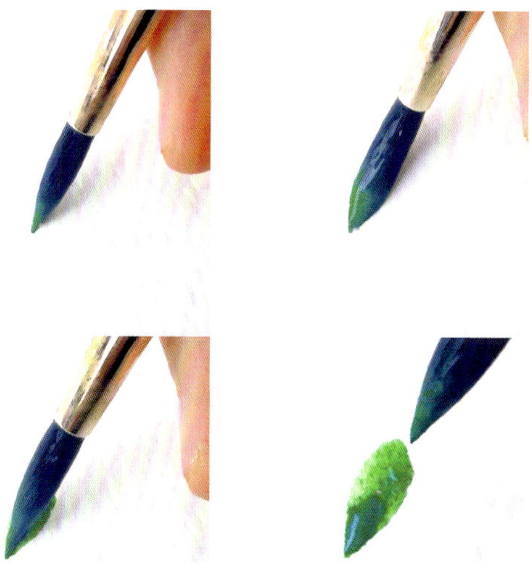

Long Rounded-Base Leaf

This leaf starts the same way as the rounded-base leaf. You press your brush down to make a wide base, then pull the stroke forward to form a long smooth shape. You can also use this same motion to make long pointy leaves like the one-stroke and two-stroke leaves you learned earlier. The difference comes from how you lift the brush at the end. For this leaf you will finish with a soft rounded tip.

How to Paint It

1. **Start with the tip**
   Touch only the tip of your brush to the paper to begin the leaf.
2. **Press to make the rounded base**
   Press down until more than half of the bristles meet the paper. This creates the wide rounded base.
3. **Pull the stroke forward**
   Without lifting your brush, slowly pull the stroke forward in one smooth motion. Keep your pressure even so the sides stay clean.
4. **Lift straight up to finish**
   At the end of the stroke, lift your brush straight up to make a soft rounded tip.

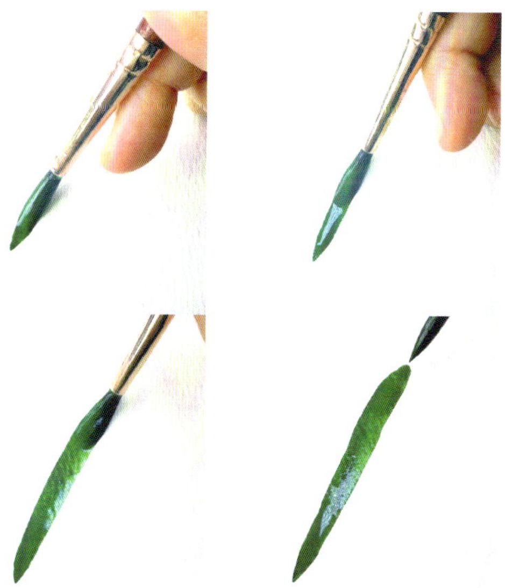

Simple Leaf Stem

This exercise shows you how to paint a thin stem and add simple leaves along it. I used rounded-base leaves here, but you can paint different types of leaves using the same steps. Try to keep the leaves smaller at the top and a little bigger as you move down.

How to Paint It

1. **Paint the stem**
   Use the tip of your brush to paint a thin curved line. Keep the pressure light so the stem stays smooth.
2. **Add the first small leaves**
   Start near the top. Touch the tip of your brush to the stem, press once to make a small, rounded leaf, then lift straight up. Leave a little space and add one or two more small leaves near the top.
3. **Add more leaves down the stem**
   Move lower on the stem and add leaves on both sides. Start with the tip touching the stem, press to make the shape, then lift straight up. Leave small spaces between each leaf so they do not touch.
4. **Make the lower leaves bigger**
   As you move toward the bottom, press a little more so the leaves become slightly larger. This gives the stem a natural and balanced look.

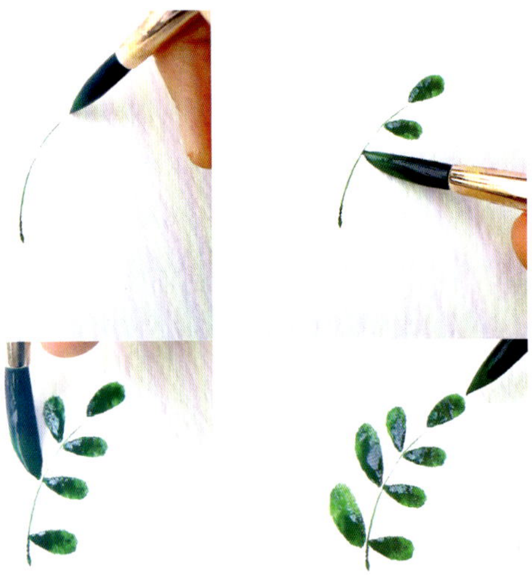

Pine Leaf Branch

Pine strokes are made with tiny, light marks that spread out from a thin curved stem. These simple little dashes create soft, delicate greenery that works beautifully in winter scenes or as filler greens.

How to Paint It

1. **Start with the tip**
   Load just the tip of your brush. Touch it lightly to the paper so you have a fine point to work with.
2. **Paint the stem**
   With a steady hand, paint a thin curved line. Keep the stroke gentle and slightly angled so the branch feels natural.
3. **Add the first dashes**
   Using only the tip of your brush, paint short, outward dashes along one side of the stem. Keep these small and close together near the top.
4. **Fill out the branch**
   Continue adding dashes on both sides of the stem. Let a few curve slightly and allow the strokes to get a little longer as you move down the branch.

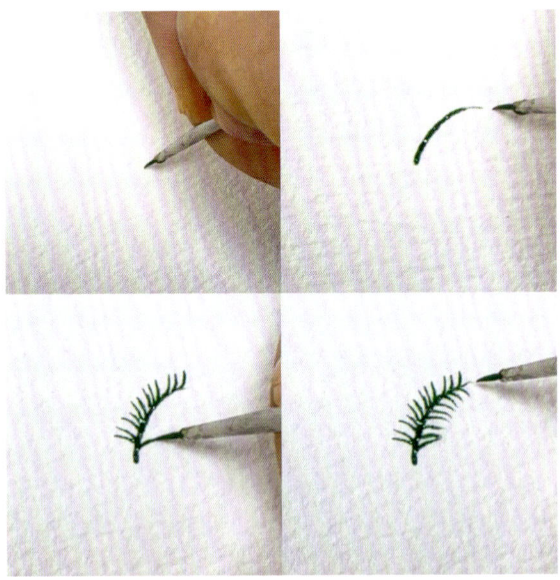

Petals

These exercises show a few basic ways to paint petals using simple brush motions. Once you learn these, you can use the same steps to create many other kinds of petals.

Dabbed Dots Flower

This flower is made by lightly dabbing small dots of paint to build the shape. You can place the dots in any loose shape you like. This is an easy way to show flowers that are made of many tiny petals.

How to Paint It

1. **Dab the first dot**
   Use the tip of your brush to make a few small dots on the paper. Keep your brush more upright so only the tip touches the paper. Keep the dots close together but not touching.
2. **Add more dots**
   Dab more small dots around the first ones to form the flower. Keep the shape loose and simple.
3. **Soften a few dots**
   Rinse your brush and tap off extra water. Your brush should be damp, not wet. Lightly touch a few of the dots so the paint moves a little and makes soft edges.
4. **Fill empty spots**
   Add a few more dots where you see gaps. Keep the edges uneven so the flower looks natural.

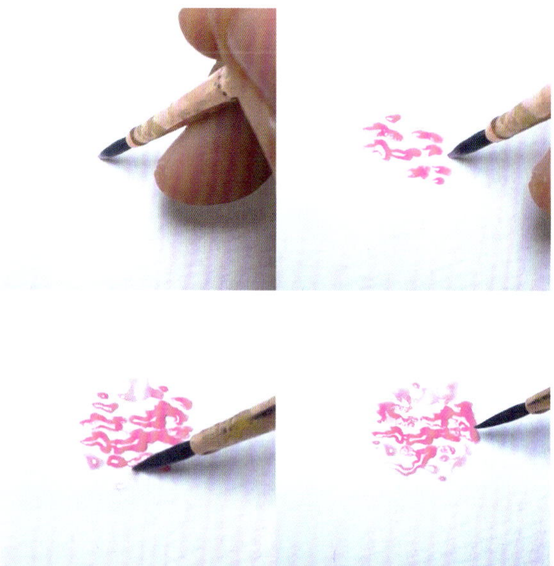

Clover-Style Petal Flower

Prepare three values of the same color for the petals: light, medium, and dark. This flower is made by repeating the same motion used for the one-stroke leaf. You are going to paint the same small strokes over and over to form a round, full flower. This motion is useful for any flower that has lots of thin petals.

How to Paint It

1. **Make the first small petal**
   Load your brush with the light value. Point the tip down, press gently, pull up a little, and lift, just like a tiny one-stroke leaf.
2. **Add more small petals around the center**
   Keep making these small leaf-shaped strokes as if they are coming from a center point. As you move outward, make some of the petals a little longer and angle a few slightly downward to shape the flower.
3. **Add the medium value**
   Switch to your medium value and place it in a few areas to give the flower depth. Add some near the center and a little on the tips or just under a few petals to show depth.
4. **Add a few darker accents**
   Use your darkest value lightly in only a few small spots. These tiny accents add contrast and help the petals stand out.

You can also add a small touch of yellow to the center when everything is dry.

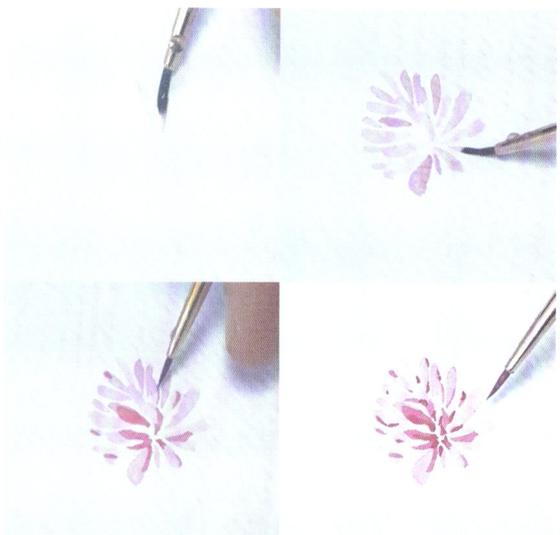

Rose-Style Flower

This flower starts with a few curved lines in the center and then uses water to pull the color outward. The petals stay soft and loose, so there is no need to make a perfect shape.

How to Paint It

1. **Paint the center**
   Use the tip of your brush to paint small, curved C shapes that slowly grow outward from the center. Leave tiny spaces between them.
2. **Soften into loose petals**
   Rinse your brush and tap off extra water so it is damp, not wet. Gently pull the color outward from a few of the C shapes to form loose petals. Keep the edges soft and free.
3. **Add darker color**
   While the paint is still damp, add a little more color where the C shapes meet the petals. This will create some shadows and deepen the center.
4. **Lift for softer edges**
   Use a clean Q-tip to gently lift a bit of color from the edges or inside the petals. This creates soft highlights and keeps the rose light and airy.

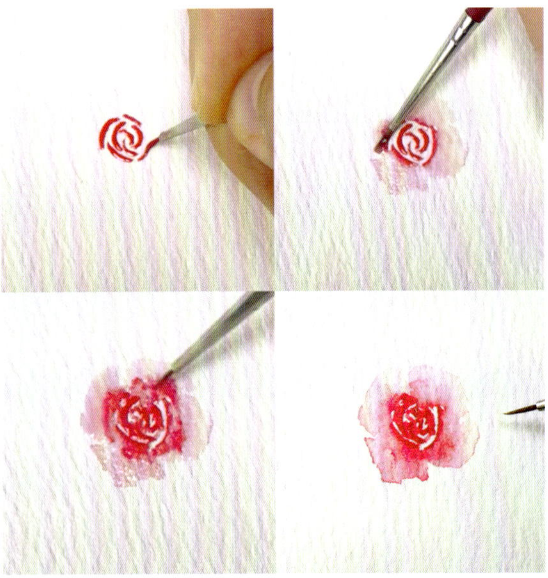

Round Petal Flower

This flower is made with two smooth strokes for each petal. The motion is similar to the two-stroke leaf you learned earlier, but the end of each petal stays soft instead of pointed. This method is versatile, and you can change the number of petals depending on the look you want.

How to Paint It

1. **Start with the center dots**
   Use the tip of your brush to make a few small dots in the middle. These dots guide where the petals will sit.
2. **Paint the first side of the petal**
   Touch the tip of your brush near the center, then press down and pull outward to form one side of the petal. Lift your brush gently at the end so the tip stays soft.
3. **Paint the second side**
   Start at the center again and paint the other side the same way. Pull the stroke outward with a slight curve and lift at the end. Let the two sides meet in a rounded shape with a slight inward curve at the center.
4. **Add the rest of the petals**
   Continue painting the other petals the same way. Small differences in shape help the flower look natural.

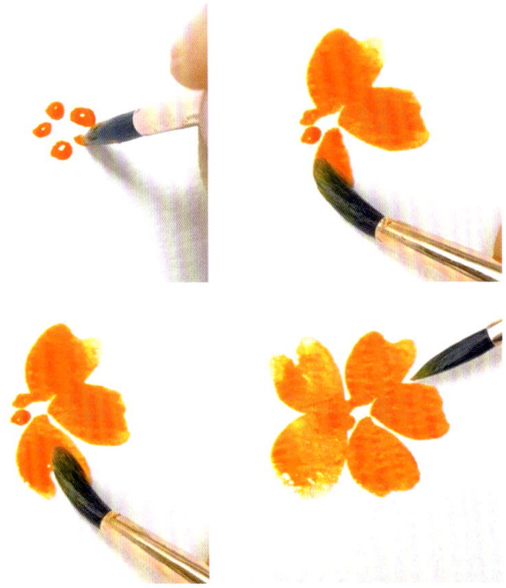

Tiny Round Petal Flower

This small flower is made with simple round strokes. You can paint it on its own or group several together for a small bouquet. It also makes a great filler flower because it fits easily between larger blooms and helps fill empty spaces.

How to Paint It

1. **Make the first petal**
   Load your brush with color and place the tip on the paper. Use a tiny circular motion to make a small, rounded shape.
2. **Add more petals**
   Add five petals around the center, spacing them out evenly.
3. **Lift a little color**
   Use a Q-tip to gently lift a bit of paint from the petals near the center to keep the middle soft.
4. **Outline the center**
   Use a darker value of your petal color to lightly outline the middle so the center of the flower stands out.

You can add a small touch of yellow in the center after everything is dry.

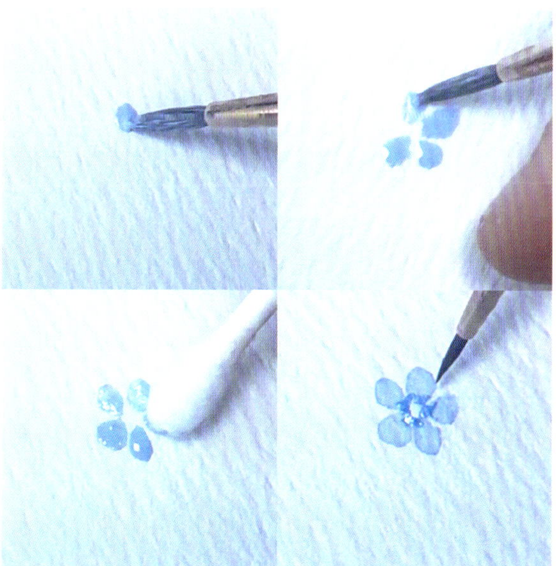

Side Petal Flower

We are painting a sideways, daisy-inspired flower. Each petal uses the same motion as the long rounded-base leaf you painted earlier. The petals can end in a round tip or a pointy tip, depending on how you lift the brush. Imagine a small invisible circle in the middle to guide where each petal starts. This flower shape is easy to change and works for many different flowers.

How to Paint It

1. **Paint the first petal**
   Start at one end of your invisible half circle. Press the tip of your brush to the paper, pull the stroke outward, then lift. The end of the petal can be round or pointy.
2. **Add more petals**
   Paint more petals around the invisible circle in a fan shape. The middle petals are the longest. The petals on the sides should be shorter. This helps the flower look like it is turned to the side.
3. **Add the center**
   Paint a small oval in the middle. It is fine if the color spreads into the petals. Wait for the petals to dry if you do not want the colors to mix.
4. **Finish the flower**
   If you want to fix any areas on the petals, add a little more paint or smooth the edges. You can also use a Q-tip to lightly lift color in some areas to soften the look.

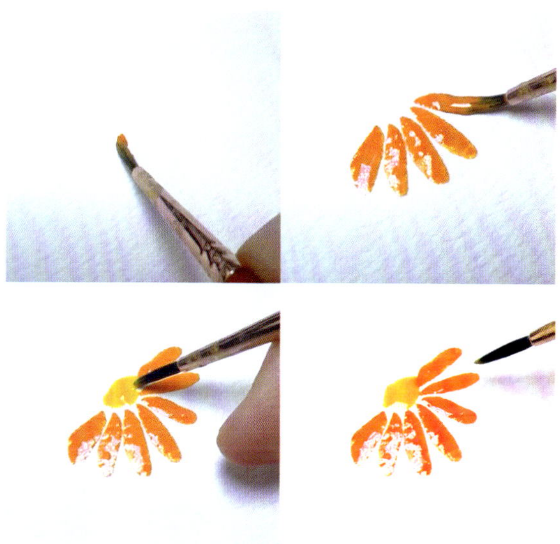

Lettering Made Easy

If you have ever thought you have bad handwriting, lettering is different. Handwriting is quick and automatic. Lettering is slow and intentional. Instead of writing words in one motion, you draw one letter at a time, which makes lettering much more forgiving.

Lettering is also different from traditional calligraphy. Calligraphy is usually created using smooth, flowing strokes with pressure sensitive pens or brushes. Lettering is built step by step. You form the letters first, then adjust and refine them as you go.

A Few Simple Lettering Terms

Downstroke
Any part of a letter where your pen moves down. These are the strokes we make thicker.

Upstroke
Any part of a letter where your pen moves up. These stay thin.

Cross stroke
The small horizontal line in letters like t. This always stays thin.

Tools You Will Need

Pencil and Eraser
Use a pencil to lightly sketch your word first if you want a guide, and an eraser to remove the lines once the ink is fully dry.

Pen
I often use the term fineliner, which is simply a pen with a thin, firm tip made for drawing smooth, precise lines. I use the Sakura Micron 005, but any similar thin pen or fineliner you already have will work beautifully.

Ruler
A simple ruler helps you draw a light pencil guideline, so your letters stay straight and don't drift up or down. You can erase it afterward, but it makes practicing and connecting letters so much easier.

Thicker Pen (optional)
If you want to fill in the downstrokes faster, you can switch to a slightly thicker pen or a brush pen for that step.

Brush Markers (optional)
Great for adding color and creating a more playful, expressive lettering style.

Faux Calligraphy

In this book, we use a simple lettering method called faux calligraphy. Faux calligraphy gives you the look of calligraphy without special pens or pressure techniques.

You write your word normally, then thicken only the parts of each letter where your pen naturally moves downward. This small change makes your writing look more hand lettered and polished.

Here is the simple idea:

1. **Write your word normally.**
   Use regular pressure and write in whatever style feels comfortable.
2. **Look for the downstrokes.**
   These are the parts of the letters where your pen moves downward. Those are the strokes we will thicken.
3. **Add a second line along each downstroke.**
   This creates a little space that shows where the thicker part will go. Pick one side and stay consistent so everything looks even.
4. **Fill in the space.**
   Color in the little gap to make the downstroke thicker.

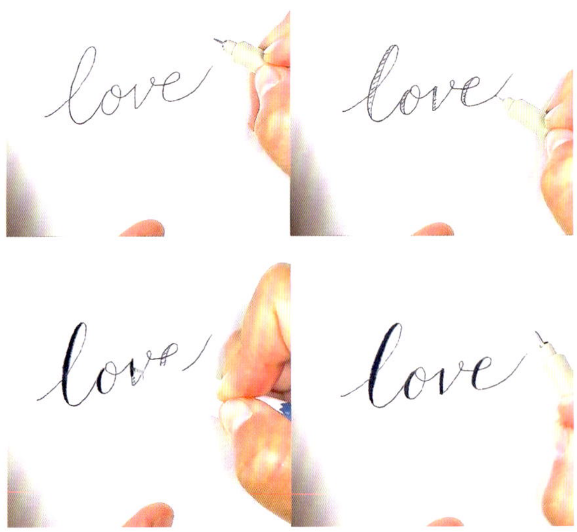

Sometimes I skip thickening completely and leave everything thin. Soft, delicate letters can look whimsical and airy, especially on cards.

A HELPFUL LITTLE TIP

When thickening your downstrokes, add the extra line on the inside of the letter rather than the outside. This keeps the outer edges smooth and helps your word look cleaner and more even.

Try This

Here are a few easy words to practice with. Start small, go slowly, and focus on spotting those downstrokes.

hello · love · joy · happy · thank you

A few tips as you try these:

- **Write the word a little bigger than your normal handwriting.** Bigger letters make it easier to see where the downstrokes are.
- **Leave a little space between letters.** It gives you room to add your thicker strokes later.
- **Say the word "down" in your head whenever your pen moves downward.** It helps you notice the downstrokes more clearly (a trick many lettering teachers use).
- **Try the same word twice — first lightly, then a little slower and more intentional.** You'll see the difference right away.
- **Do not worry about perfect spacing.** Faux calligraphy is forgiving. The goal is simply to get comfortable thickening the right strokes.

As you keep practicing, the downstrokes will start to jump out naturally and thickening them will feel less like "steps" and more like a smooth part of writing.

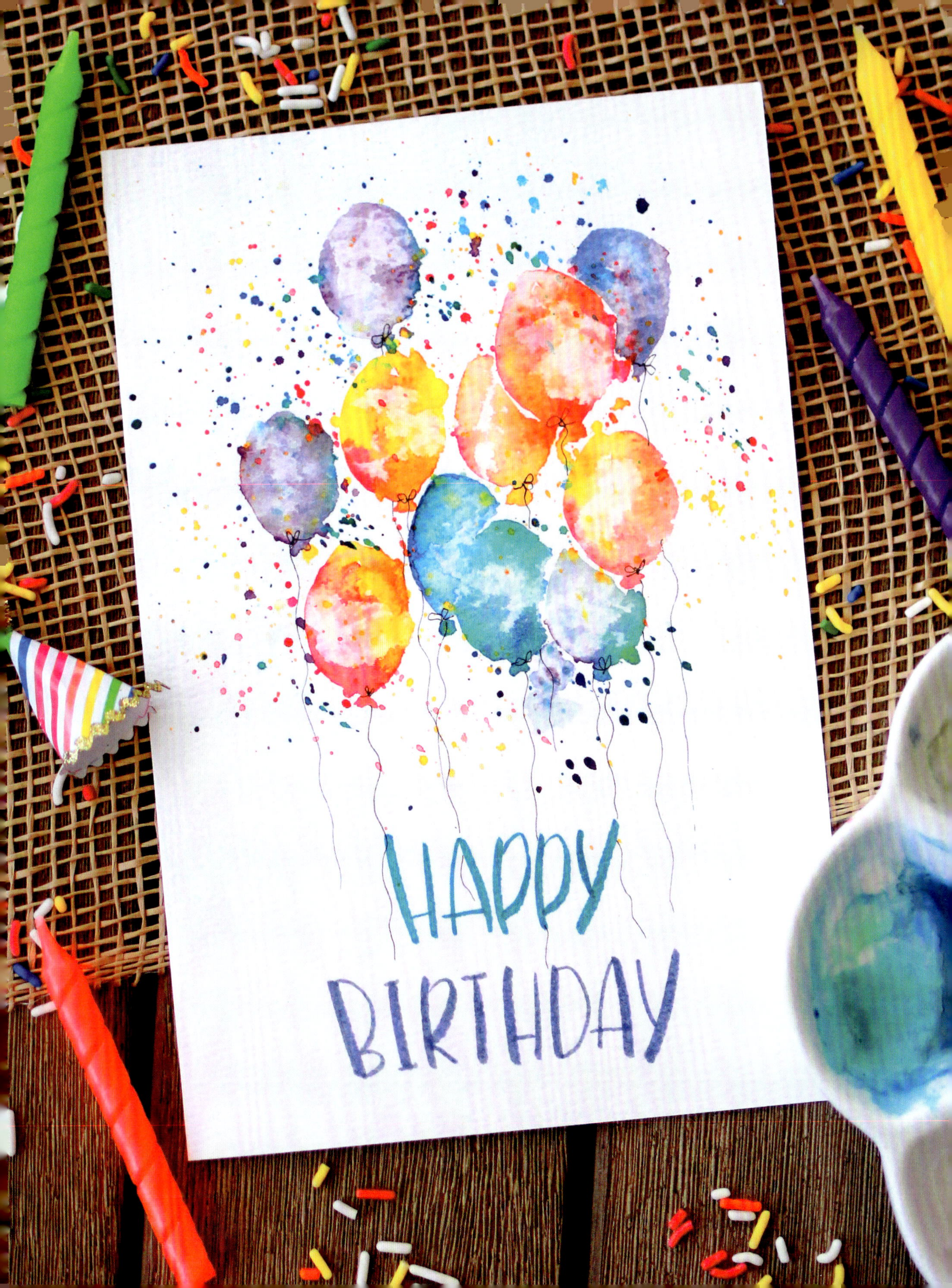
HAPPY
BIRTHDAY

CHAPTER 3

Everyday Cards

Birthday Card: Balloons

Paint Colors

(Feel free to substitute similar shades; you don't need to match the exact names.)

- Cadmium Yellow
- Cadmium Red
- Cobalt Blue
- Cadmium Orange
- Sap Green
- Violet

Tools

(Feel free to use similar supplies; these are just suggestions!)

- Medium round brush (size 6–8)
- Small round brush (size 2-4)
- 005 black fineliner
- Brush markers

Balloons are a bright and joyful way to celebrate someone's birthday. In this project, we'll paint them in a loose watercolor style, starting with playful splatters of color and shaping them into soft balloon forms.

To keep the colors looking fresh and vibrant, we'll begin with warm tones like yellow, orange, and red. Once those layers are dry, we'll add cooler colors on top. Working this way helps the hues stay bright instead of blending into muddy shades.

Step 1: Splatter Yellow

Now we will create a loose, playful base using the splattering technique (see Splattering, page 17). Add cadmium yellow splatter across your paper, keeping the pattern light and uneven. Leave some open areas for additional colors later.

If you are using the tear-out card, splatter directly over the sketch and skip any shaping steps.

Step 2: Splatter Orange

While the yellow is still slightly damp, splatter cadmium orange in and around the yellow areas. Let the colors touch and blend naturally but avoid covering everything. Keep the splatter loose and spontaneous.

Step 3: Splatter Red

Add cadmium red splatter in smaller amounts, focusing on a few areas to create depth and variation. Try not to overdo it. These warmer colors will form the first layer of balloons.

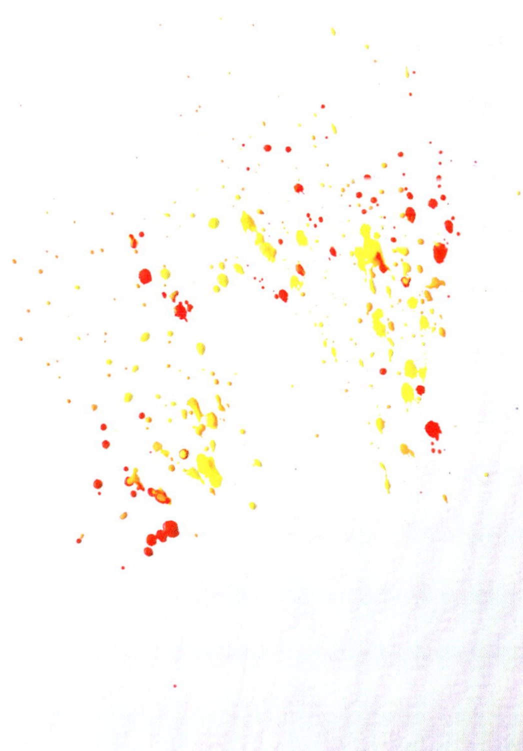

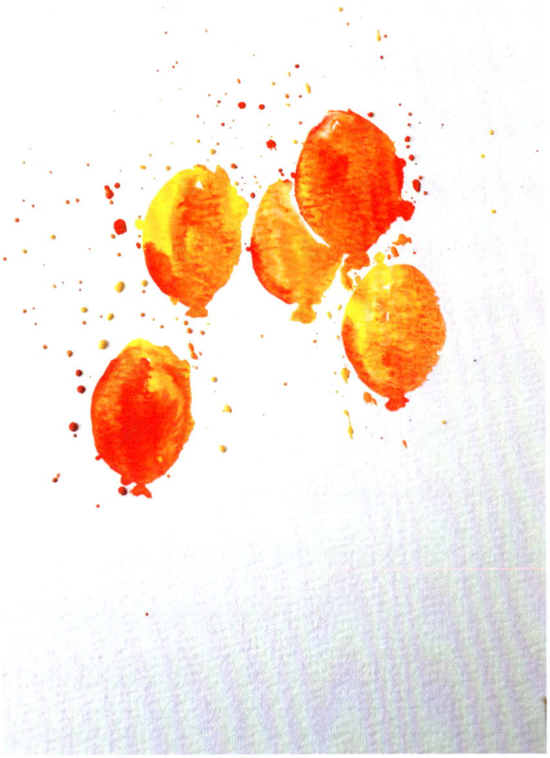

Step 4: Shape the Balloons

While the paint is still wet, use a small brush to gently shape the splatters into balloon forms. Curve one side, then the other, to create rounded ovals. They don't need to be perfect. As a finishing touch, add a small, rounded triangle at the bottom of each balloon to suggest the knot.

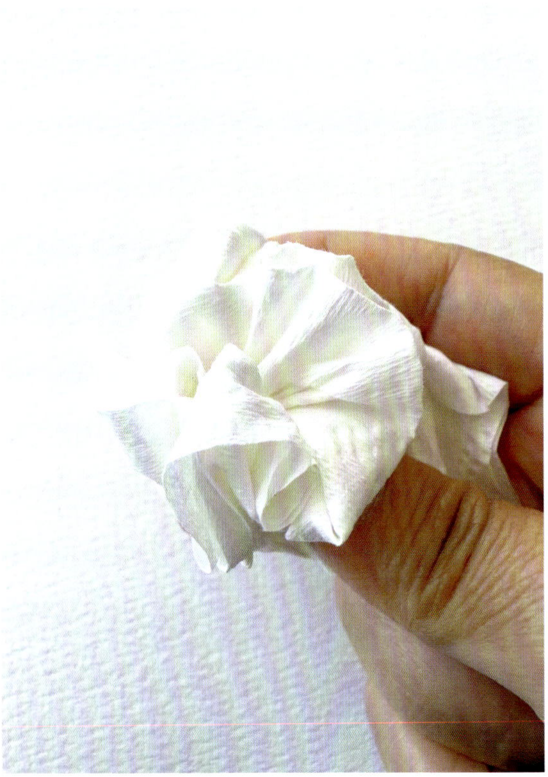

Step 5: Blotting Buddy

Crumple a clean paper towel or napkin into a soft shape. Do not flatten it. This will be used to lift color and create texture in the next step. It might not look like much, but paper towels are surprisingly effective!

Step 6: Blot the Balloons

Take the crumpled paper towel and gently press it onto each balloon once or twice while the paint is still wet. This lifts a small amount of color and creates soft texture, helping the balloons feel lighter and more playful. Use a clean spot on the paper towel for each balloon so the colors do not smear.

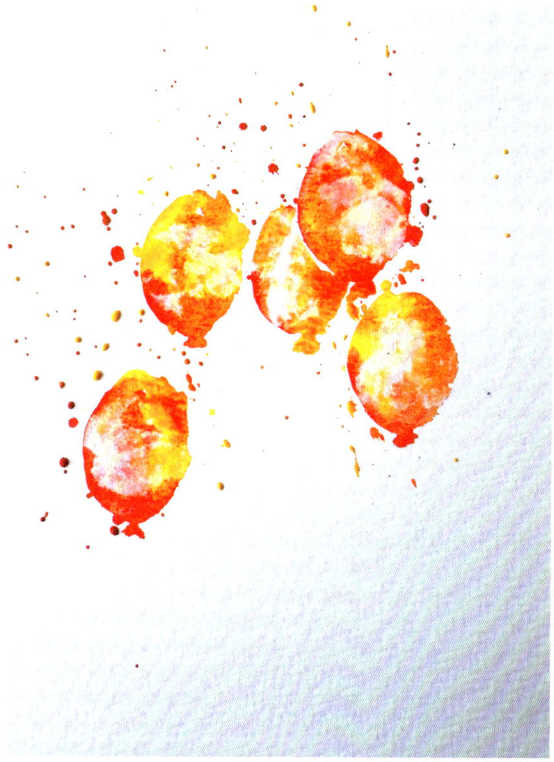

Step 7: Cover the Balloons

Let the warm colored balloons dry completely. Then lightly cover them with scrap paper or soft, torn paper towels; anything that won't stick. This keeps the warm colors safe while you work on the next layer.

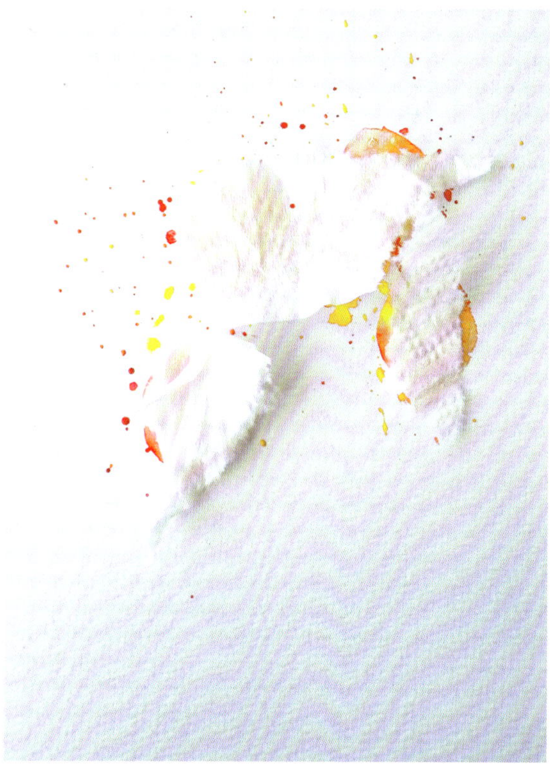

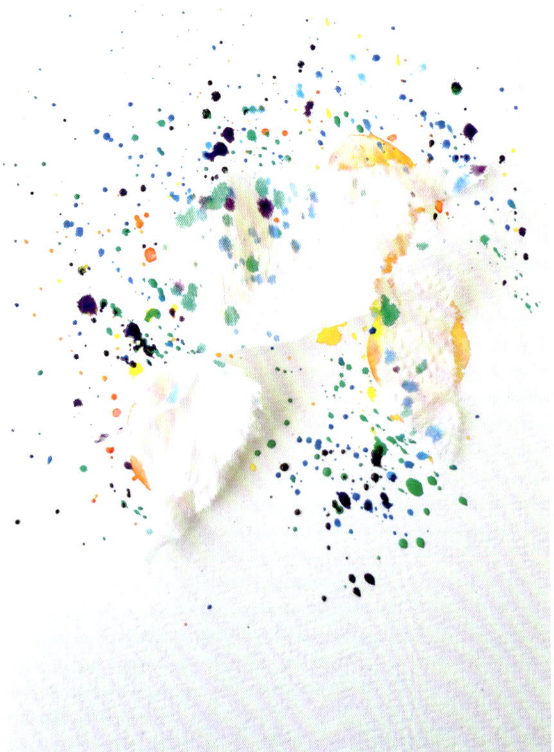

Step 8: Splatter Cool Colors

Using the same splattering technique from the warm colors, add cool colors such as cobalt blue, sap green, and violet. Splatter where you want the next balloons to appear. Let the paint fall loosely and enjoy the process.

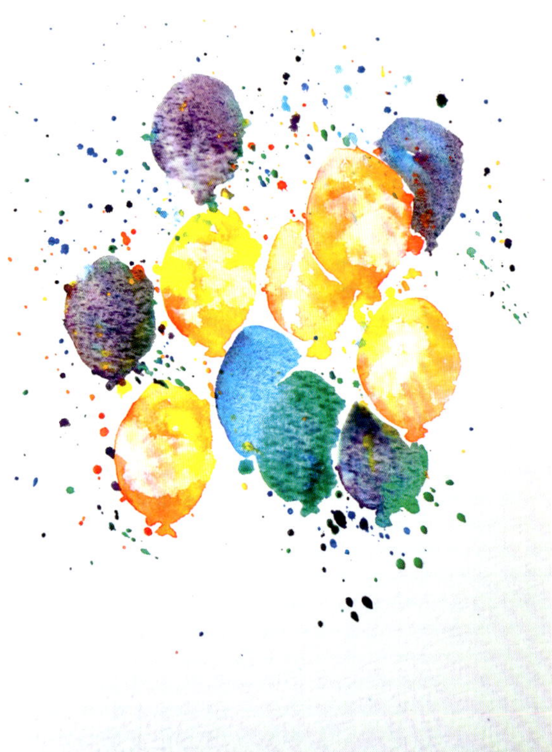

Step 9: Shape the Balloons

While the cool paints are still wet, use a small round brush to shape each splatter into a balloon just like in step 4. Curve one side, then the other to form the round shape, and add a small tail at the bottom. To make a balloon look like it's behind another, let the shapes overlap slightly but leave a very thin gap between them. That small space helps your eye see one balloon as being behind the other. It's a simple trick that adds depth and makes the painting feel more layered and fun!

Step 10: Blot the Balloons

Just like in Step 6, crumple a clean paper towel or napkin and gently blot each balloon just once or twice while the paint is still wet. This lifts a bit of the color and creates fun, uneven textures. To keep the colors bright and clean, switch to a fresh spot on the paper towel for each balloon.

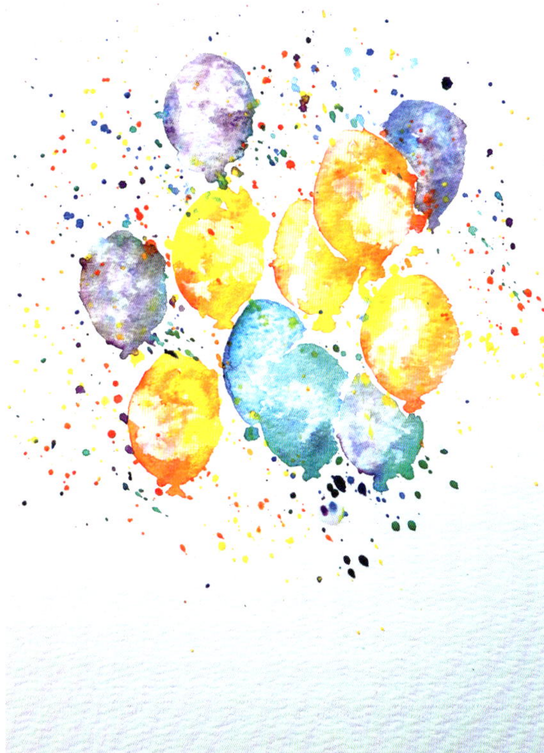

Step 11: Letter Happy Birthday

Once everything is dry, use brush markers to write "Happy Birthday" in a style that matches the playful feel of the balloons. Lightly sketch the words in pencil first if needed, then trace with marker. Keep your hand relaxed and let the letters feel natural.

TIP:

- **Press slightly on downstrokes to make them thicker, and lighten your pressure on upstrokes to make them thinner.**
- **Keep your hand relaxed.**
- **Erase your pencil lines once the ink is dry.**

This final step ties it all together and adds a cheerful finish to your card!

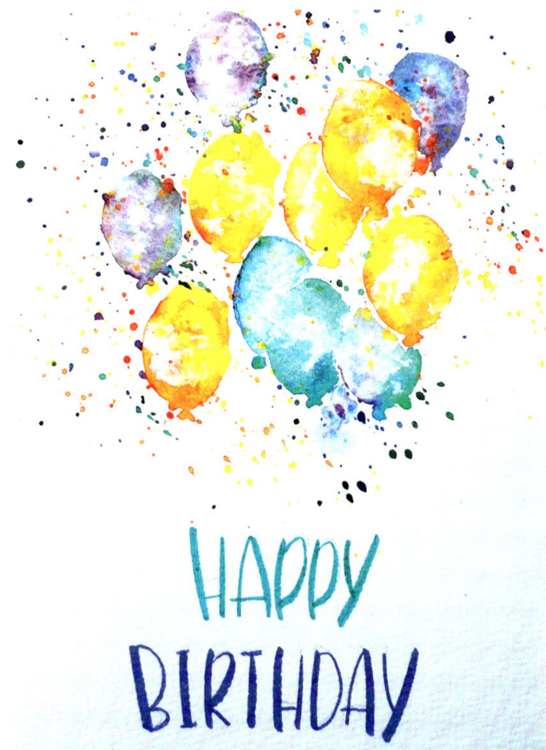

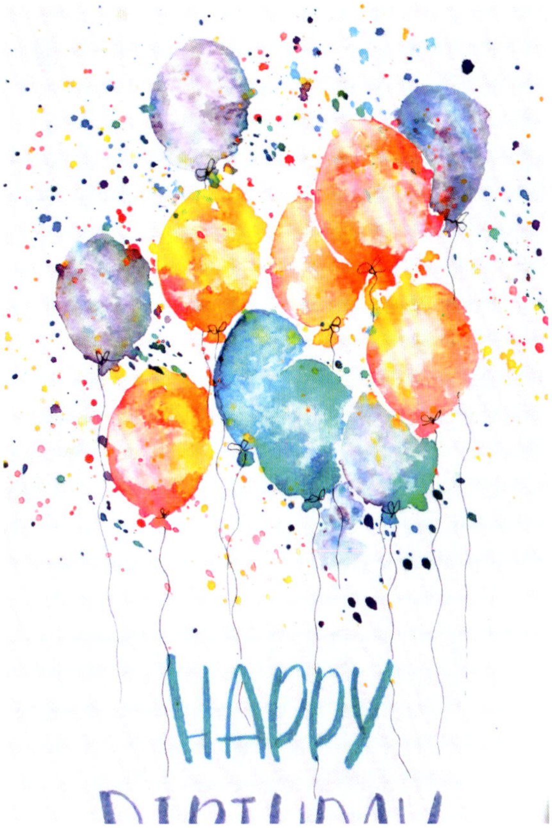

Step 12: Balloon Strings

When the paint and lettering are completely dry, use a 005 black fineliner to draw the balloon strings. Let your hand move freely and allow gentle curves rather than straight lines. Some strings can disappear behind balloons and reappear below to create depth and a layered look.

Try This!

Here are some easy ways to change it up:

- Use just cool colors or just warm colors for a different vibe.
- Try just one color for a simple, clean look.
- Add a little metallic splatter for some shine.
- Use the design on a tag, postcard, or gift bag.
- Add someone's name to make it extra personal.

Small changes can totally change up the card!

What to Write

Simple words for your handmade card. Here are a few ideas to get you started:

- Let the good times float
- Have a sweet and colorful birthday
- Hooray for you!
- Celebrate big
- Make a wish
- Up, up, hooray!
- Sweet birthday wishes
- Wishing you a colorful day
- Wishing you all the fun
- It's your day to shine

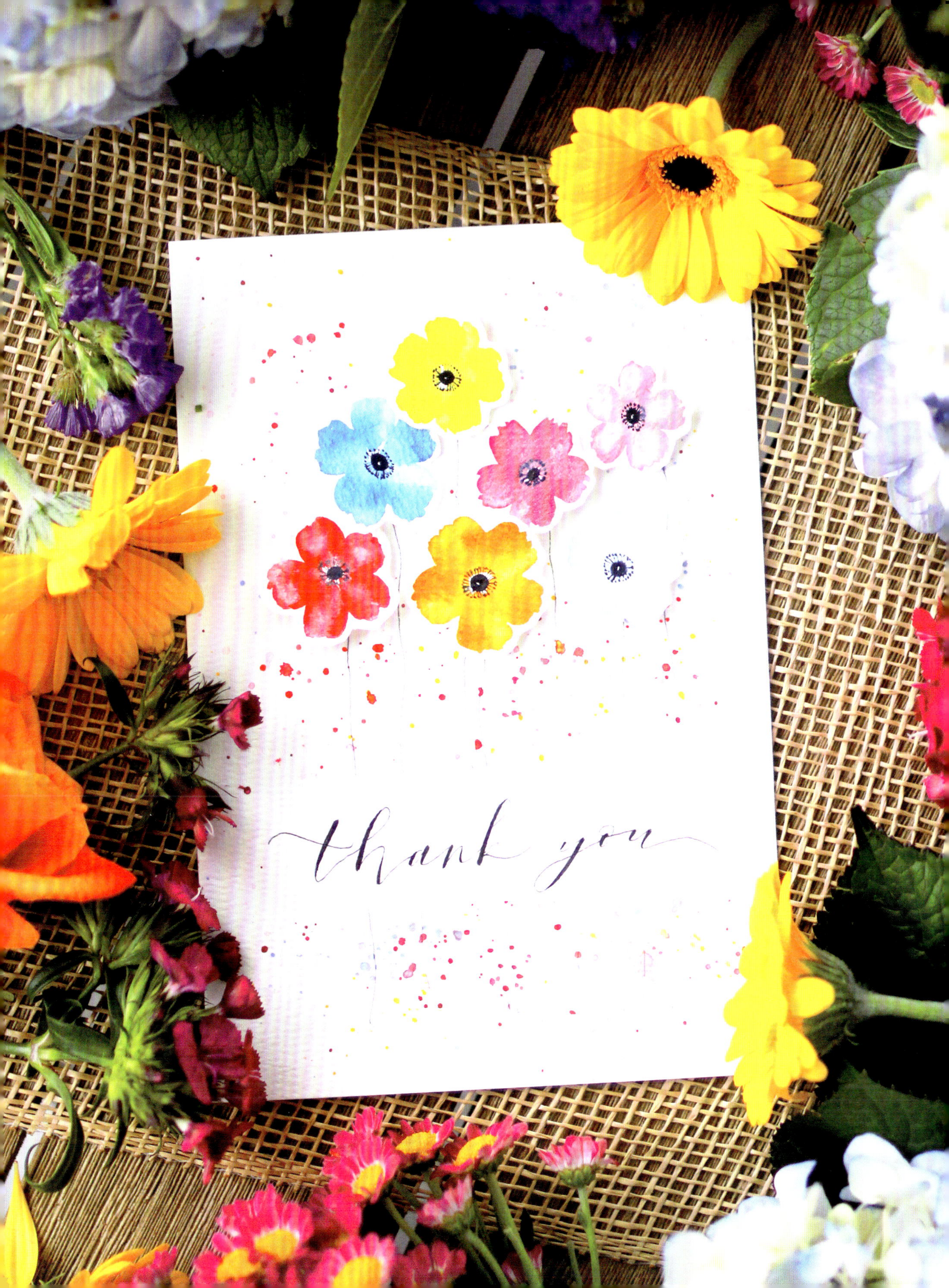
thank you

Thank You Card: Layered Flowers

Paint Colors

(Feel free to substitute similar shades; you don't need to match the exact names.)

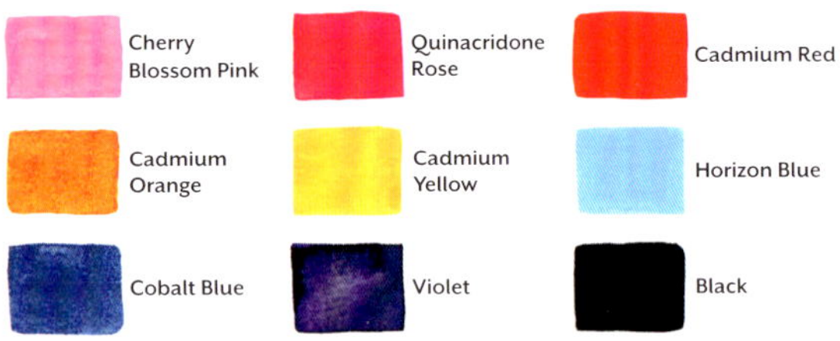

I used a rainbow set of colors, but you can choose any shades you like from your own palette. Look at your color swatches and pick the ones that feel joyful to you.

Tools

(Feel free to use similar supplies; these are just suggestions!)

- Medium brush (size 6–8)
- Small brush (size 2–4)
- Detail brush (size 0 or smaller)
- 005 black fineliner
- Double-sided tape
- Masking tape

Flowers are such a classic way to say thank you, and in this project, we're giving that idea a playful and handmade twist. You'll paint simple watercolor flowers, cut them out, and layer them on a card to create a sweet little 3D bouquet. Add some splatter, write a message, and you've got a card that feels just as thoughtful as fresh flowers on a doorstep.

You can make this card for a friend, a loved one, a family member, or anyone who made your day a little brighter. Use any colors you love, like bright yellow, soft pink, bold red, or a mix of a few. Try one flower in multiple colors or keep it simple with just one. There is no right or wrong here. Just have fun and paint what makes you smile.

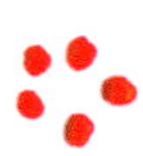

Step 1: Red Dots

With red paint and the tip of a medium round brush, paint five small dots in a loose circle. These dots will act as placeholders for the petals you'll paint next. Leave a little space between each one so your petals have room to form around them. If you are using the tear out card, simply paint over the printed sketch and skip the steps about painting and cutting out flowers.

If you're using the tear-out card, skip any sketching or shaping steps and begin painting where appropriate.

Step 2: Petals

With your brush still loaded with red paint, gently pull each dot outward into a petal shape (see Round Petal Flower, page 28). Use soft, curved strokes to stretch the paint from the center dot, creating five rounded petals.

Step 3: Highlights

While the petals are still damp, use a clean cotton swab to gently dab or roll over a small area of each petal to lift a bit of color (see Lifting, page 13). This creates soft highlight spots and adds a gentle sense of depth to your flower.

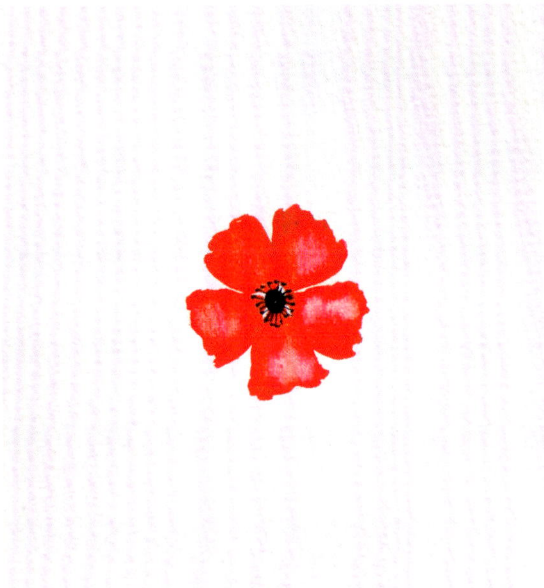

Step 4: Add Details

Make sure your flower is dry or mostly dry before adding the center. Use a detail brush and black paint to make a tiny circle in the middle. Then use just the tip of your brush to dab small dots around the circle. Keep your brush fairly dry so the dots stay clean. Finish by painting a few thin lines that stretch from the center outward to connect with the dots. These little details help the center look lively and textured.

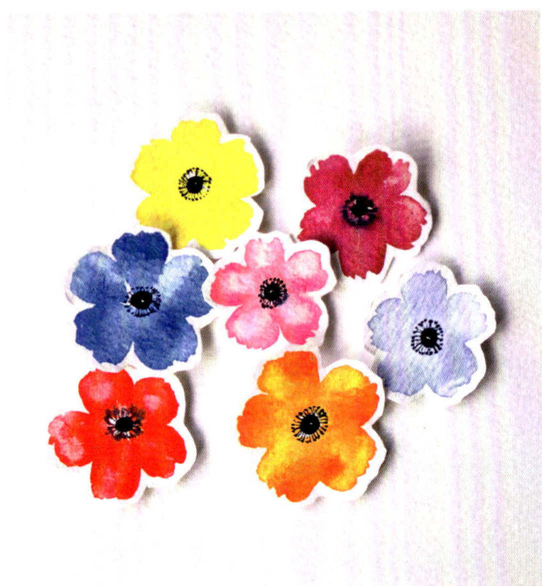

Step 5: Paint More Flowers

Using the same steps as before, paint additional flowers in different colors like yellow, pink, blue, orange, and purple. Once they're completely dry, use scissors to carefully cut around each flower, leaving a small white border around the edges.

Step 6:
Taping and Splattering

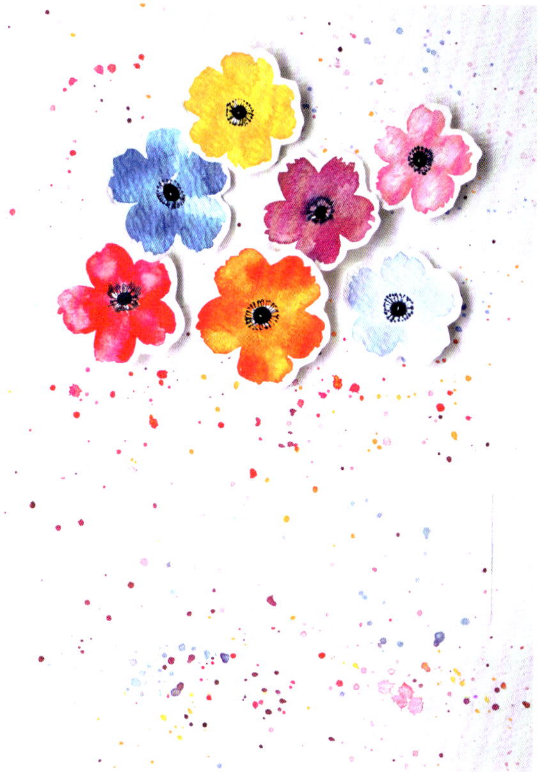

Tape off a small rectangle near the bottom of your card to keep space clean for your message (see Taping, page 17). Then splatter paint across the rest of the card for a playful background (see Splattering, page 17). Load your medium round brush with watery paint, tap it gently over your finger, and let the tiny dots fall across the page.

TIP:

- **Match the splatter colors to your flowers so everything feels connected.**
- **If your tape isn't wide enough, place two strips slightly overlapping and trim the edges for a clean rectangle.**
- **Don't line the flowers up too perfectly. It looks more natural when they're spaced a little unevenly.**

Step 7:
Attach Flowers and Stems

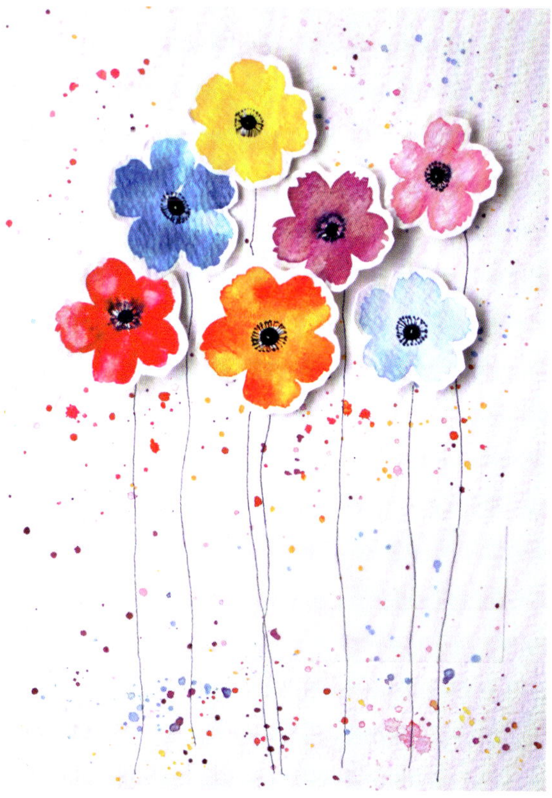

Once the splatters are dry (you can use a heat tool if you're in a hurry), stick on your cut-out flowers using double-sided tape to give them a little pop and a soft 3D feel. Next, grab a 005 black pen and draw long, loose stems that trail from each flower down toward the bottom of the card.

TIP:

- **Let the stems curve or wiggle a bit for a playful feel.**
- **Use a light touch with your pen so the lines stay soft and delicate.**

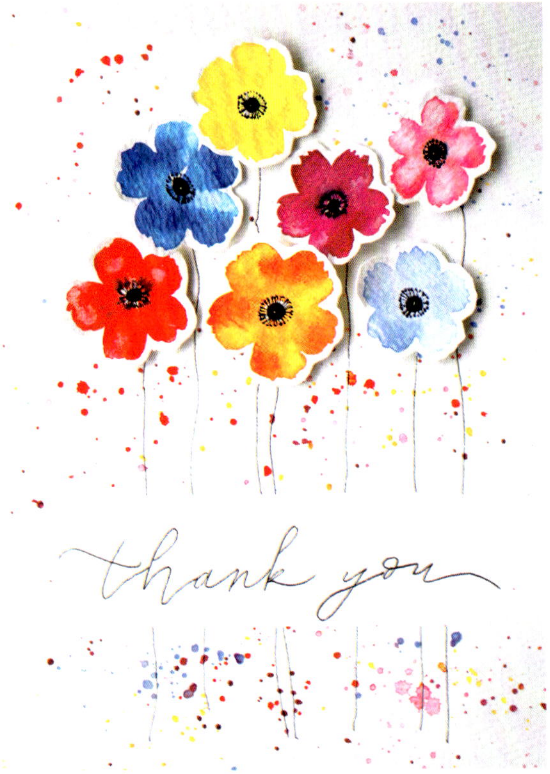

Step 8: Lettering

Gently peel off the tape to reveal the clean space you saved for your words. Lightly sketch your message in pencil first if that helps, then go over it with a pen once you're happy with the placement. For a simple styled look, thicken only the downstrokes (see Faux Calligraphy, page 30).

TIP:

- **Keep your lettering centered or balanced with the flowers so everything feels polished.**

Try This!

Here are some fun and easy ways to change it up:

- Use just cool colors or just warm colors for a different vibe.
- Try just one color for a simple, clean look.
- Add a little metallic splatter for some shine.
- Use the design on a tag, postcard, or gift bag.
- Add someone's name to make it extra personal.

What to Write

Simple words for your handmade card. Here are a few ideas to get you started:

- Thanks so much
- Grateful for you
- You made my day
- Appreciate you
- Many thanks
- Thanks a bunch
- Sending thanks
- With all my thanks
- So very thankful
- Thanks a bloom

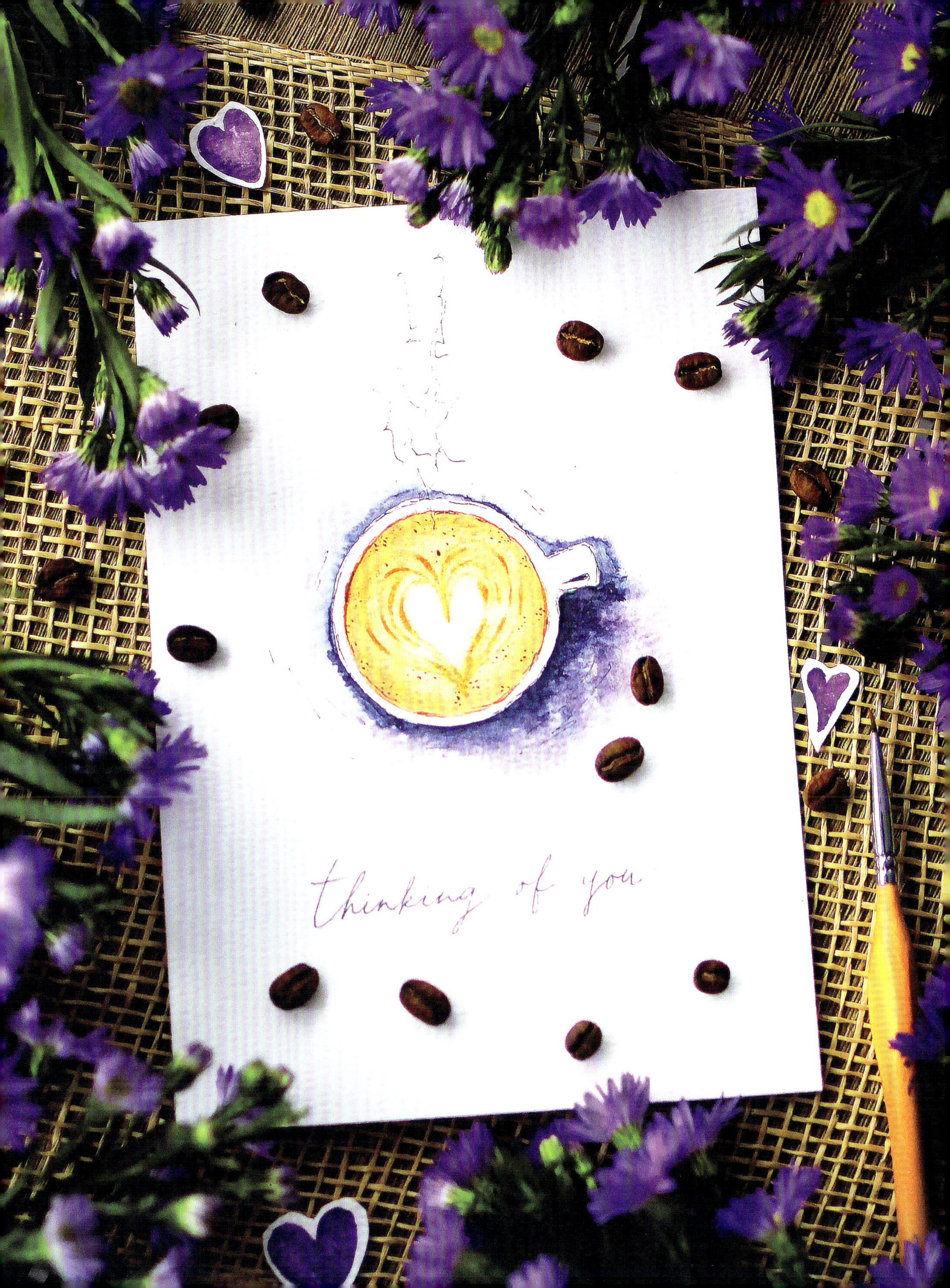
thinking of you

Thinking of You Card: Latte Love

Paint Colors

(Feel free to substitute similar shades; you don't need to match the exact names.)

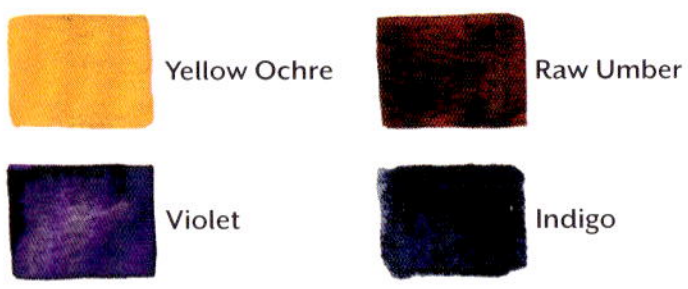

Tools Used

(Feel free to use similar supplies; these are just suggestions!)

- Pencil
- Medium round brush (size 4–6)
- Detail brush (size 0 or smaller)
- 005 black fineliner

You don't need a holiday or big event to send a card. Sometimes, the most meaningful gestures are the small ones. The kind that show up quietly and say, "I see you," "You matter," or "I'm thinking of you today."

A "Thinking of You" card is a gentle way to offer comfort, encouragement, or connection. You might send one to a friend who's having a tough week, someone you haven't talked to in a while, or someone who just popped into your mind.

I chose a latte for this project because it's something ordinary and comforting. It's something we reach for on a slow morning or in the middle of a busy day. That's what this card is meant to be too: a little pause, a little calm, a little kindness.

To create the heart in the foam, we'll use one of watercolor's most popular techniques: wet on wet. It just means your paper is a little wet when you paint on it, which helps the colors spread softly without sharp edges. It's perfect for this kind of design because it creates that soft, blended look you see in real latte art, where the milk and coffee gently swirl together before they settle.

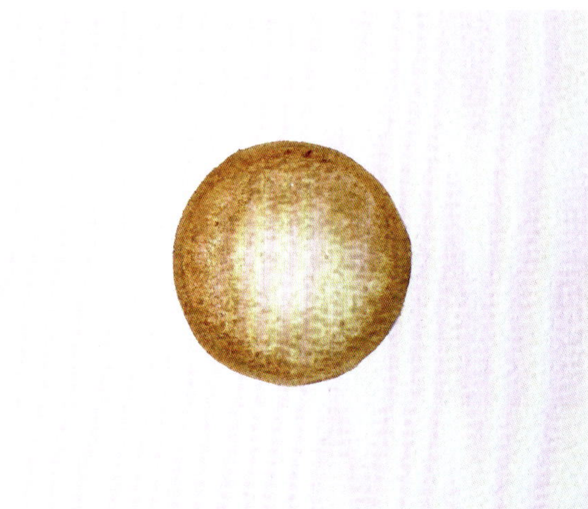

Step 1: Create the Latte Base

Lightly sketch a circle in the center of your card. You can trace a lid, jar, or anything round. Or use the tear-out card as your start.

Mix a warm coffee color using mostly raw umber with a small touch of yellow ochre (see Color Mixing, page 12). Adjust with a little more yellow ochre or water until you reach a soft coffee-brown you like, then fill the circle with a smooth wash.

While the paint is still damp, gently lift color from the center with a cotton swab (Q-tip) to create a soft, lighter glow (see Soft Center Glow, page 13).

If you're using the tear-out card, skip any sketching or shaping steps and begin painting where appropriate.

Step 2: Add the Heart Design

When the circle is damp but no longer shiny, use a detail brush and raw umber to paint a small heart in the center with soft curved strokes. Then add a few more hearts around it, each one slightly larger than the last. The shapes do not need to be perfect or fully connected. Small gaps between strokes help the design feel natural, like real latte art.

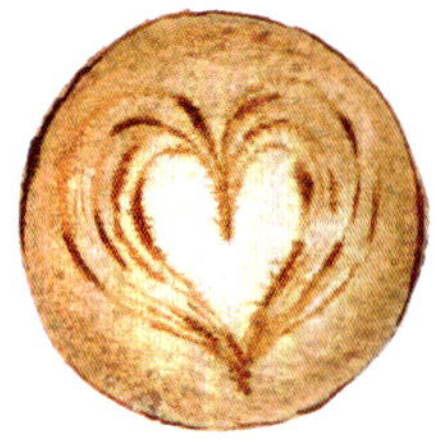

For more contrast, add another layer of raw umber in a few areas of the hearts. Once everything is dry, use the same detail brush to lightly outline the edge of the circle. Keep your hand relaxed.

Step 3: Sketch the Cup

Once the circle is completely dry, lightly sketch the outline of the cup around it. Use the painted circle as your guide, leaving a small, even space around it to suggest the thickness of the cup's rim. Follow the curve all the way around and add a small handle on one side. I waited to sketch the cup until after painting the circle so I could base the shape on what I had already painted. But if you traced your circle with something like a lid or cookie cutter and already know the size, you can sketch the cup first, before painting. Keep your pencil lines light.

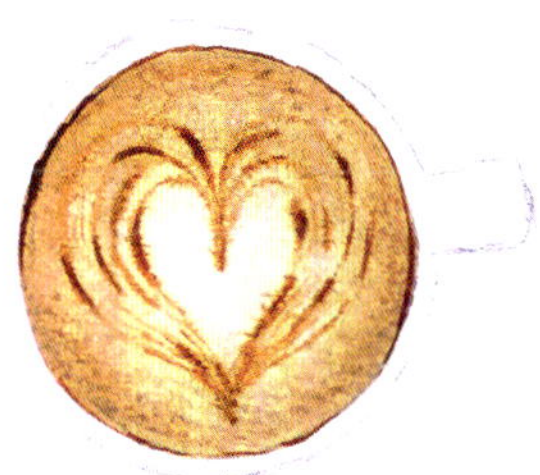

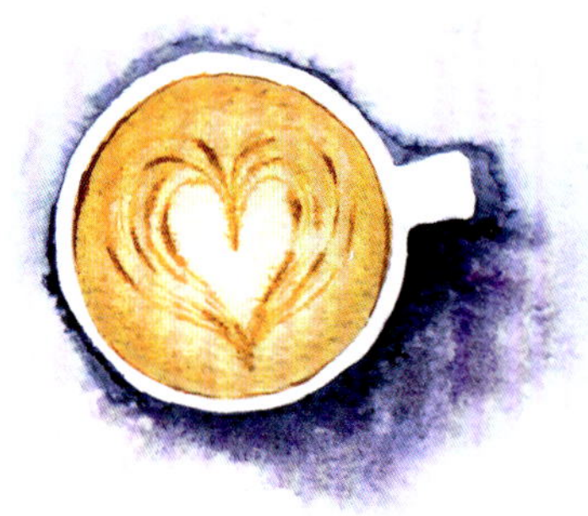

Step 4: Add the Shadow

Wet the area just outside the pencil line with clean water and a medium round brush. While the paper is still damp, drop in a light purple mix made from violet. Add plenty of water so the color looks soft and gentle. Touch the paint near the cup and let it spread outward into the damp paper.

If you want more depth, mix a little Indigo into the purple and add it closer to the base of the cup and under the handle. Keep the darkest color nearest the cup so the shadow feels natural.

If the shadow feels too strong, gently soften the edges with a clean damp brush or a Q-tip.

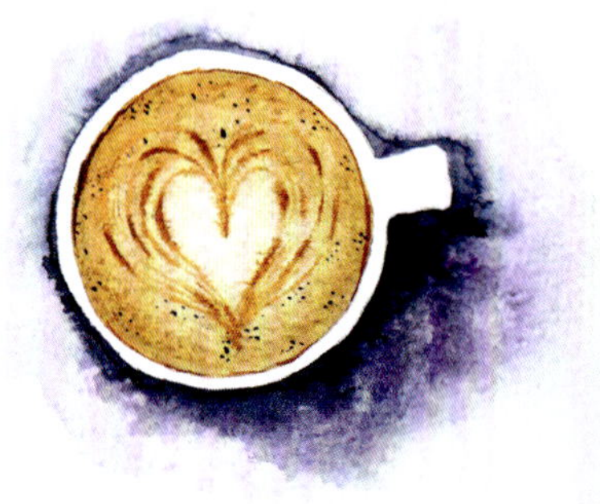

Step 5: Add Tiny Dots

When the painting is dry, load a detail brush with raw umber, using more paint and less water for a richer color. Gently tap the surface of the drink to create small dots that suggest tiny bubbles in the foam.

Vary the size by pressing slightly harder or softer. A mix of small and slightly larger dots helps the drink feel more realistic.

Step 6: Add Ink and Steam

When everything is completely dry, take a thin black pen and outline the cup. Trace the inside and outside edges of the rim and handle, keeping your touch light. It is okay to leave small gaps. Broken or uneven lines add character and help the drawing feel more natural.

Above the cup, draw a few wavy lines to suggest steam. Let your pen move upward in a soft curving motion. The lines can be slightly scribbly or uneven to give the steam a gentle, drifting feel.

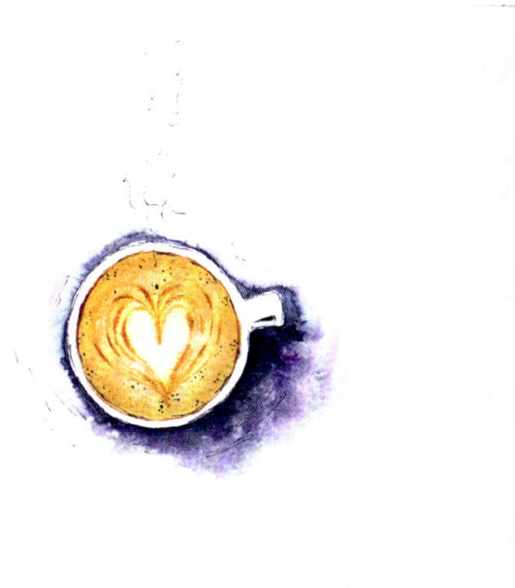

Step 7: Lettering

Make sure your painting is completely dry before you begin. Lightly sketch your words in pencil first so you can adjust the size and placement before using ink. To help keep the letters straight, draw a faint guideline and erase it after the ink has dried. If you want your message centered, find the middle of your page and make a tiny pencil dot. Start your message just a little to the left of that dot so the full phrase sits nicely beneath the cup.

I chose a simple lowercase script because it matches the cozy handmade feel of this card. Use a thin black pen and write slowly, letting your letters stretch and curve in a relaxed way. Keep your touch light and let the letters flow. Just keep it simple.

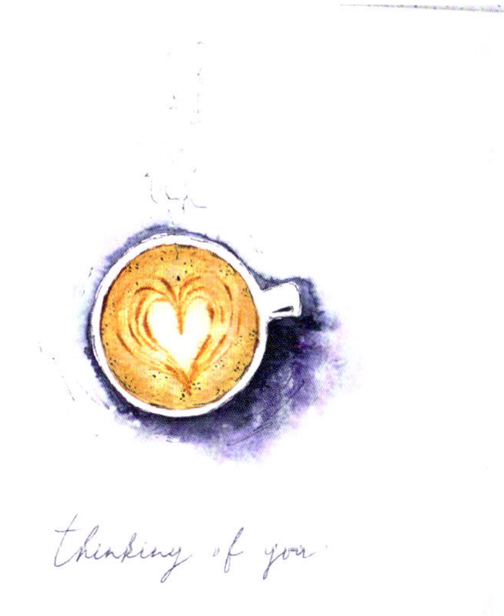

Try This!

Want to give your latte card a new twist? Here are some fun ways to change it up:

- Add a small sprig of lavender or a daisy beside the cup.
- Turn the steam into soft lettering with words like hi or love in a curvy, drifting style.
- Change the pattern in the foam to a smiley face or word instead of hearts.
- Add a cinnamon stick or berries beside the cup.
- Write your message along the curve of the saucer.

What to Write

Simple words for your handmade card. Here are a few ideas to get you started:

- Just because
- You've been on my mind
- A little hello
- Miss you
- Sending a hug in a mug
- A little love, one cup at a time
- Coffee soon?
- Let's catch up soon
- You warm my heart
- I brewed up a little happy for you

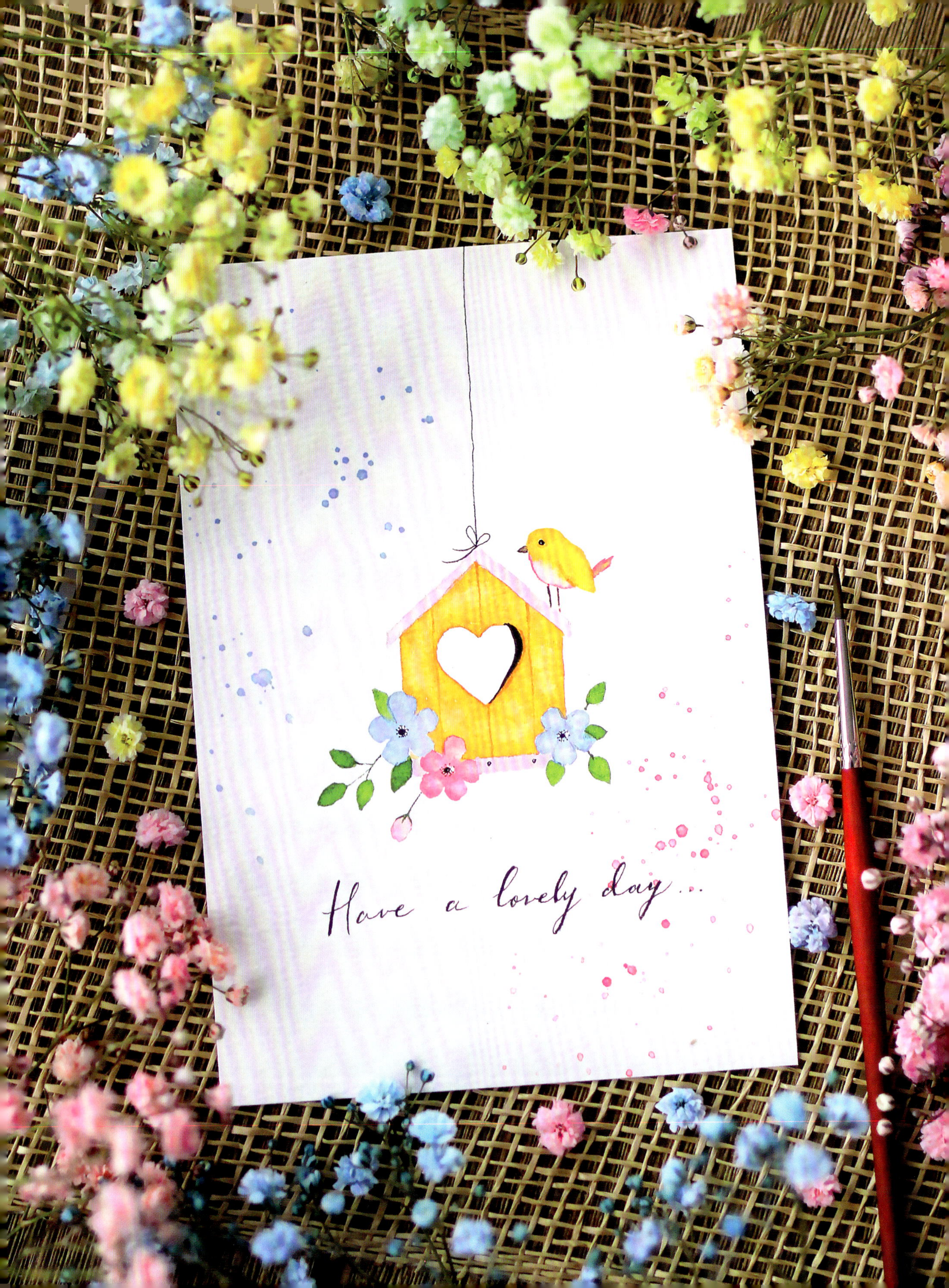
Have a lovely day...

Anytime Card: Birdhouse

Paint Colors

(Feel free to substitute similar shades; you don't need to match the exact names.)

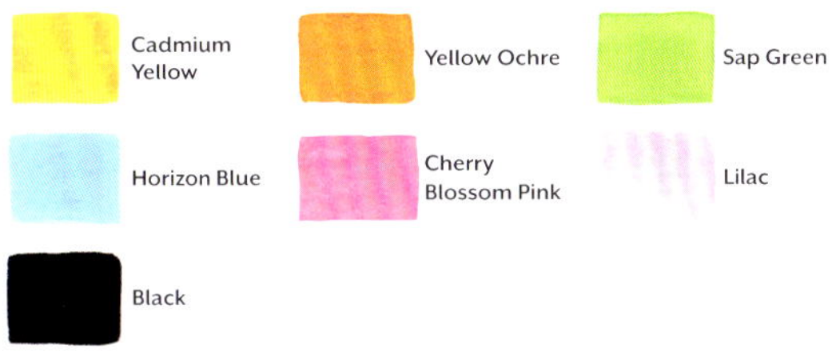

Tools Used

(Feel free to use similar supplies; these are just suggestions!)

- Pencil
- Medium round brush (size 6-8)
- Small round brush (size 2–4)
- Detail brush (size 0 or smaller)
- 005 black fineliner

This cheerful birdhouse card is a thoughtful way to send a kind message for any occasion. The birdhouse and bird form a gentle, charming image that pairs naturally with a "Have a Lovely Day" greeting. This beginner friendly project focuses on simple shapes and clear steps rather than perfect drawing skills, making it easy to follow and personalize as you paint.

Step 1: Light Sketch

Use a pencil to lightly sketch a small birdhouse in the center of your card. Begin with a square or rectangle for the house, then add a triangle on top for the roof. Inside the house, draw a heart shape for the opening. Add a line above the roof so it looks like the birdhouse is hanging. Place a little bird on one side of the roof so it feels natural. Around the bottom of the house, sketch a few flowers and leaves in different sizes. Let some leaves stretch out a little longer to the sides. This will give the card a soft and flowing look, as if the house is surrounded by a real cluster of plants.

If you're using the tear-out card, skip any sketching or shaping steps and begin painting where appropriate.

Step 2: Paint the Flowers

Paint a few flowers around the base of the birdhouse using light watery colors. Start with the horizon blue flowers. If you sketched the flowers, fill in each petal. If not, create each flower by pressing the tip of your brush into rounded petal shapes turning your paper as needed (see Tiny Round Petal Flower, page 29). Paint the cherry blossom pink flowers the same way and add one pink bud by making a single petal shape, then gently lift a little color from the center with a Q-tip to keep it soft.

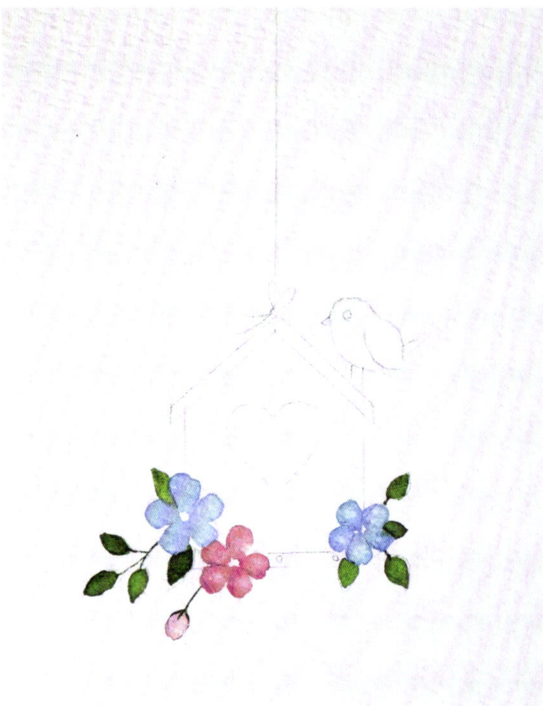

Step 3: Paint the Leaves

Paint the leaves around the flowers using a small round brush and sap green. Follow the shapes of your sketch or add them in freely, keeping your brushstrokes light and smooth. To make each leaf, paint one curved stroke for one side, then add a second curved stroke that meets it at the tip. This creates a soft rounded leaf shape (see Two-Stroke Leaf, page 24). Try making a few leaves longer or angled in different directions so they feel natural and let a few extend outward to give the cluster a flowing look. Paint a few of the leaves and stems with a bit of stronger sap green, a mix with more paint and less water.

Step 4: Paint the Birdhouse

Paint the main part of the birdhouse with yellow ochre. Start with a light layer, then add a bit more color along the edges while the paint is still damp so the house looks softly shaded. Keep the center lighter and gently lift a little paint with a Q-tip if you'd like a softer look. Lifting creates a soft, natural texture (see Lifting, page 13).

Leave the heart-shaped opening white and let the house dry completely.

Step 5: Paint the Roof and Base

When the house is dry, paint the roof and bottom trim in lilac. Paint one section at a time and let each part dry before moving to the next so the colors stay clean. If any area looks too strong, you can gently lift a little paint with a Q-tip as needed to keep the color soft and even.

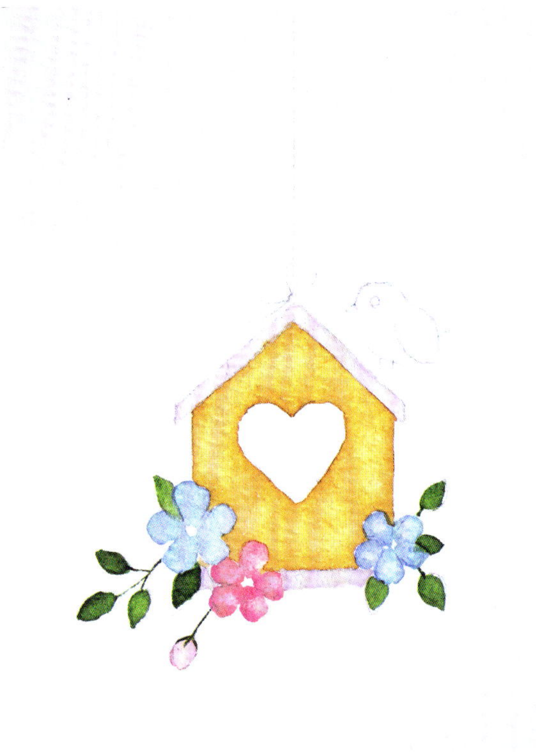

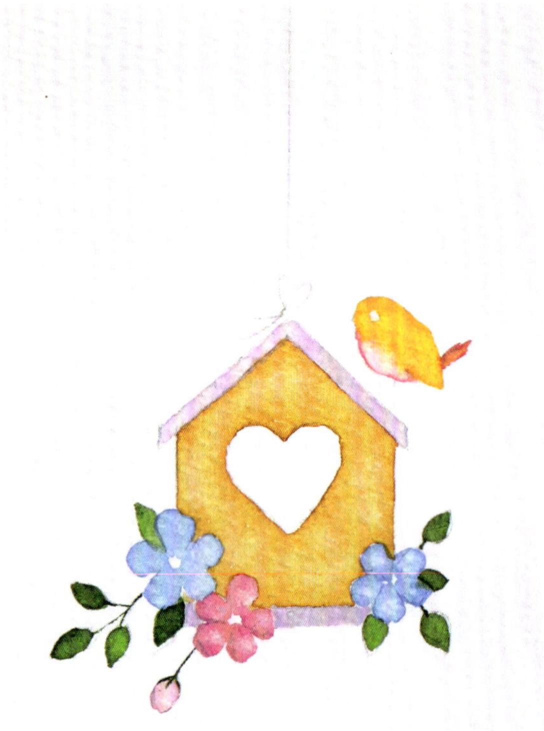

Step 6: Paint the Bird

Paint the little bird on the roof using cadmium yellow for the body. Leave a tiny white spot for the eye so the bird looks bright and full of life. For the belly, use cherry blossom pink and let it meet the yellow so the two colors blend softly where they touch. While the paint is still damp, use a Q-tip to gently lift some color from the belly and parts of the yellow body. This keeps the center areas light while the edges stay darker, giving the bird a soft rounded look. Once the body is dry, add a small pink tail in cherry blossom pink.

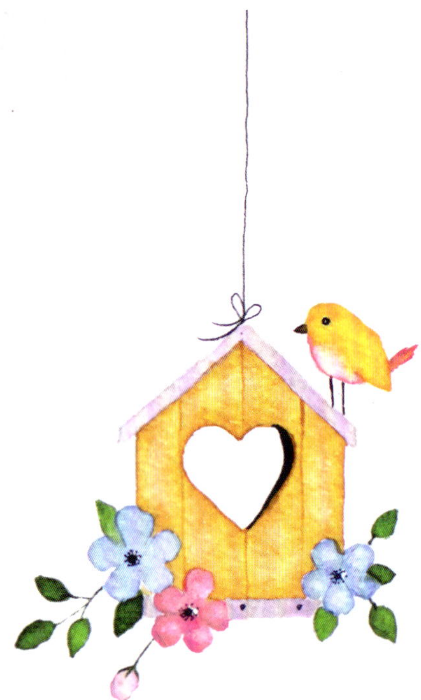

Step 7: Add Ink Details

Once everything is completely dry, use a 005 fineliner and keep your touch light. Outline part of the heart opening and softly fill it in to suggest a gentle shadow inside the birdhouse. Add two thin lines for the bird's legs so it appears perched on the roof.

For the flowers, draw a small circle in the center of each bloom, then lightly connect a few thin lines outward. These marks don't need to be exact, just a few simple lines will bring the flowers to life.

Trace over the hanging string where it meets the roof and add a tiny bow so it looks tied in place. Add a small circle for the bird's eye, leaving it white, and lightly define the beak if needed. If you like, add a few tiny dots along the bottom of the birdhouse to suggest small nails. These final details are optional but add a sweet, handmade finish.

Step 8: Splattering

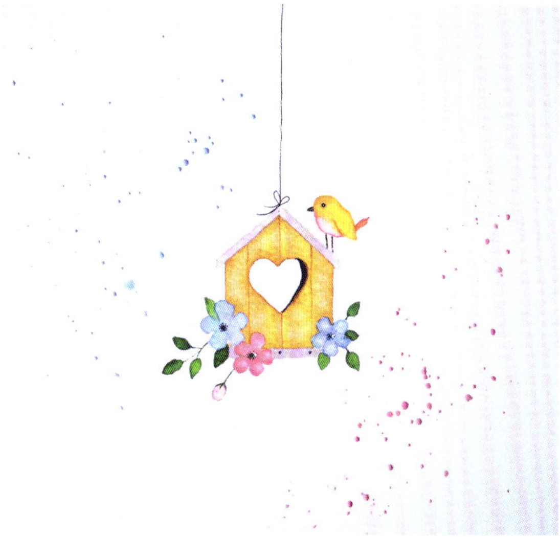

Add a playful background with splattering. Dip your brush into watery horizon blue and tap it gently to make light splatters in the top-left corner. Then use cherry blossom pink to add a few soft splatters in the bottom-right corner. A bigger brush will make larger drops, and a smaller brush will make finer ones. If you want to keep the splashes off the main painting, place a torn paper towel or scrap paper over the birdhouse and flowers.

The amount of paint on your brush also changes the look. A wetter brush will create darker splatters, while less water will create lighter splatters. For more ideas on splattering (see Splattering, page 17). Do not worry about making them even or exact. The random spots are what make this step feel playful and full of life.

Step 9: Lettering

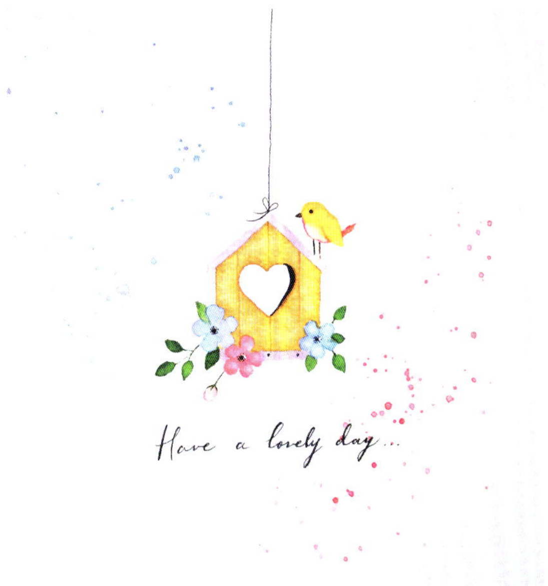

Finish your card by adding the words "Have a lovely day" or any message you like under the birdhouse. Lightly mark the center of your card with a pencil. Sketch the words first to check spacing, then trace over them with a pen. Simple script with soft, rounded strokes feels warm and handmade. Plain print letters look clean and sweet.

If you would like to try a calligraphy look, you can gently thicken the downward strokes of your script (see Faux Calligraphy, page 30). Most important of all, keep it relaxed. Your own writing will make the message personal and full of heart.

Try This!

Want to give your card a new twist? Here are some fun ways to change it up:

- Paint the birdhouse in a different color such as soft blue or bright red.
- Add more flowers or change the colors to match the season.
- Add tiny clouds or a light blue wash in the background.
- Use splatters in one color for a softer look or mix two colors for extra playfulness.
- Fill the heart opening with a soft color instead of leaving it blank.

What to Write

Simple words for your handmade card. Here are a few ideas to get you started:

- With heartfelt sympathy
- Wishing you healing and calm
- May each new day bring more healing
- You make me smile
- So glad we are friends
- You brighten my day
- Holding you in my heart
- A little note for you
- Hope today feels bright
- You are on my mind

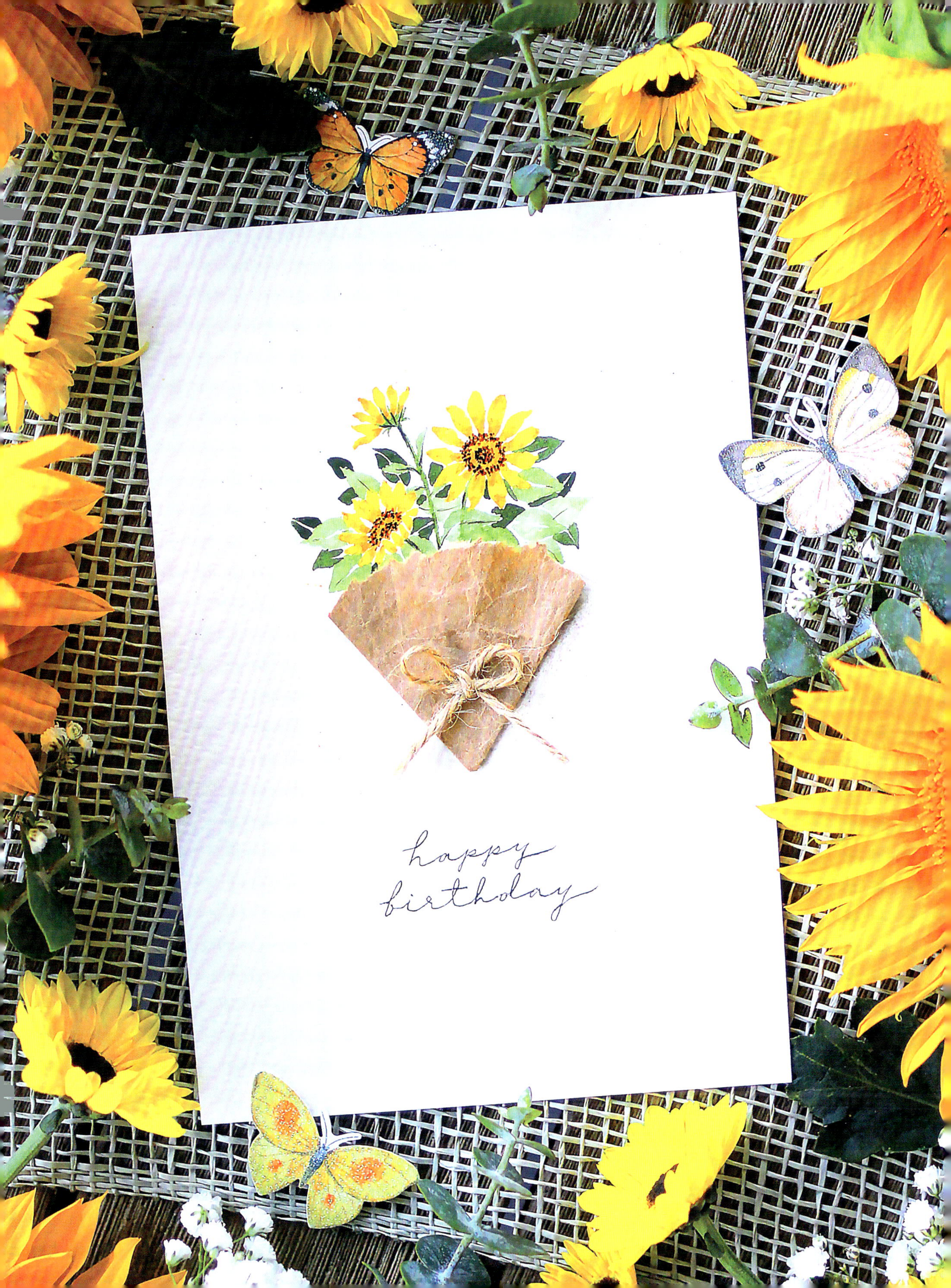
happy
birthday

Birthday Card: Sunflower Bouquet

Paint Colors

(Feel free to substitute similar shades; you don't need to match the exact names.)

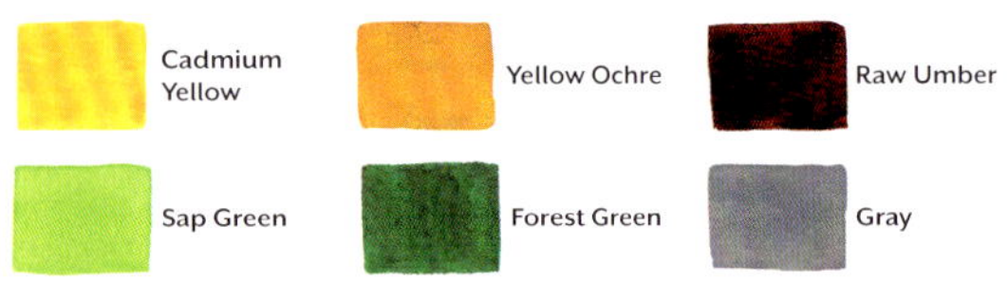

Tools Used

(Feel free to use similar supplies; these are just suggestions!)

- Pencil
- Medium round brush (size 6-8)
- Small round brush (size 2–4)
- Detail brush (size 0 or smaller)
- 005 black fineliner
- Kraft paper or grocery bag
- Jute string or thin twine

There is something about sunflowers that instantly feels like a celebration. They turn toward the light and symbolize warmth, hope, and positivity, which makes them a lovely choice for a birthday card.

In this project, we will paint a simple sunflower bouquet using light pencil shapes to plan the flowers before letting the watercolor flow. The loose petals, soft greens, and brown paper wrap all come together in an easy and relaxed way that beginners can follow without pressure.

Let your brushstrokes stay light and natural because sunflowers look their best when they are not too exact. This keeps the bouquet feeling warm and full of life.

Step 1: Light Sketch

The tear-out card already includes lightly sketched sunflowers for you. If you are drawing your own, lightly sketch small circles to mark the centers of the sunflowers. Use this circle as a guide and sketch a larger circle around it to mark the size of the petals. For the sunflower that is turned slightly, draw the center as a soft, flattened circle, then add a larger shape that follows the same curve. This helps show the flower from an angle. Above these shapes, draw a half circle to show a fully side-facing flower. At the bottom, sketch a simple triangle to show where the paper wrap will go. Keep all pencil lines light so they disappear under the watercolor.

If you're using the tear-out card, skip any sketching or shaping steps and begin painting where appropriate.

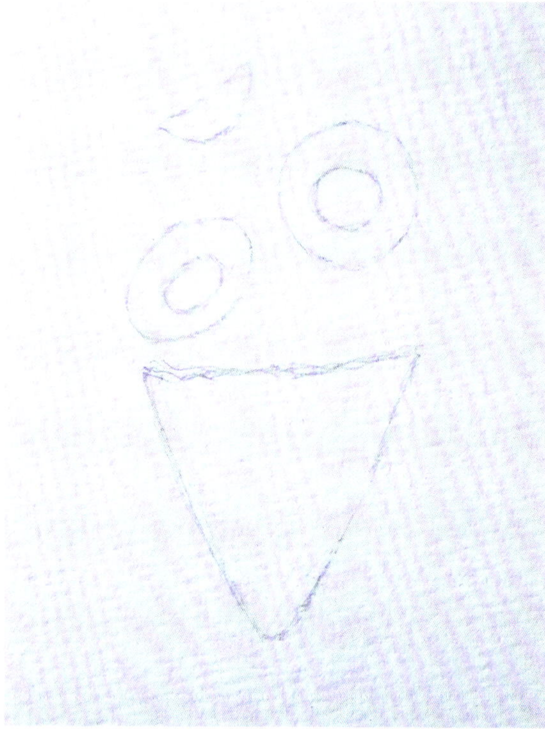

Step 2: Paint the Flower Center

Mix yellow ochre with a small touch of raw umber to create a warm brown (see Color Mixing, page 12). Load your brush with this color and use just the tip to fill in the small center circle from your sketch. Keep the edges soft and natural. The circle does not need to be exact.

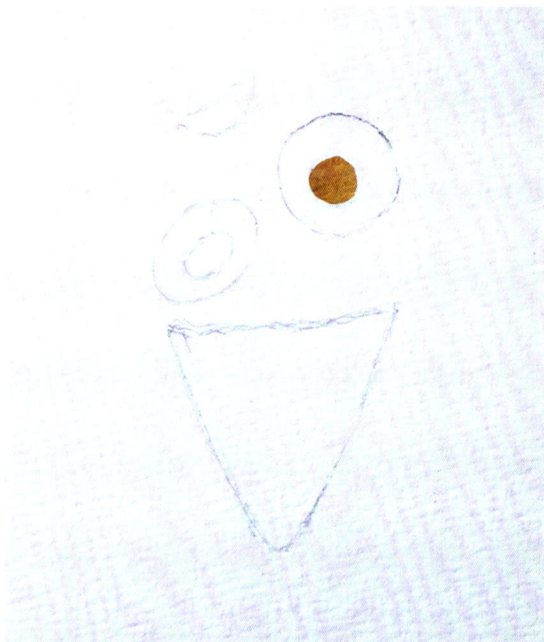

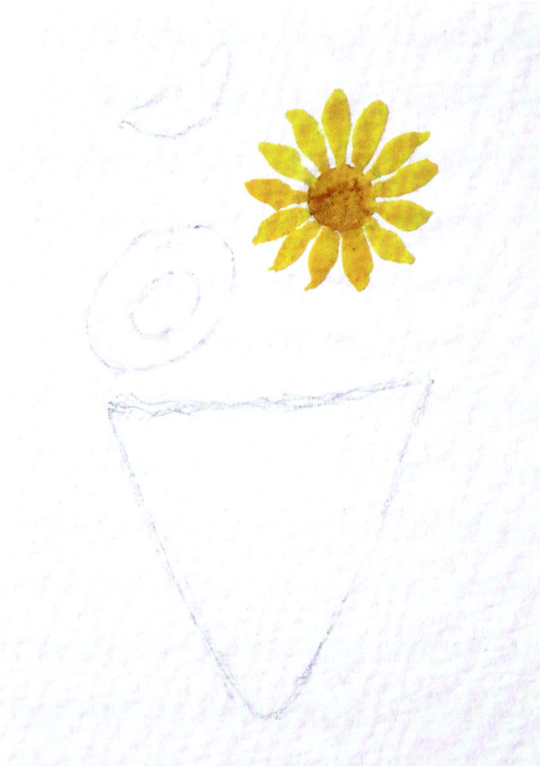

Step 3: Paint the Petals

Using a small round brush and cadmium yellow, paint each petal with one smooth outward stroke (see One-Stroke Leaf, page 23). Start at the edge of the center and pull your brush outward so the base stays narrow and the tip becomes slightly wider. Lift your brush at the end of the stroke to make a soft point. Leave a thin bit of white space between the bases of the petals to keep them separate and give the flower a bright, open look. It is fine if the center is still slightly wet. A little blending at the base will make the petals look soft and natural.

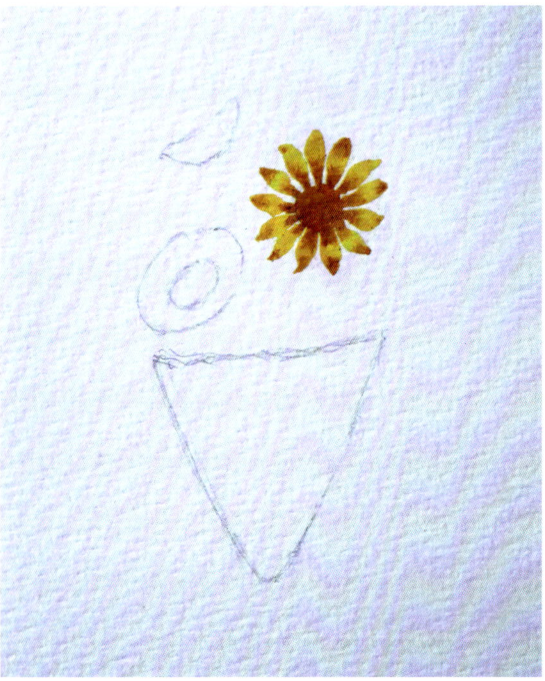

Step 4: Deepen the Petals

While the petals are still slightly damp, pick up a small amount of the same warm brown you used for the center. Touch this color lightly to the base of a few petals and let it spread on its own. You can also place a small touch near the tips for gentle variation. Then use a clean Q-tip to lightly lift a bit of paint in the center of the petals to bring back a lighter area (see Lifting, page 13). This step also helps if any areas look too dark.

Step 5: Add Center Dots

When the center of the flower is completely dry, load a detail brush with a stronger value of raw umber (use more paint and less water). Use just the tip of your brush to place tiny dots around the outer edge of the center (see Dotting, page 21). Add a few more dots inside the center to form a soft, round cluster. You can also place a few dots just outside the center on the base of the petals. This helps the center blend naturally into the petals. Keep your pressure light so the dots stay small and delicate.

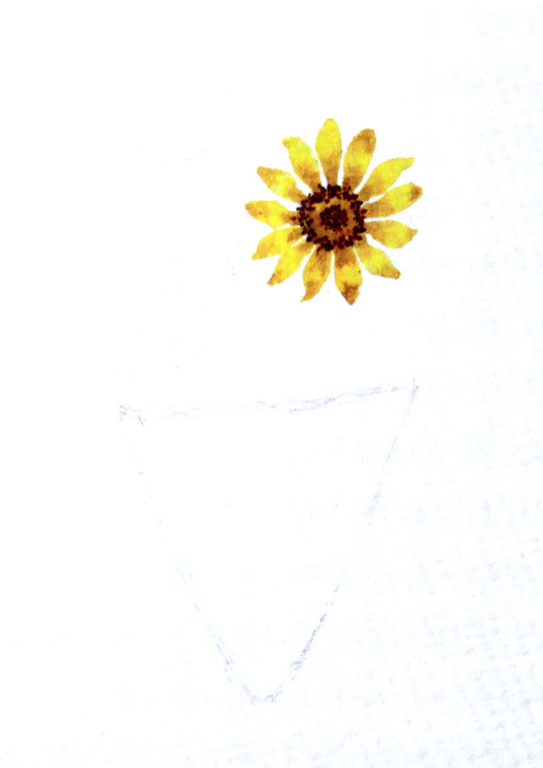

Step 6: Side-Facing Flower

Use cadmium yellow and place the center slightly off to one side. Paint the front petals and the back petals longer to show the flower turning. It is completely fine if the shorter front petals end up a bit shorter than your original sketch. The sketch is only a guide, and you can adjust the petal lengths as you paint. Use one smooth outward stroke for each petal and leave a thin white space at the base. It is fine if the tips of the petals touch or slightly overlap.

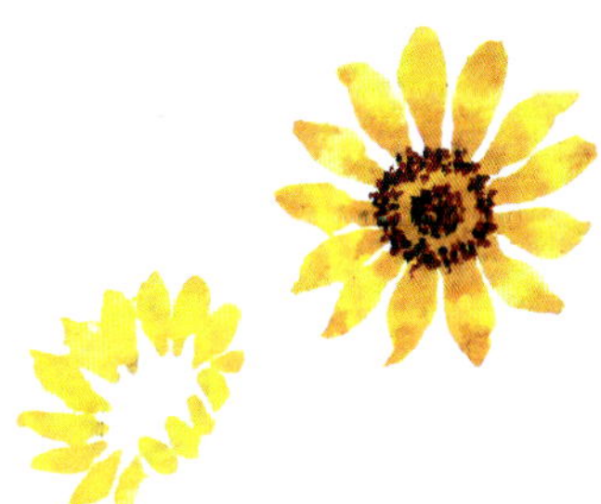

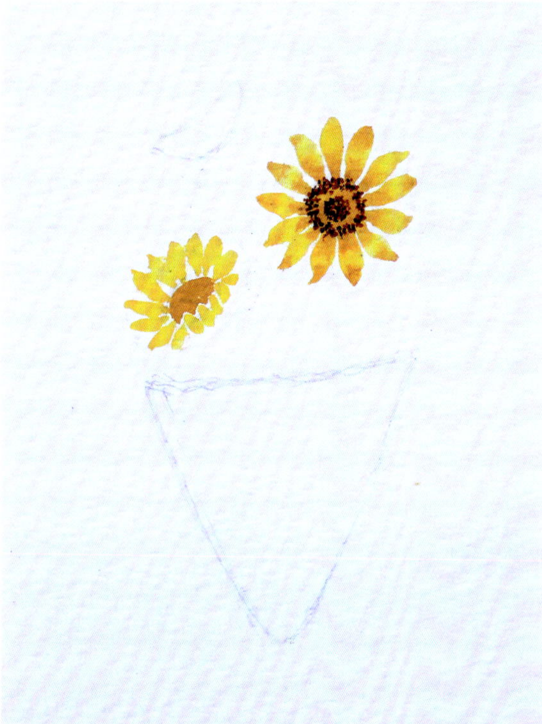

Step 7: Side-Flower Center

Use a small round brush and the same warm brown to paint the center of the side flower. Paint carefully around the bottom petals so you don't cover them. Since this flower is turned a little, the center will look more like an oval than a circle. Keep your brushstrokes light so the color blends softly into the petals.

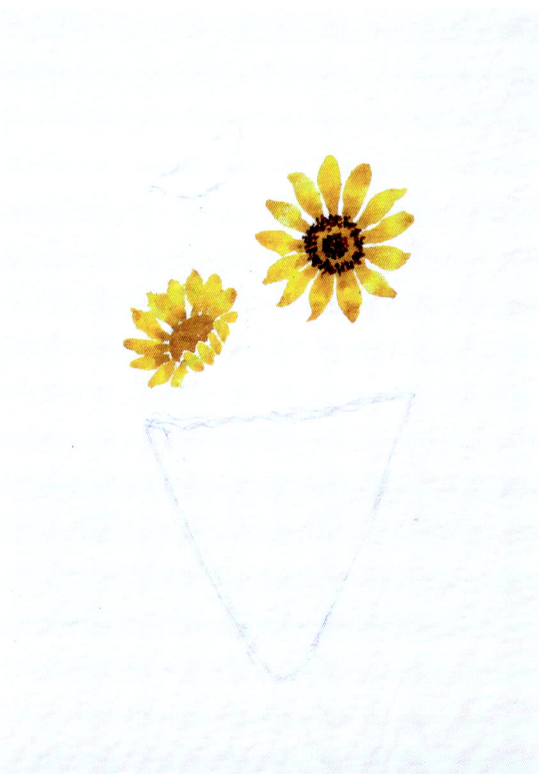

Step 8: Add a Little Depth

Use the same warm brown you used for the center, and drop a small amount of that color at the base of a few petals. Let the paint spread on its own. You do not need to touch every petal, just add it in a few places for gentle variation. If the petals are dry, lightly wet them with a clean damp brush first so the color blends smoothly. You can lift a little paint from the center of the petals the same way you did in Step 4 to bring back a soft lighter area. This keeps the petals looking bright and natural.

Step 9: Add Center Dots

Once the center of the side flower is dry, load a detail brush with raw umber using more paint and less water. Hold your brush straight up and gently tap the tip to make small dots around the outer edge of the center, just like you did in Step 5. Add a few more dots inside the middle in a loose round shape. Try to keep your hand steady and use a light touch so the dots stay soft. It is perfectly fine if some of them go a little past the edge and touch the petals. This helps the center blend in naturally.

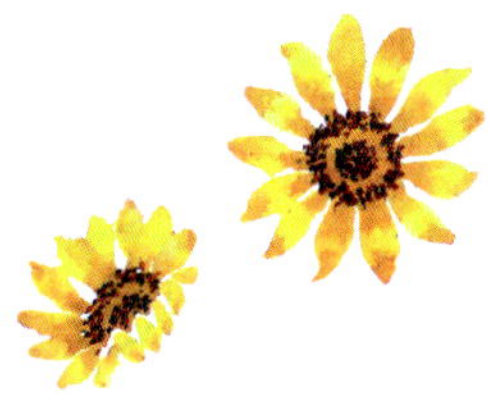

Step 10: Paint the Turning Flower

This sunflower is facing slightly away from us and turned to the side, so the petals in the middle appear taller while the ones on the sides are shorter. That small difference gives the feeling that the flower is turning away. Using a small round brush and cadmium yellow, pull each petal out from the center, leaving a bit of white space near the base to help the petals stand apart and keep the flower feeling light and natural. While the paint is still damp, drop a touch of yellow ochre at the base and tips of a few petals. The soft blend of colors adds depth and makes the sunflower feel full of life.

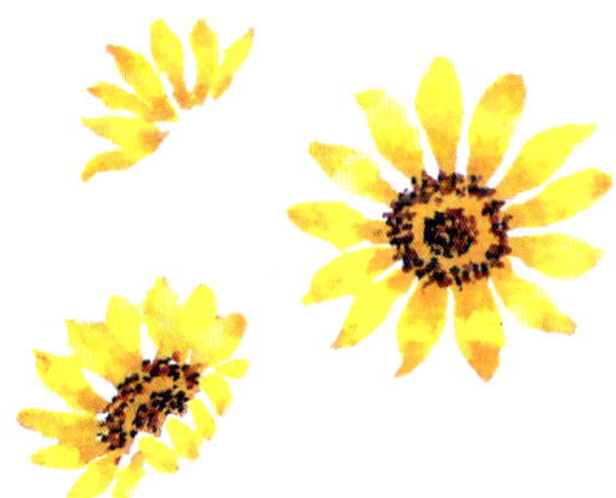

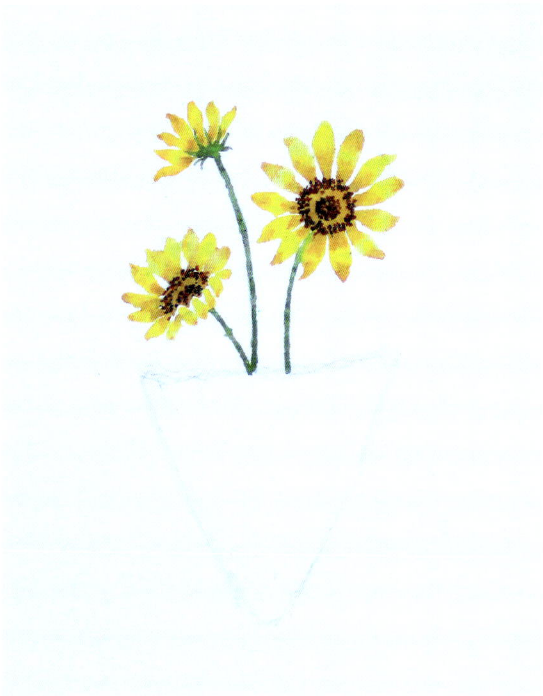

Step 11: Add Stems

Use a detail brush and sap green to add the stems. Start from the base of each flower and draw the stem down toward the triangle shape. Keep your touch light so the lines stay thin and flow naturally (see Thin Lines, page 21). Add a few tiny leaves right under the top flower where the base is visible, using quick curved strokes. While the paint is still damp, drop in a bit of forest green at the base of each flower and near the top edge of the triangle. You can use a clean Q-tip to lightly dab some areas while the paint is still damp. This lifts a little color and creates soft natural variations in the green, giving your bouquet a light fresh look.

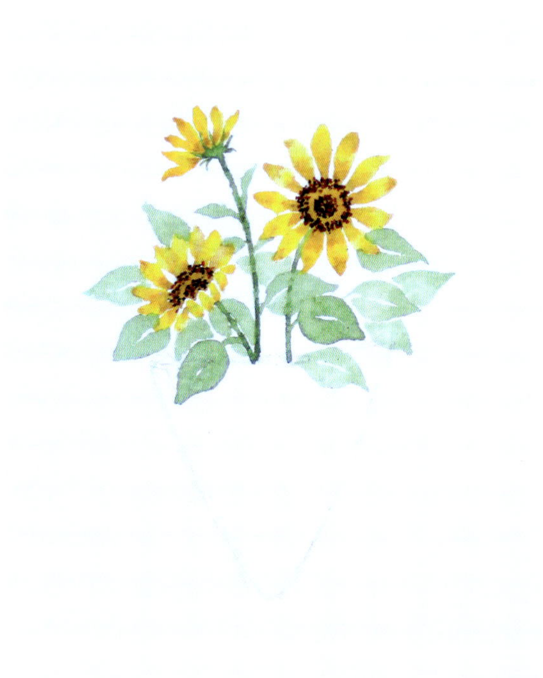

Step 12: Paint the Leaves

Use a medium round brush and sap green to paint the leaves. Start at the base of each leaf and paint one side at a time, leaving a thin white line in the middle for the vein (see Two-Stroke Vein Leaf, page 24). Add a little extra water to your sap green for the leaves in the back so they appear softer and farther away. Paint a few leaves that overlap or sit behind others to make the bouquet feel more natural. Leave a bit of white space between the leaves so your painting stays open and airy.

While the paint is still damp, take a clean Q-tip and gently dab a few spots to lift a little color, just like you did earlier. This adds soft highlights and makes the leaves look fresh and full of light.

Step 13: Add Dark Leaves

Now it's time to make your bouquet feel fuller by adding a few darker leaves behind the lighter ones. Use forest green to paint these background leaves between and behind the others. Paint these darker leaves the same way you did in Step 12, one side at a time, leaving the center vein unpainted.

If any leaf looks too dark, use a Q-tip to gently lift a little color. This softens the leaf and adds depth. Keep your brushstrokes light and relaxed so the darker leaves blend naturally into the background.

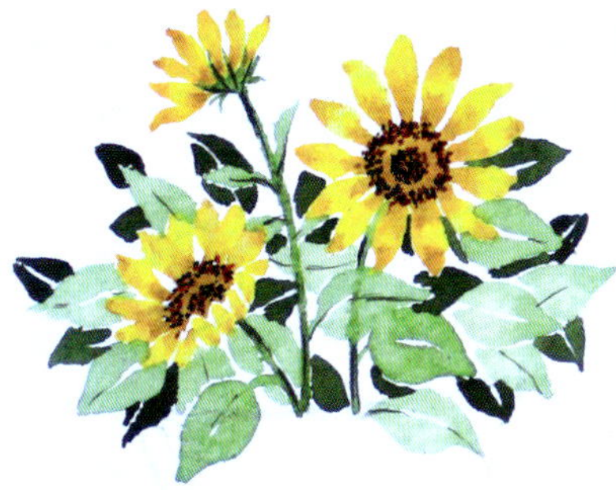

Step 14: Paper Wrap

Cut a piece of kraft paper or a brown paper bag into a rectangle. The size of your rectangle will determine how large your bouquet looks. Use a pencil to gently draw the lines as shown in the picture. Cut along the two straight side lines. Gently tear along the curved line at the top for a softer edge. The torn edge gives it a softer and more natural look.

Once you have torn the shape, lightly crinkle the paper with your hands to add texture. Fold the sides inward so they overlap slightly at the bottom to form a cone shape. Place it over your bouquet to check the fit and make any adjustments if needed. When you are happy with the size and shape, glue the paper wrap down so it sits neatly under the flowers.

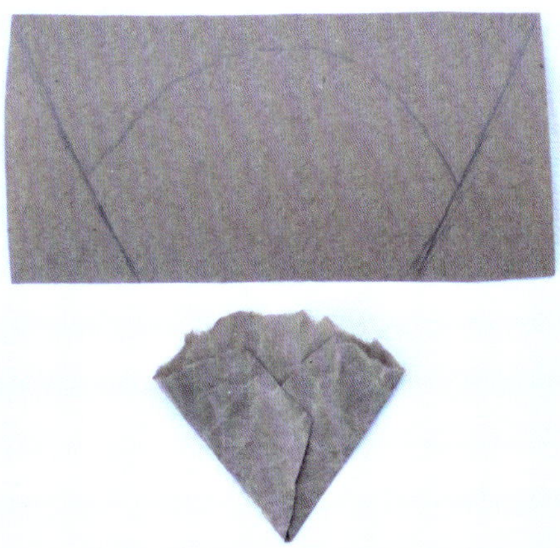

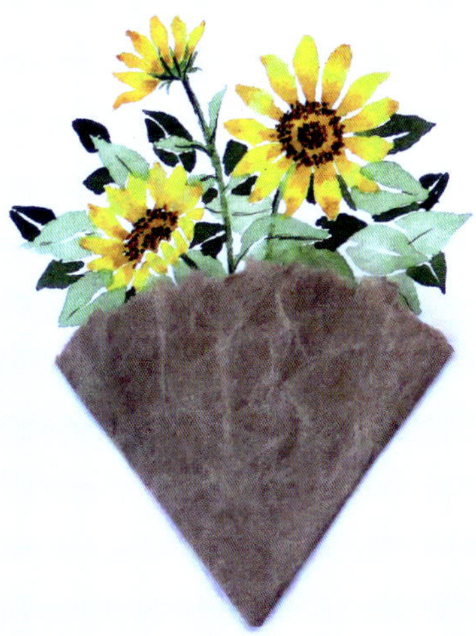

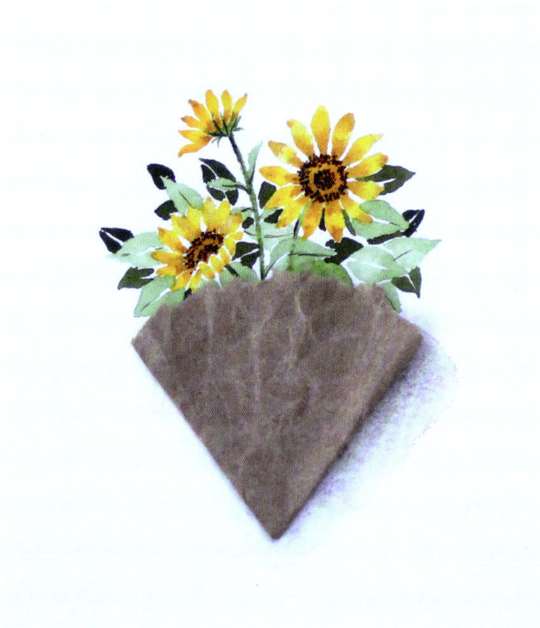

Step 15: Paint the Shadow

To make your bouquet look more three dimensional, start by lightly wetting the area where you want the shadow with clean water. Then mix a little gray with a touch of raw umber. Using the same raw umber from your flower centers helps the shadow blend naturally with the rest of your painting.

While the paper is still damp, gently drop the color into the wet area and let it spread on its own (see Soft Shadows, page 18). Use the tip of your brush to softly guide the paint so the transition looks smooth and natural. You can add a stronger value of the same color right along the edge of the paper wrap, since this is where the shadow is darkest. Keep the rest of the shadow lighter and let it fade as it moves outward. This soft shadow adds depth and makes the paper wrap look like it is gently lifting off the page.

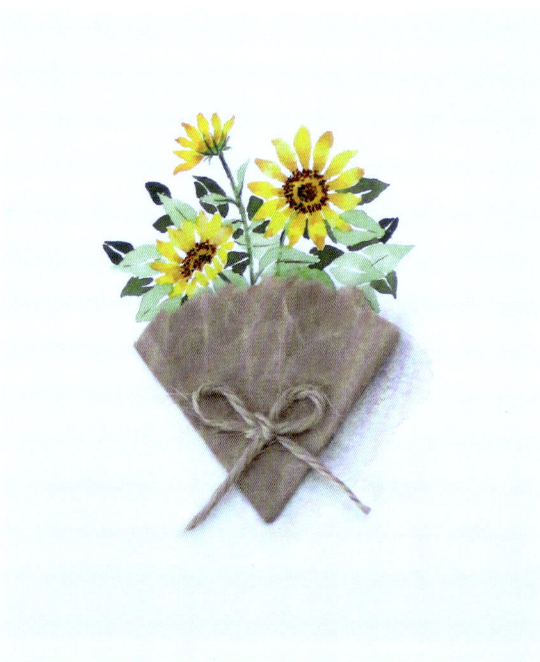

Step 16: Add the Twine Bow

Cut a piece of jute twine about 10 inches long. It's better to start a little longer so you have room for adjustment later. Make a small knot in the center of the twine first to help hold the bow in place. Make a small loop on each side and tie them together, like tying shoelaces. Adjust the loops until they look even and trim the ends to the length you like.

Use a tiny dab of glue or even a glue stick to attach the bow about one third of the way up from the bottom of the paper wrap. Placing it here helps balance the bouquet and makes it look more natural. Press it down gently and let it dry. The little bow adds a sweet handmade touch that ties the whole bouquet together.

Step 17: Lettering

Now it is time to add your lettering. Start by lightly marking two small pencil dots to show where you want your words to begin and end. These little guide points help you place your writing so it stays centered under the bouquet. You can lightly sketch "happy birthday" in pencil first to check the size and spacing before you use your pen.

Use a 005 fineliner or any thin pen you feel comfortable with. Keep your letters small and evenly spaced and try writing in lowercase for a soft and friendly look. Move your hand slowly and let your strokes stay relaxed so the letters flow across the page. It does not need to look perfect. Simple, natural handwriting gives your card a warm and personal touch.

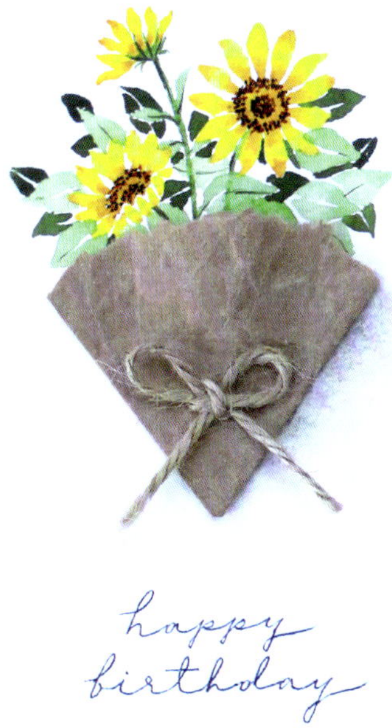

Try This!

Want to give your Birthday Sunflower card a fun twist? Here are a few easy ways to make it your own:

- Try different flowers like daisies or wildflowers for a fresh look.
- Add a little gold mica ink or metallic pen on the flower centers for a subtle shimmer.
- Use colored twine or ribbon instead of jute for a softer or more festive touch.
- Add a few watercolor butterflies or bees fluttering near the flowers for a lively touch.
- Tear a piece of old book paper or sheet music to use as the wrap for a vintage look.

What to Write

Simple words for your handmade card. Here are a few ideas to get you started:

- Wishing you a bright and happy birthday
- May your day bloom with joy
- Sunshine and laughter on your birthday
- You make every day brighter
- A little sunshine for your birthday
- Hope your birthday shines bright
- Wishing you sunshine and smiles
- Bloom bright on your special day
- May your birthday be warm and bright
- Sending sunshine and joy your way

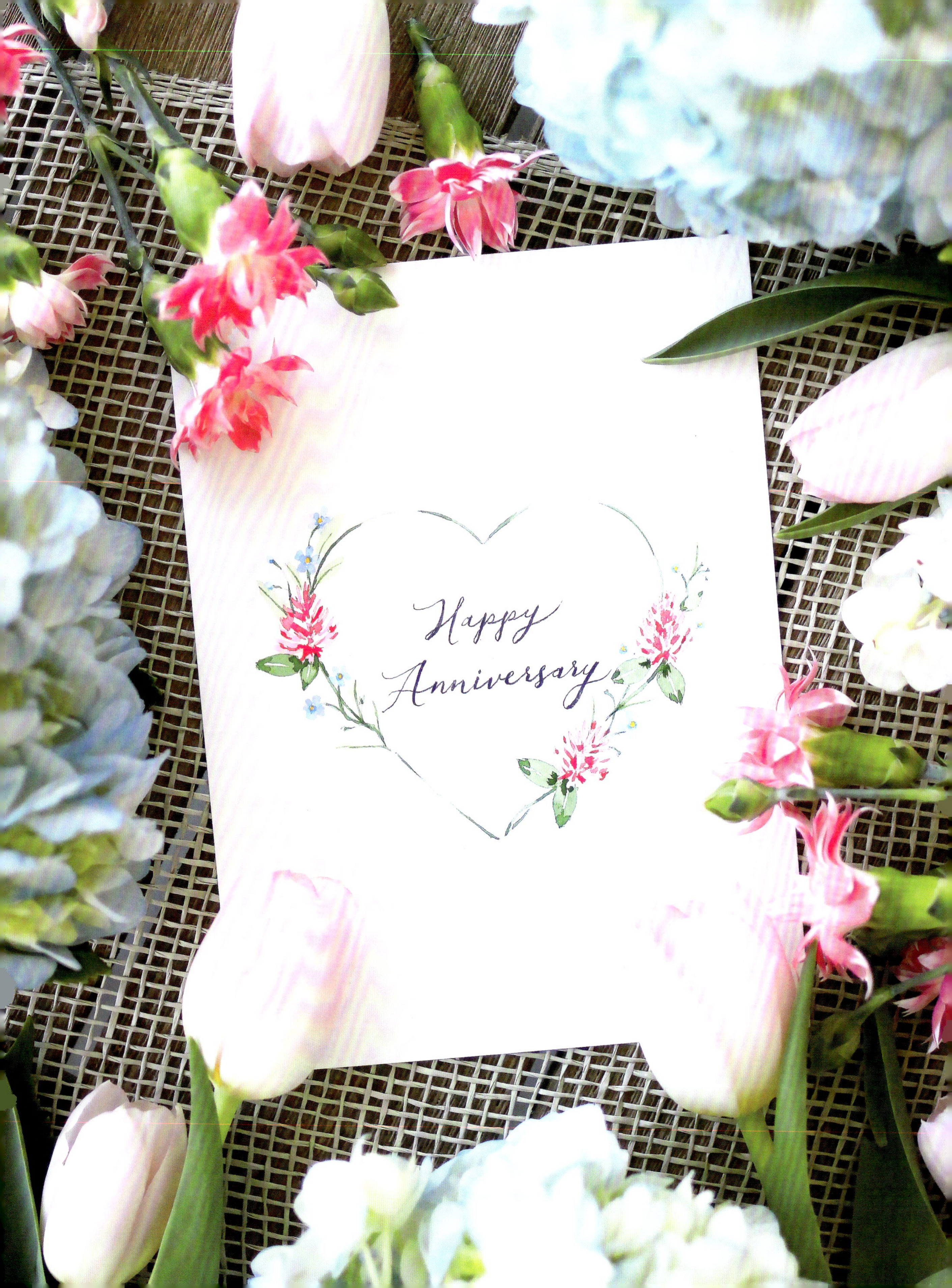
Happy
Anniversary

Anniversary Card: Floral Heart

Paint Colors

(Feel free to substitute similar shades; you don't need to match the exact names.)

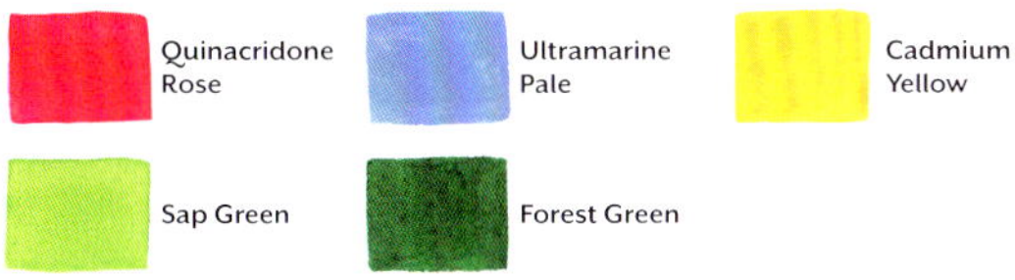

Tools Used

(Feel free to use similar supplies; these are just suggestions!)

- Pencil
- Medium round brush (size 6-8)
- Small round brush (size 2–4)
- Detail brush (size 0 or smaller)
- 005 black fineliner

Anniversaries remind us how love grows through the small everyday moments that make life together feel steady and full. For this card, we will paint a heart made of clovers and forget-me-nots. I chose these flowers because their meanings fit this project in a gentle and simple way. Clovers represent luck, faith, and hope. Forget-me-nots stand for loyalty and lasting connection.

These flowers are also beginner friendly. Their shapes are soft and easy, and the heart will look beautiful even if your petals are not perfect. Keep your strokes light and relaxed. A handmade card always feels special because of its tiny imperfections.

Step 1: Light Sketch

Lightly sketch a simple heart in the center of your card. You can trace a cookie cutter or stencil or make a heart on paper first. To make a paper heart, fold a piece of paper in half, draw half a heart along the fold, cut it out, then open it. Use this paper heart as your template and trace it with soft pencil lines so they erase easily.

If you're using the tear-out card, skip any sketching or shaping steps and begin painting where appropriate.

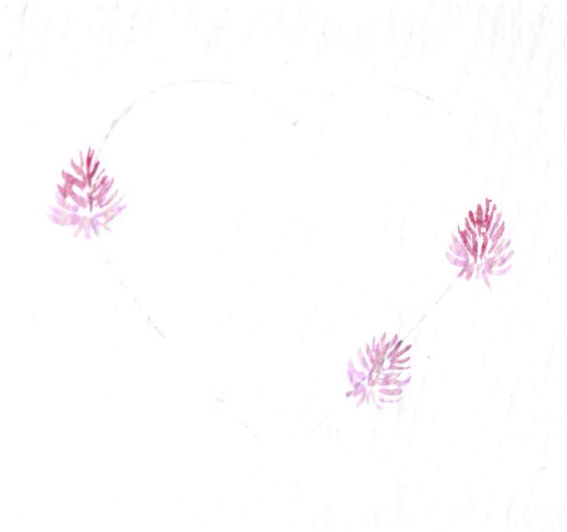

Step 2: Paint Light Clovers

Using a light wash of quinacridone rose, paint three small clovers around the heart. Place one clover at the bottom point and two halfway up on each side, leaving room for the other flowers and leaves.

To paint each clover, use the tip of your brush to make short dashes. Start at the top and add more rows as you move down, letting each row get a little wider. Keep the center strokes straight and angle the side strokes outward. At the bottom, curve a few strokes downward so the clover looks like it is growing. Use light pressure to keep the petals soft (see Clover-Style Petal Flower, page 27).

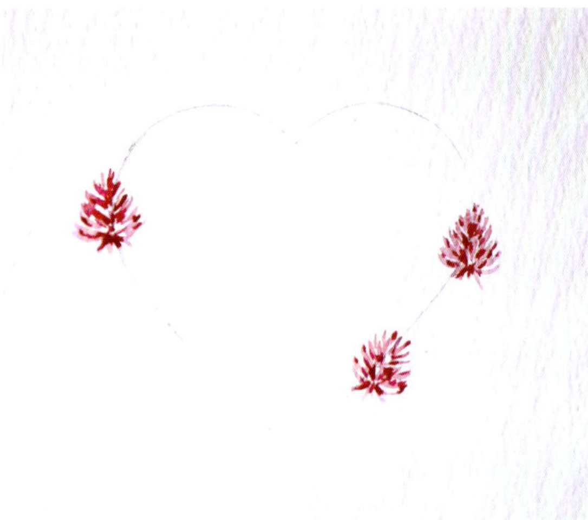

Step 3: Paint Dark Clovers

When the first layer is almost dry, use quinacridone rose with less water to create a darker value. Use the tip of your brush to add a few short strokes in the center of each clover. Then touch a little of this pink onto the tops or tips of a few petals. Do not cover the whole flower. Let most of the lighter color show so the clovers keep their soft natural depth. Work gently so the colors blend on their own.

Step 4: Paint Leaves and Stems

Paint the leaves using a small round brush. Mix sap green with a small touch of ultramarine pale to create a medium green. Paint two or three leaves at the base of each clover. Vary the sizes and directions of the leaves so the design feels natural. Leave a little space between each leaf so the painting stays light.

Paint the leaves with two strokes, leaving a thin white center vein (see Two-Stroke Vein Leaf, page 24).

Finish with a thin, slightly curvy stem connecting each clover to the heart.

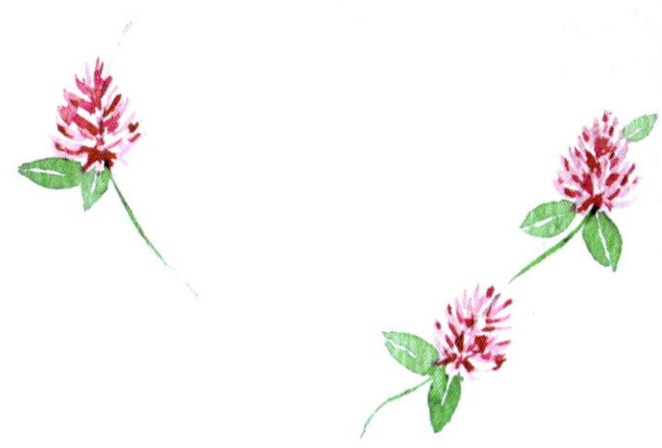

Step 5: Add Darker Green

While the medium green is still a little damp, use forest green and drop it near the base of each leaf where it meets the flower, and at the bottom tip. Let the forest green spread softly into the medium green on its own to create natural shading. You can also add a little forest green to the stem, especially near the flower. Keep your brush light and use just a few touches so the greens stay soft and fresh.

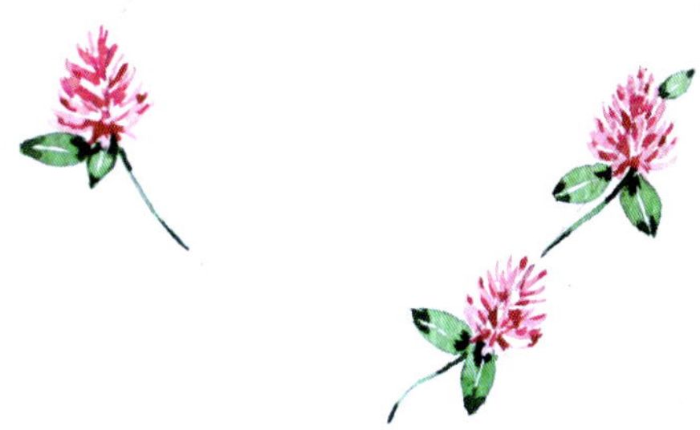

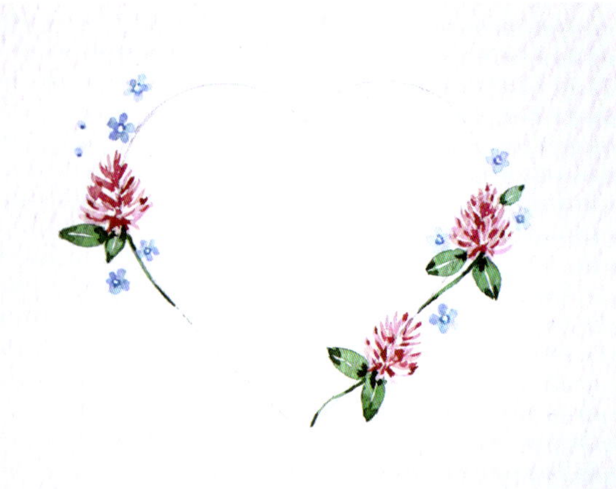

Step 6: Paint Forget-Me-Nots

Use ultramarine pale, or any light blue you have, to paint the forget-me-not flowers. Add a little extra water to keep the color soft and light. Paint the flowers using the tiny round petal flower from the Watercolor Toolbox chapter (see Tiny Round Petal Flower, page 29). Form each petal with a small circular stroke. Vary the sizes a little and add a few small buds or dots to fill open spaces.

While the petals are still damp, add a slightly darker blue to the center of each flower. If needed, mix in a tiny touch of a deeper blue to create more contrast. Lightly outline the inside of the flower and dot the base of each bud for a little depth. Leave the center white for the yellow we will add later.

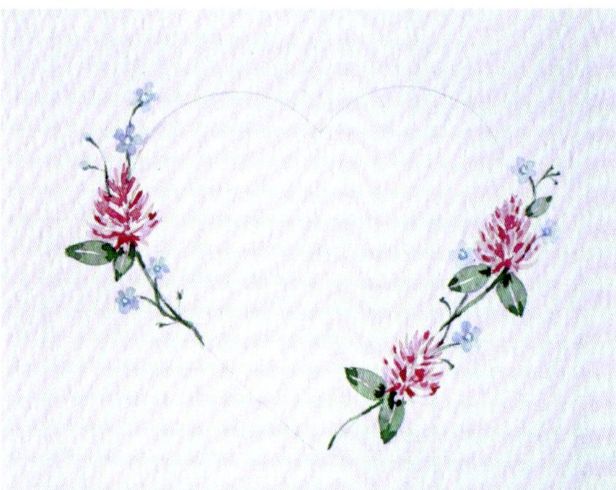

Step 7: Paint Stems

Use the same medium green to paint the thin stems for the forget-me-nots. Paint gentle, curved lines that loosely follow the heart shape. Keep the stems thin and soft. Add a few small, forked stems so the flowers and buds look like they are growing naturally. While the paint is still slightly damp, add a small touch of forest green near the base or tip of a few stems for added depth.

Step 8: Adding Details

When the blue petals are dry, use a detail brush and cadmium yellow to dot the centers of the forget-me-nots. Keep the dots tiny and gentle.

Paint a few light, diluted green leaves to suggest background leaves that sit farther back (see Controlling Values, page 12).

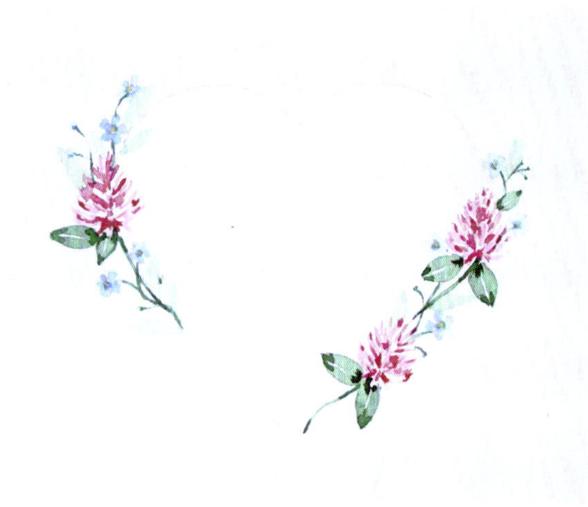

Step 9: Outline and Add Veins

Use the same medium green to outline the heart shape. Paint the line slowly so it stays soft and even.

With this same medium green, add a few simple veins to some of the lighter leaves.

To keep the heart outline from looking flat, add a tiny touch of forest green in a few spots. Keep these touches light so everything still feels soft and natural.

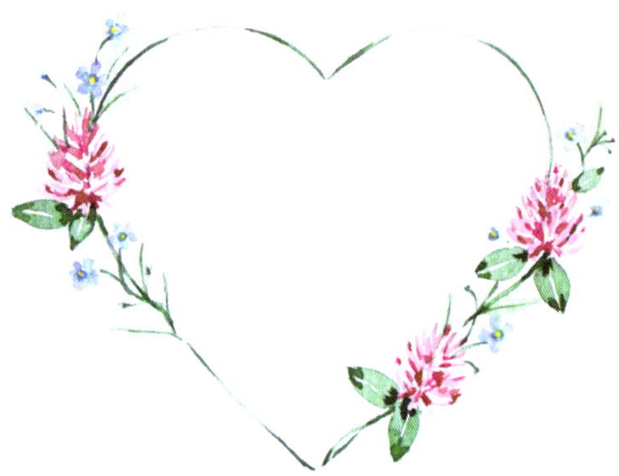

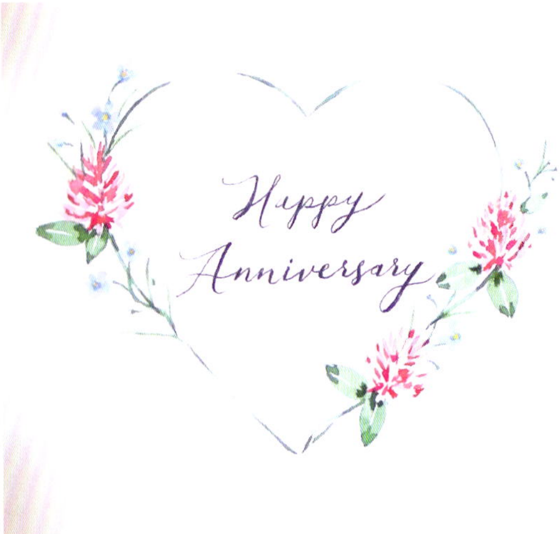

Step 10: Lettering

When the painting is completely dry, lightly sketch "Happy Anniversary" in pencil to plan your spacing. Start by finding the center of the heart and place the middle of your phrase there so the lettering feels balanced.

Keep your pencil lines soft and simple. Aim for smooth, slightly rounded letters because they pair well with the gentle style of the flowers. If you prefer, write the phrase on scrap paper first and place it over the heart to test size and placement before writing on your card.

When you are ready, trace over your pencil lines with a black fineliner. Write slowly and keep your hand relaxed. Rest your wrist lightly on the table for stability and move your hand from your arm rather than only your fingers to keep your lines steady. If you want the letters to look a little more styled, gently thicken the downward strokes after you outline them. This creates a simple faux calligraphy effect (see Faux Calligraphy, page 30).

A soft cursive works nicely for this project, but clean print letters are just as beautiful if that feels easier.

Try This!

Want to give your anniversary card a new twist? Here are some fun ways to change it up:

- Choose your favorite colors to give the heart your own style, using soft pastels for a gentle look or bright, bold tones for something cheerful.
- Use different flowers instead of clovers and forget-me-nots, such as daisies, wild roses, or lavender sprigs.
- Replace the flowers with leaves and greenery for a simple botanical heart.
- Paint the heart outline with gold watercolor or a metallic pen for a soft shimmer.
- Try a new shape like a circle or oval of flowers for a fresh twist on the design.

What to Write

Simple words for your handmade card. Here are a few ideas to get you started:

- Grateful for another year together
- So thankful for us
- Blessed to share this life with you
- Here's to lasting love
- Together through it all
- Our love keeps growing
- Another year, another blessing
- A lifetime of love and laughter
- Thankful for every year with you
- Love you then, love you still

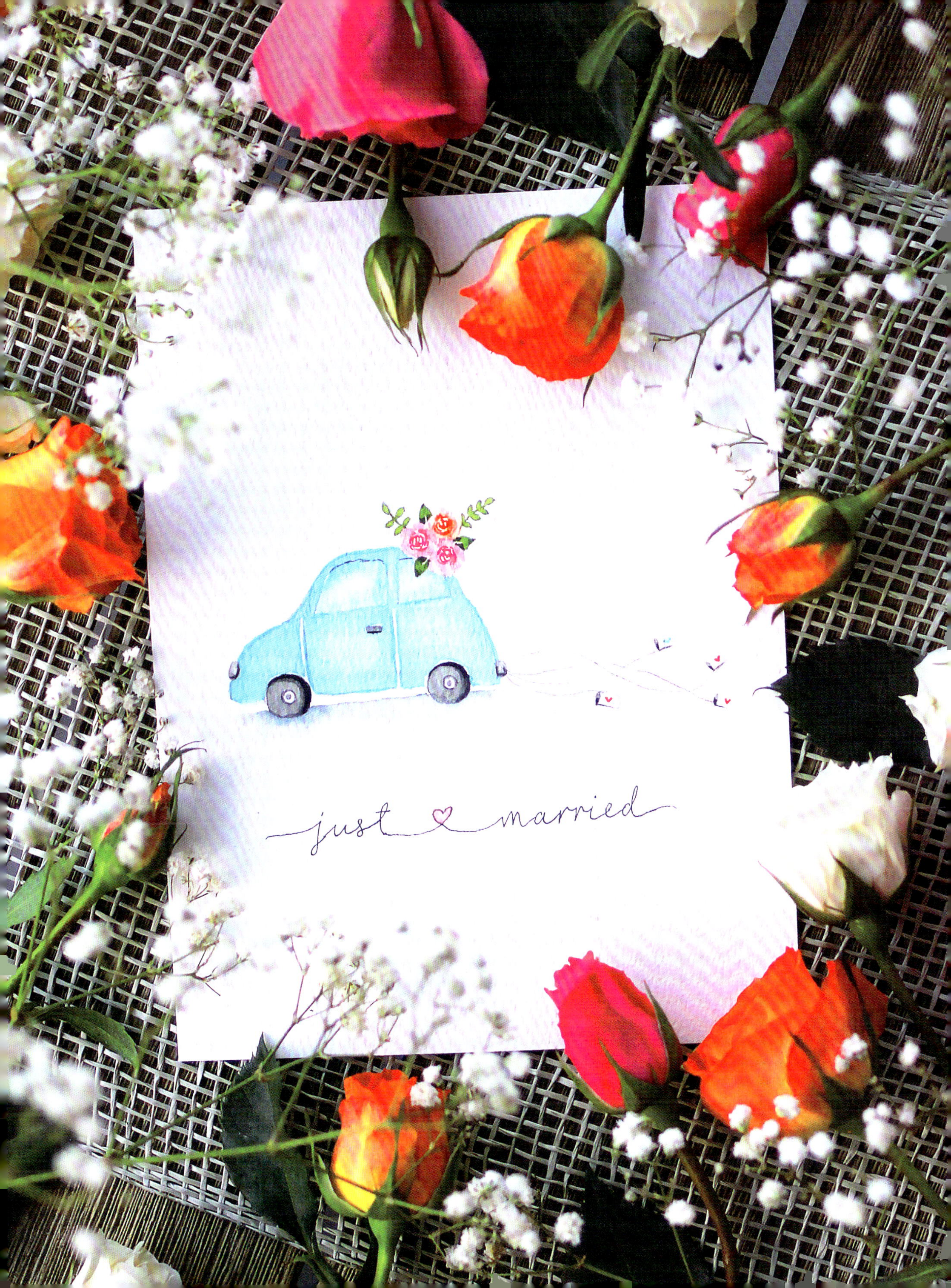
just ♡ married

Just Married Card: Getaway Car

Paint Colors

(Feel free to substitute similar shades; you don't need to match the exact names.)

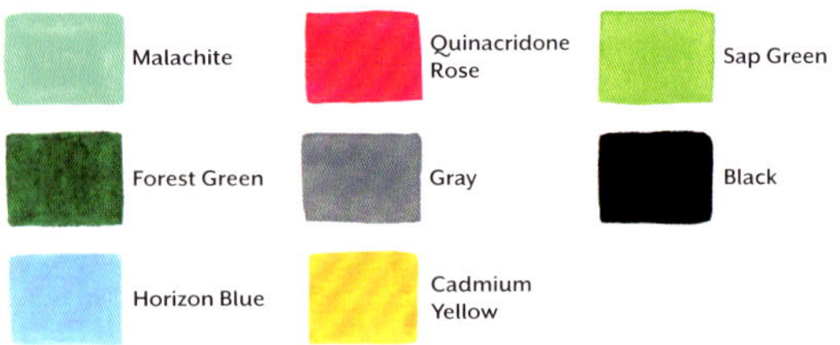

Tools Used

(Feel free to use similar supplies; these are just suggestions!)

- Pencil
- Medium round brush (size 6-8)
- Small round brush (size 2–4)
- Detail brush (size 0 or smaller)
- 005 black fineliner

There is something really sweet about a small car driving away with flowers and cans trailing behind it. This comes from a long wedding tradition where friends decorate the couple's car after the ceremony. The little cans make a cheerful clinking sound as the newlyweds drive off, celebrating their new beginning and bringing good luck.

I created this card to capture that happy moment. The design is simple and gentle. A small teal car, loose flowers on top, and the words "just married" written below. For the flowers, we will paint easy watercolor roses using a few soft dashes of color and then a clean damp brush to pull the paint outward into a loose rose shape.

This card is relaxed and fun, and it works well for weddings, engagements, or anniversaries. Lines do not need to be perfect. Soft washes and loose blooms give it plenty of charm, and it is a great project for beginners.

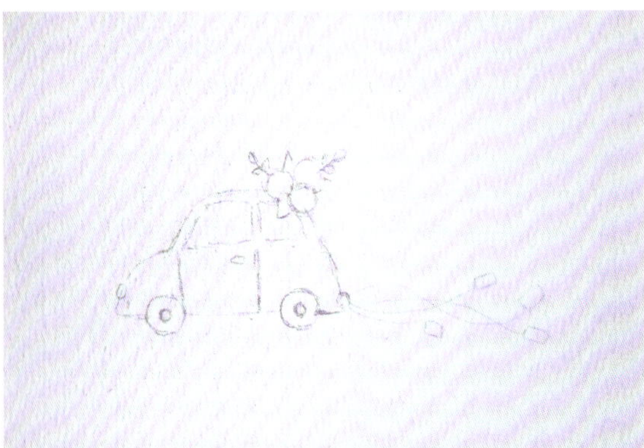

Step 1: Light Sketch

Start by sketching the car using simple shapes. Lightly draw a rounded rectangle for the body and a soft curved rectangle on top for the roof. Add two circles for the wheels and a small, curved rectangle for the window. On the roof, sketch three loose circles for the roses and add a couple of single leaves and a couple of thin stems with tiny leaves. Draw a few light lines flowing behind the car and add small rectangles at the ends to suggest the cans. Keep the sketch soft because it is just a guide.

If you're using the tear-out card, skip any sketching or shaping steps and begin painting where appropriate.

Step 2: Paint the Roses

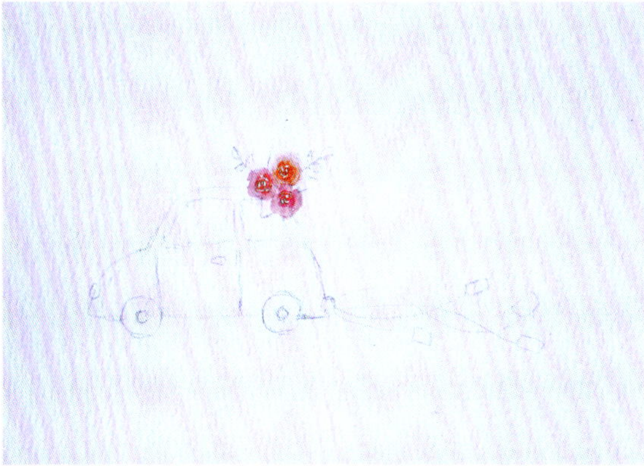

Using a detail brush, paint small roses on top of the car with quinacridone rose (see Rose-Style Flower, page 28). Keep the strokes loose and light. Form soft petals by pulling the color outward with a damp brush.

For variety, create a soft peach tone by mixing a small touch of cadmium yellow into quinacridone rose. If the paint feels too wet, lightly lift with a Q-tip. Keep the flowers simple and relaxed.

Step 3: Paint the Leaves

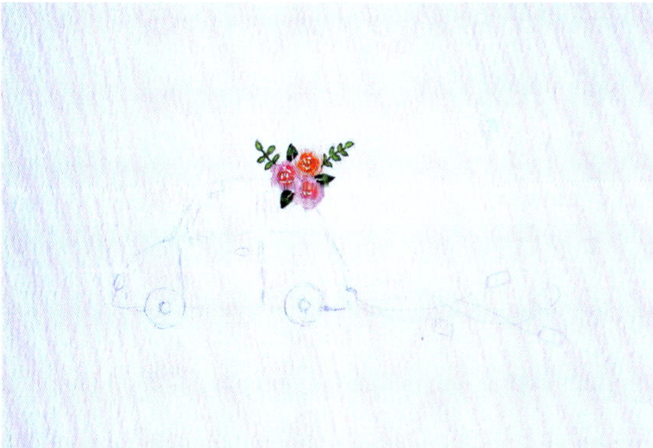

Use sap green to paint two kinds of leaves around the roses. For the single leaves, press your brush down lightly to form a simple leaf shape, then lift at the end to create a gentle point. Leave a thin line of white in the middle for a soft vein (see Two-Stroke Vein Leaf, page 24). Before the leaf dries, drop a touch of forest green at the tip and base to add natural depth.

For the tiny stem leaves, paint a thin line for the stem, then use a detail brush to add small leaves on each side by pressing and lifting the tip of your brush. Keep these simple and balanced.

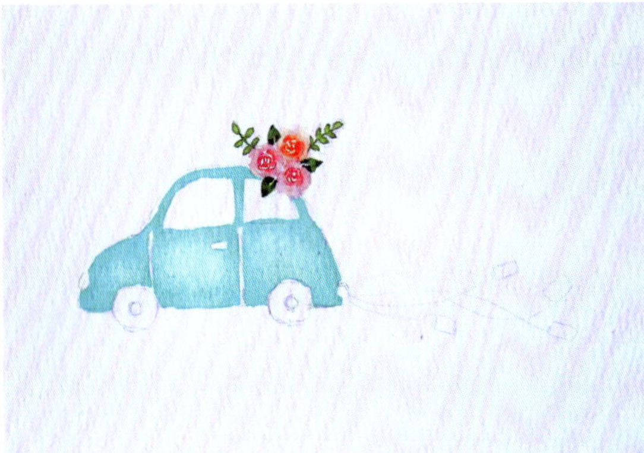

Step 4: Paint the Car

Load your round brush with a light wash of malachite and paint the car body. Leave a thin white line on both sides of the door and a tiny white space for the door handle. Keep the color soft and even.

While the paint is still damp, use a Q-tip or a clean damp brush to gently lift a little color from the center areas of the car. This creates a soft highlight and keeps the edges naturally darker (see Lifting, page 13).

To add depth, mix a stronger value of the same color by using less water and more pigment. Drop this slightly deeper malachite along the bottom edges of the car and near the door. Keep the touches light so the style stays soft and airy.

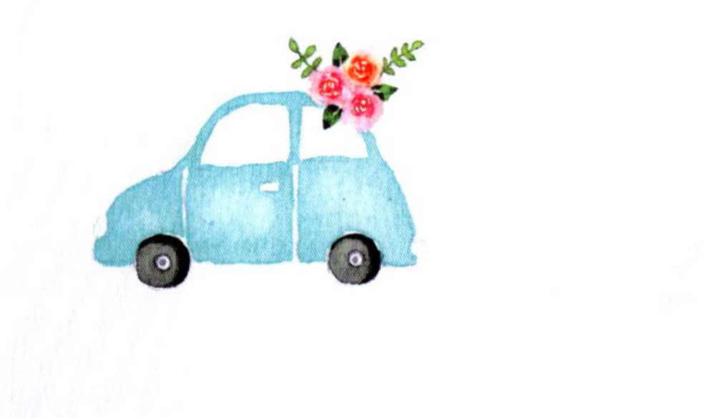

Step 5: Paint the Wheels

Make a light wash of gray by using more water than paint so the color looks soft and pale. Use this light gray to fill in each wheel and leave the center circle white.

When the first layer is dry, use the light gray to paint a small circle in the center of each wheel. This keeps everything soft and matches the gentle style of the card.

Next, use your detail brush to paint a thin black outline around that gray inner circle. Keep your hand relaxed so the line stays light and simple.

Finish by adding a small black crescent on the right side of each wheel, like a tiny curved moon, to suggest a soft shadow.

Step 6: Paint the Window and Door Handle

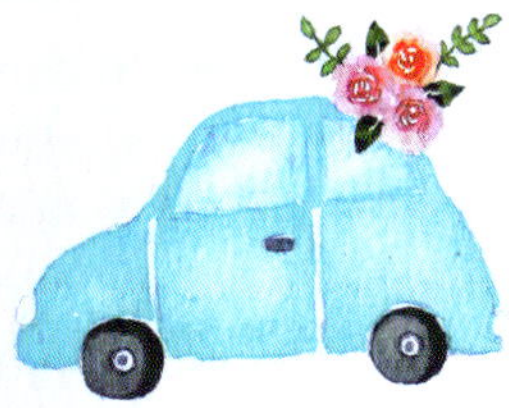

Mix a light wash of horizon blue by adding plenty of water so the color stays soft. Use this wash to paint the window. While the paint is still damp, gently lift a little color from the center with a Q-tip or a clean damp brush, just like you did in earlier steps, so the middle stays light and the edges slightly darker.

Next, use the same gray you mixed for the wheels in Step 5 to paint the tiny door handle. While the gray is still fresh, touch a tiny bit of black along the lower edge to add a soft shadow. Keep the handle small and simple so it blends with the gentle look of the car.

Step 7: Paint the Cans

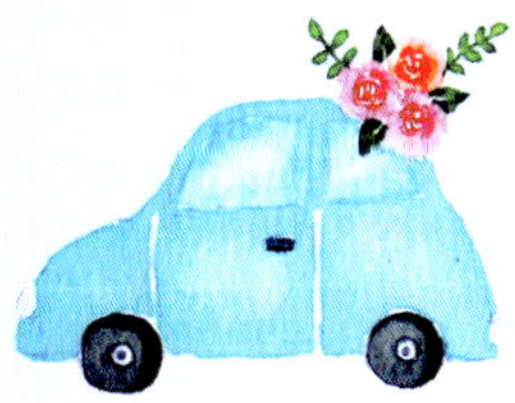

Use a very light gray wash to paint each can. Slightly round the corners as you paint so the cans feel soft rather than like perfect rectangles.

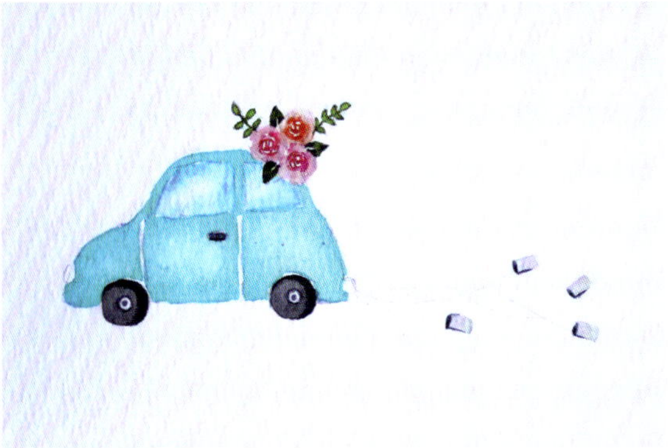

Step 8: Add Details to the Cans

Once the gray is dry, use a tiny bit of black to add a thin shadow along the bottom edge of each can. Then add a thin dark oval on one side of each can for dimension. Keep these details light so the cans stay soft and simple.

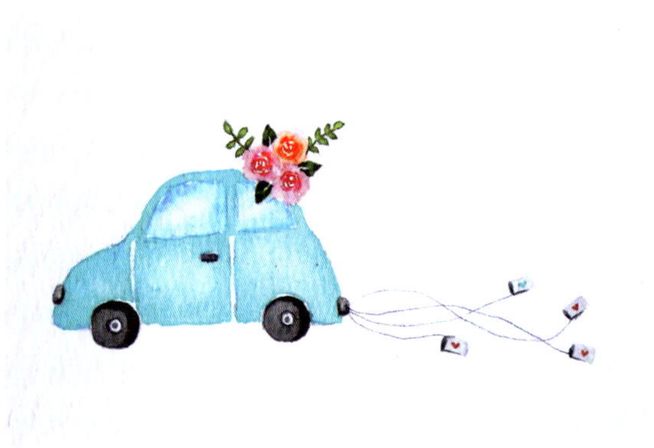

Step 9: Paint the Bumper and Add Hearts

Use a very light gray wash to fill in the bumper shape. Keep the color pale and even so it blends naturally with the car.

Once dry, add a tiny touch of black along the lower edge and where the bumper meets the car to suggest depth. With a detail brush, paint tiny hearts on the cans using quinacridone rose. Keep the hearts small and simple so they feel like sweet finishing details.

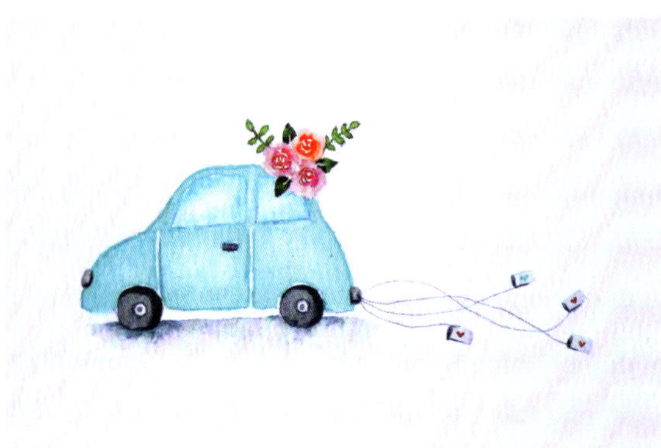

Step 10: Paint the Shadow

Make sure the car is completely dry before adding the shadow. Use a medium round brush to lightly wet the ground beneath the car. Keep the damp area close to the bottom of the car so the shadow stays tucked underneath. The paper should look slightly shiny but not puddled.

Drop in a light gray wash to form the shadow. While the area is still damp, mix a slightly darker gray and add it right under the wheels to deepen the shadow (see Soft Shadows, page 18). Let the paint soften and fade naturally into the paper so the shadow stays light and subtle.

Step 11: Lettering and Final Touches

Lightly sketch your lettering in pencil so you can adjust the spacing and make a faint guideline with a ruler if you want the words to stay straight. Trace over it slowly with your fineliner, keeping your hand relaxed and steady. Write *"just married"* and add a small heart where the words connect. Fill the heart with the same pink used in the flowers to tie everything together. If you want the windows to look a bit more realistic, brush a tiny touch of gray along the top edge of the glass for a soft shadow.

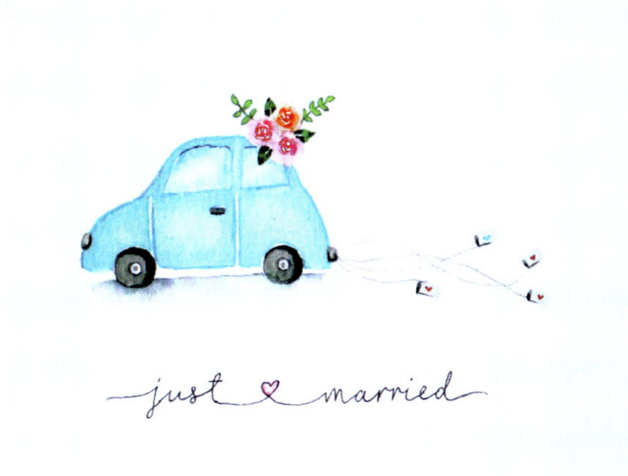

Try This!

Want to make your wedding car card even more personal and fun? Here are a few ideas to try:

- Paint a small string across the back window and add little triangle flags. Write the couple's initials on the flags for a sweet, personalized touch.
- Write one letter on each can so they spell LOVE as they trail behind.
- Add a tiny dotted map line behind the car for a whimsical, travel-inspired look.
- Use little hearts instead of flowers for a modern, sweet version.
- Hang a tiny heart banner from the bumper in place of the cans.

What to Write

Simple words for your handmade card. Here are a few ideas to get you started:

- You two are perfect together
- You two make love look easy
- Wishing you both the sweetest beginning
- Congrats to you both
- Happily ever after starts now
- Mr. and Mrs.
- Love is in the air
- Here's to a lifetime of happiness
- May love lead your way

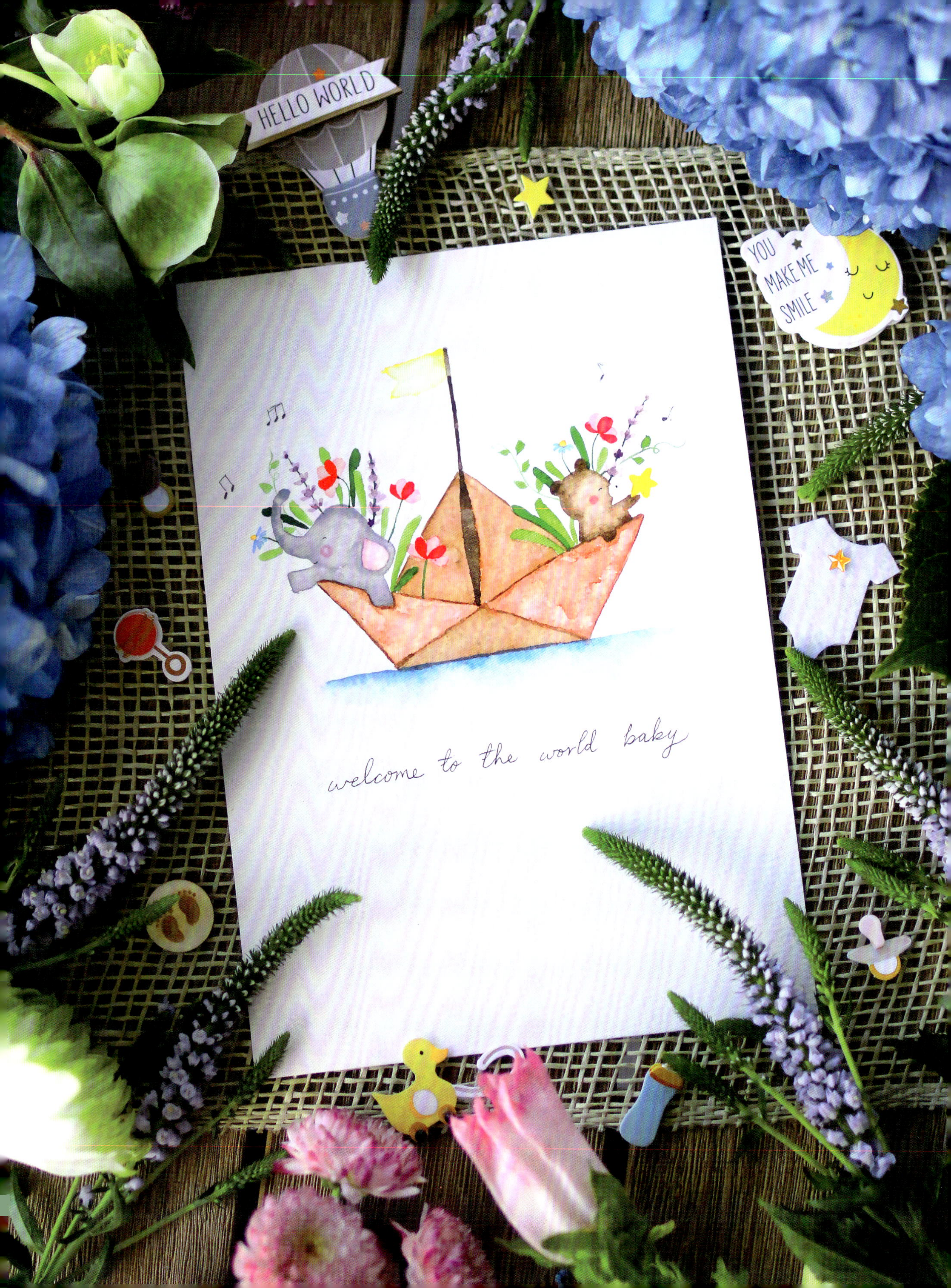
HELLO WORLD
YOU MAKE ME SMILE
welcome to the world baby

Baby Card: Sailing into the World

Paint Colors

(Feel free to substitute similar shades; you don't need to match the exact names.)

Cherry Blossom Pink	Cadmium Red	Cadmium Yellow
Sap Green	Forest Green	Horizon Blue
Lilac	Violet	Yellow Ochre
Raw Umber	Gray	Natural Beige

Tools Used

(Feel free to use similar supplies; these are just suggestions!)

- Pencil
- Medium round brush (size 6-8)
- Small round brush (size 2–4)
- Detail brush (size 0 or smaller)
- 005 black fineliner

A new baby brings so much joy, with tiny fingers, sleepy smiles, and all the love in the world wrapped in something so small. I wanted this card to capture that feeling of softness, tenderness, and gentle happiness. The little paper boat carrying animal friends and flowers feels like a symbol of new beginnings, sailing into a bright new life.

We'll take this one step at a time. Start with the simple boat, then add the little friends, and finish with the flowers. Each part is easy and relaxing, and before you know it, you'll have a cheerful scene that feels full of life and love.

This is a lovely project for anyone who wants to paint something from the heart. Keep your brush light, enjoy the colors flowing on paper, and take your time. Each stroke adds warmth and love, a handmade welcome into the world that will be treasured for years to come.

Step 1: Light Sketch

Lightly sketch the paper boat in the center of your card. Keep the shapes simple by breaking them into basic triangles and folded sections so it feels like a little paper boat. Add the elephant on one side and the bear on the other, using gentle rounded shapes for the bodies and heads. Sketch a small flag and flagpole at the top and a tiny star in the bear's paw.

Draw a few simple flower shapes and tall lavender stalks behind the animals, keeping everything soft and loose. Your pencil lines are just a guide, so keep them light so they will blend in or erase easily later.

If you're using the tear-out card, skip any sketching or shaping steps and begin painting where appropriate.

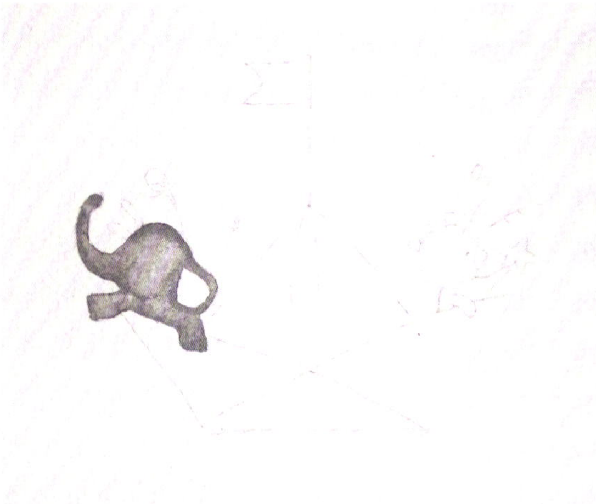

Step 2: Paint the Elephant

Mix a gentle wash of gray and use a medium round brush to fill in the elephant with a light, even layer of color. Keep the paint soft but not too wet so it stays easy to control, and leave the inside of the ear blank for now.

While the gray is still damp, lightly dab the center of the body and the head with a Q-tip to lift a little color. This creates a soft highlight and makes the elephant look round and full (see Soft Center Glow, page 13). You can also drop a bit more gray along the edges while it is still wet so the darker paint spreads softly and adds natural shading without hard lines.

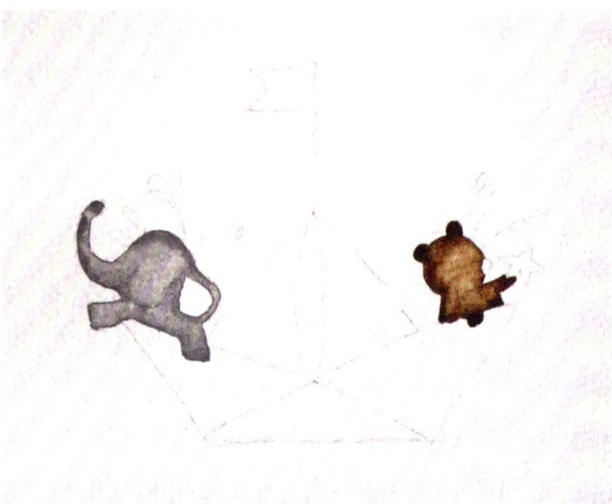

Step 3: Paint the Bear

Mix raw umber with a little yellow ochre to create a warm brown for the bear. Use smooth, even strokes to fill in the body and head.

While the paint is still damp, gently touch the center of the face and body with a clean Q-tip to create that same soft glow. The middle will stay lighter while the edges remain slightly darker, just like you did for the elephant in Step 2.

Drop a touch more raw umber along the ears, arms, and bottom so the edges look slightly deeper and blend softly into the lighter center.

Step 4: Paint the Boat

Mix yellow ochre with a little raw umber to create a lighter warm brown. Use smooth, even strokes to fill in the paper boat. Keep your brush light as you move across the folds and add a bit more raw umber to the middle section to make it look deeper. While the paint is still damp, lightly dab a few spots with a clean Q-tip to lift a little paint, just like you did in the earlier steps.

When it is almost dry, use a detail brush and a deeper raw umber mix to go over the fold lines. Keep the lines light and loose and do not press too hard. This adds definition while keeping the edges soft and natural.

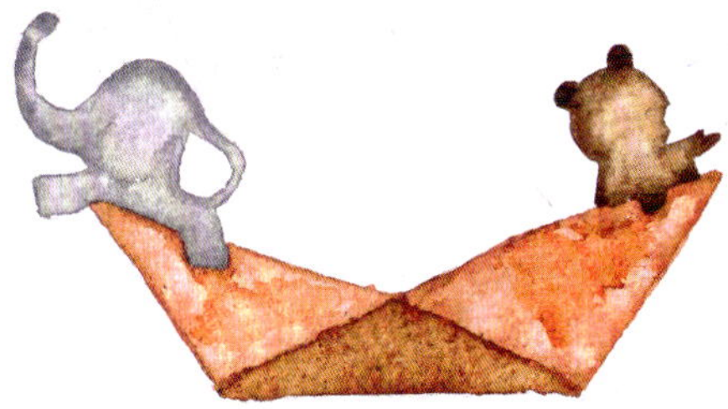

Step 5: Paint the Flowers

Use a light wash of cherry blossom pink to paint small oval shapes for the flowers around the animals. Let the ovals touch at the bottom so they come together in a loose, open bloom.

When the cherry blossom pink layer is completely dry, paint cadmium red ovals in between the pink ones. Aim for about five petals per flower, and vary the number of red and pink petals so they do not all look the same.

The mix of cherry blossom pink and cadmium red makes them look bright and cheerful, adding a lively touch around the boat.

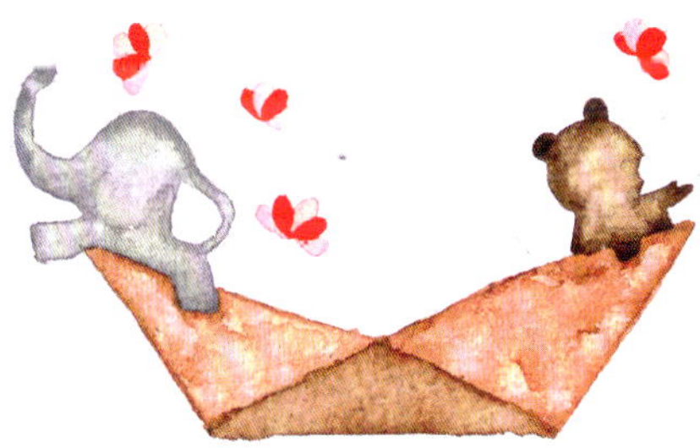

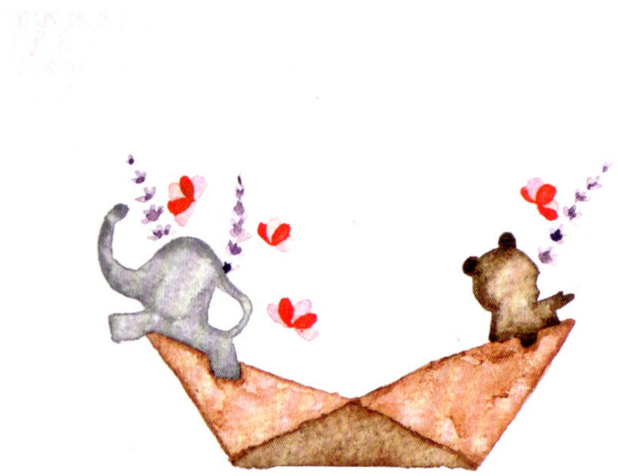

Step 6: Paint the Lavender

Lavender blooms grow on tall vertical stalks, so paint them with that shape in mind. Use a detail brush and lilac to create the blooms. Start at the top and gently press the tip of your brush down, angling the stroke toward the stem to make short dashes. As you move down the stalk, add more dashes on each side so the flowers become fuller near the bottom. Keep your strokes light and relaxed.

When the lilac layer is just starting to dry, drop a bit of violet near the center of each cluster. This adds weight and depth to the lavender without painting extra layers of petals.

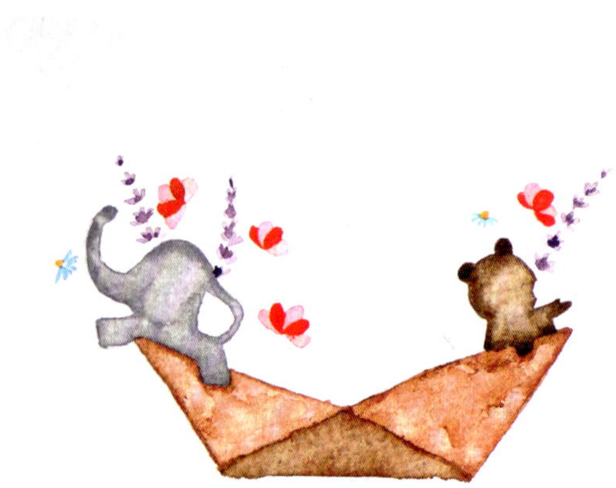

Step 7: Paint the Blue Flowers

Use a detail brush and a light wash of horizon blue to create small daisy-like flowers. Start each petal at the center and pull the brush outward to form short lines, keep the petals on the bottom half of a small circle so the flower looks like it's facing upward (see Side Petal Flower, page 29). Turn your paper if needed to make the strokes easier. The petals do not need to be perfect, just small, simple shapes that suggest the form.

When the petals are completely dry, use a detail brush and cadmium yellow to paint a tiny cone in the center. The warm yellow against the cool horizon blue adds a cheerful pop of color.

Step 8: Paint the Stems

Use a detail brush and sap green to add the stems. Start at the base of each flower and gently pull your brush downward toward the boat in one smooth motion. Use just the tip of your brush and keep your hand relaxed. If your hand feels shaky, turn your paper or rest your wrist lightly on the table for more control.

Vary the angle of the stems so they lean in slightly different directions. While the sap green is still damp, drop a touch of forest green at the base of each stem to add a bit of depth.

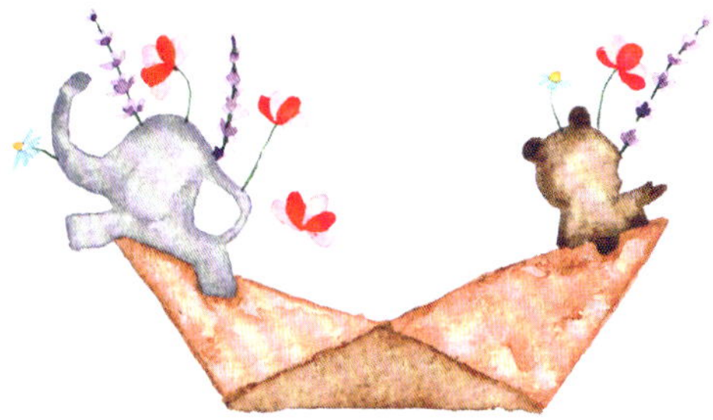

Step 9: Paint the Long Leaves

Use a medium round brush to paint each leaf in one smooth stroke (see Long Rounded-Base Leaf, page 25). Press your brush down gently to make the rounded base, then lift as you pull upward to create a long shape that comes to a soft point.

Create a mix of different greens so the leaves look natural and layered (see Color Mixing, page 12). You can make a light green by mixing sap green with cadmium yellow and plenty of water. A medium green comes from using sap green with less water. For darker leaves, use forest green and add water for adjustment.

Play on your mixing palette and explore different greens. Try the mixes on a scrap piece of paper and use the ones you like best.

Arrange the leaves in soft V or fan shapes around the flowers. Mix the directions by adding a few upright leaves and a few that lean outward so everything feels open and natural.

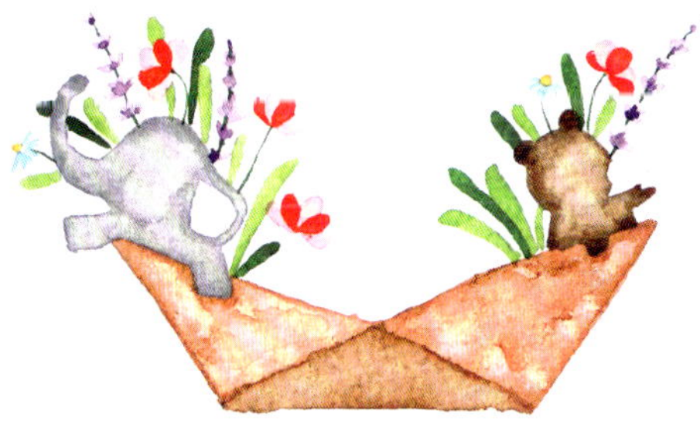

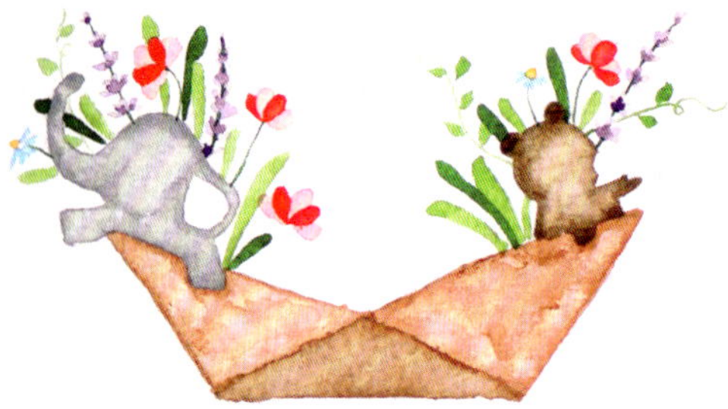

Step 10: Add Vines

Use a detail brush and the same light green mix you used in Step 9. Paint thin, flowing lines that curve gently upward around the flowers. Keep your touch light so the vines stay soft and delicate. Add small leaves along both sides of each vine. Each leaf is made with two short strokes that meet at a point (see Two-Stroke Leaf, page 24). Vary the spacing and angle of the leaves so they look light and natural. Leave small gaps between clusters so the vines stay airy and do not feel too heavy.

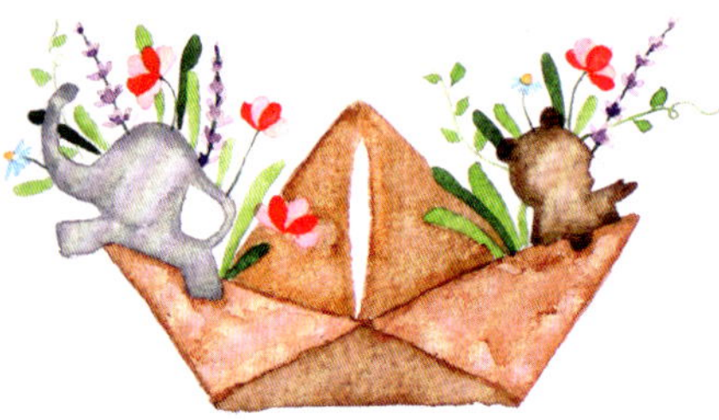

Step 11: Paint the Back Fold of the Boat

Make sure everything is dry before painting the center folded section.

Use the same lighter warm brown mix from Step 4 (yellow ochre with a little raw umber).

Use a medium round brush to fill in the fold, painting slowly around the leaves and flowers in front. Add a touch of extra raw umber near the edges so the fold looks slightly deeper.

While the paint is still damp, gently lift a little color from the middle with a clean Q-tip to create a soft highlight (see Lifting, page 13).

Step 12: Paint the Flagpole and the Bear's Muzzle

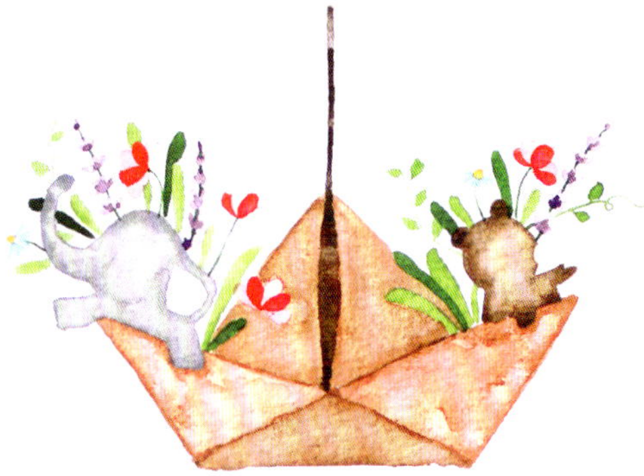

Make sure everything is dry before adding the flagpole and muzzle. Use the same brown mix you used for the bear (raw umber with a little yellow ochre) and paint a thin line upward from the top point of the boat to form the flagpole. Use a detail brush and make one slow, steady stroke. While the paint is still damp, add a tiny bit more raw umber near the base of the pole to deepen the shadow.

Next, lightly fill the bear's muzzle with natural beige. Use plenty of water so the color stays soft. This is just a gentle wash to separate the muzzle from the rest of the face.

Step 13: Paint the Flag, Star, and Face

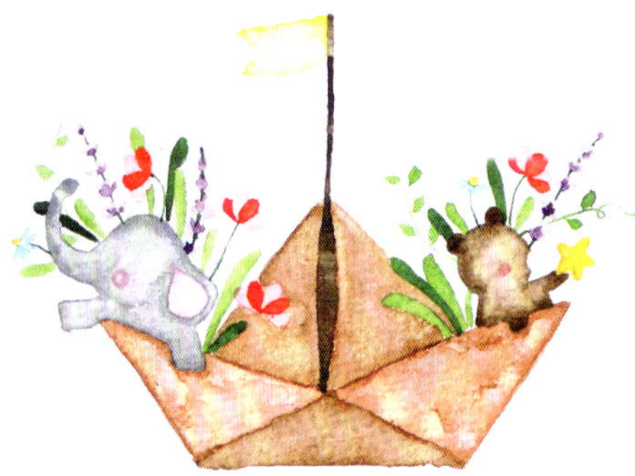

Use a small round brush and cadmium yellow to paint the flag. Add a little extra water so the yellow stays soft and light. While the paint is still damp, lift a little color from the center with a clean Q-tip to create a gentle highlight.

For the star, use cadmium yellow again, but with less water so it looks brighter. You can add a tiny touch of orange on one edge while it is wet.

Next, use cherry blossom pink for the animals' cheeks and the inside of the elephant's ear. Keep the color soft, then lift a small bit from the center to make the blush look light and gentle.

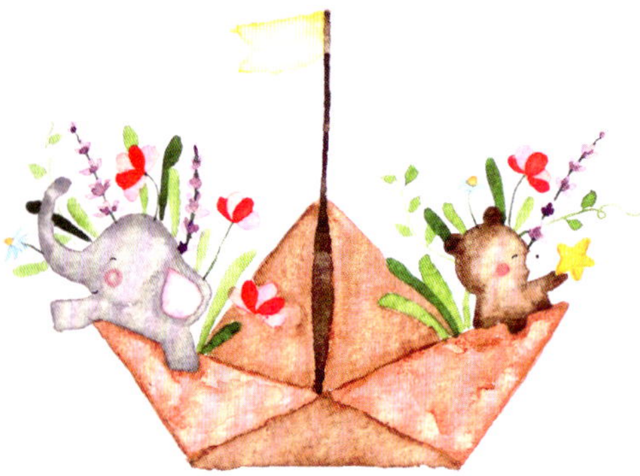

Step 14: Add Pen Details

When everything is completely dry, use a 005 black fineliner to add the small details. Start with the eyes and nose, using tiny dots so the features stay soft and cute. For the elephant, add a small, curved line for the smile and a dot for the eye. For the bear, add little dots for the eyes and nose. You can trace over your pencil lines or make simple adjustments now that the painting is finished.

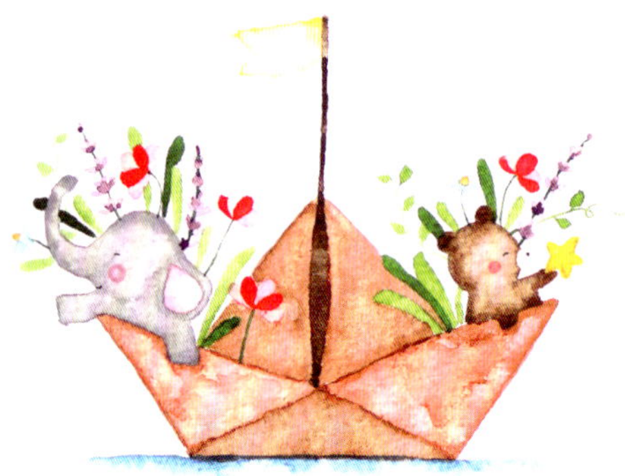

Step 15: Paint the Water

Lightly wet the area just below the boat with clean water. While the paper is still damp, use a medium round brush and a light wash of horizon blue to paint the water. Let the color spread softly on its own. Gently dab along the bottom edge with a paper towel to fade the blue so it looks light and airy.

Then use a detail brush and a stronger value of horizon blue (more paint) to paint a thin line right under the boat. This makes the area closest to the boat slightly darker, creating a soft shadow in the water (see Soft Shadows, page 18). Keep the stroke light so it blends naturally into the wash.

Step 16: Lettering

Use your 005 fineliner to write "welcome to the world baby" beneath your painting. Lightly sketch the words in pencil first so you can adjust the spacing and keep the phrase centered. When tracing with your pen, you do not need to follow the pencil lines exactly. The sketch is just a guide.

Hold the pen lightly and write slowly so your lines stay steady. Keep your hand relaxed and move from your arm instead of only your fingers. If you want smoother letters, draw a faint baseline in pencil to help keep the words straight. Write in your natural handwriting. Simple, clean letters look beautiful and keep the card feeling soft and handmade.

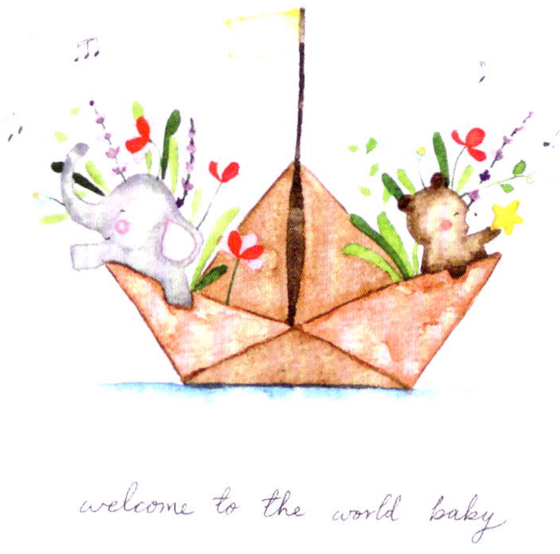

Try This!

There are so many ways to make this little boat your own!

- Switch the flowers for watercolor balloons to give it a happy, celebratory feel.
- Paint the boat in soft pastel shades for a lighter, dreamier look.
- Add the baby's initials or name on the flag for a personal touch.
- Use soft pinks or blues if you're making it for a gender reveal or baby shower.
- Replace the flowers with simple watercolor toys like blocks or stacking rings for something playful.

What to Write

Simple words for your handmade card. Here are a few ideas to get you started:

- A tiny bundle, a big joy
- The adventure begins
- A dream come true
- Hello, sweet baby
- You make the world brighter
- A new story begins today
- The best kind of miracle
- Congratulations on your beautiful baby
- Congratulations on your tiny miracle
- Congratulations on your greatest adventure yet

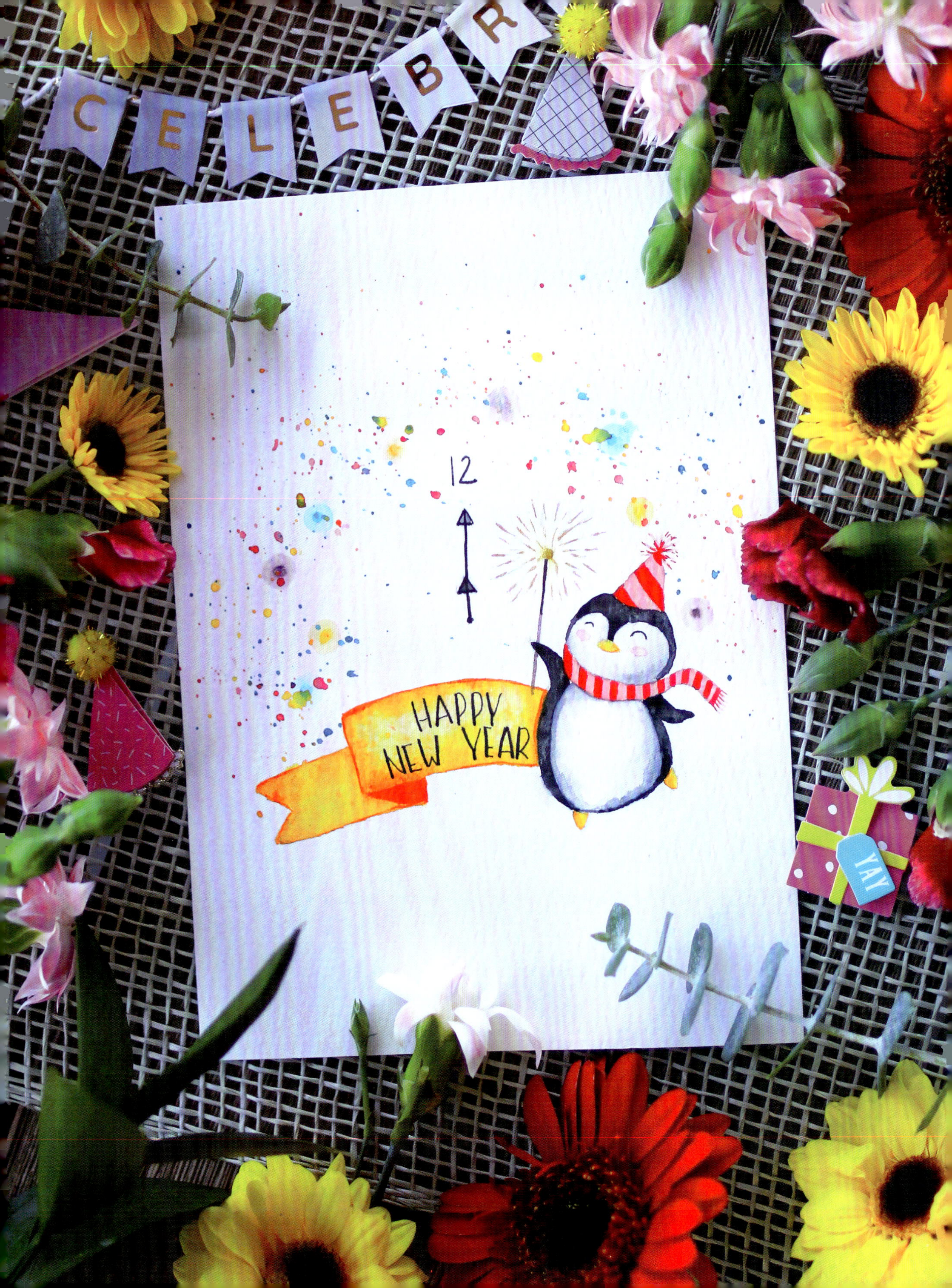
CELEBR
12
HAPPY NEW YEAR
YAY

CHAPTER 4

Seasonal and Holiday Cards

New Year Card: Firework Penguin

Paint Colors

(Feel free to substitute similar shades; you don't need to match the exact names.)

- Black
- Gray
- Cadmium Red
- Cherry Blossom Pink
- Cadmium Yellow
- Cadmium Orange

Tools Used

(Feel free to use similar supplies; these are just suggestions!)

- Pencil
- Medium round brush (size 6-8)
- Small round brush (size 2–4)
- Detail brush (size 0 or smaller)
- 005 black fineliner
- Metallic gold paint

Penguins are one of my favorite animals to paint because they start with simple round shapes. A bit of black on top and you suddenly have a penguin, even if the shape is not perfect. That is the nice thing about watercolor. Small uneven areas make your painting feel handmade and full of charm.

A New Year card is also a thoughtful project. It feels bright and hopeful and it works for anyone, even if you missed sending holiday cards in December. There is something nice about starting the year with a small painting you made yourself.

In this card, the penguin is holding a sparkler and counting down to midnight with you. The soft glowing dots and tiny bursts in the sky give it a gentle festive look without needing a detailed background. We will use simple steps such as light washes and soft blending to keep things easy. Remember, your card does not need perfect shapes or lines. Small wobbles give it a warm handmade feel.

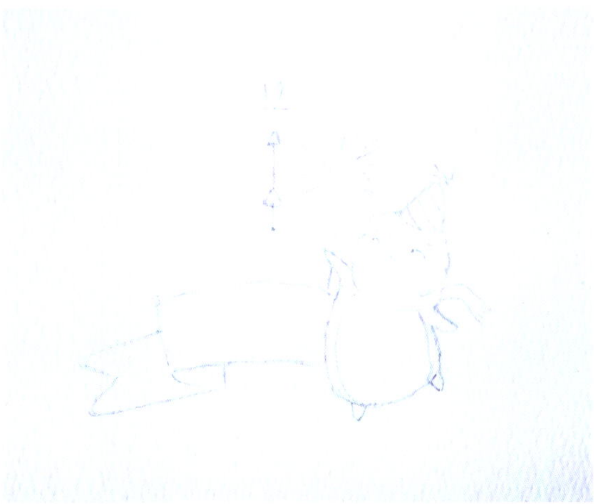

Step 1: Light Sketch

Start by sketching the penguin using a big oval for the body and a smaller round oval on top for the head. Tilt both shapes slightly so the penguin looks like it is jumping with excitement. Add two short, curved lines on each side for the wings, and small bumps at the bottom for the feet.

In the raised wing, draw a thin line for the sparkler stick. Add tiny, short dashes around the top of the stick to show the sparkling glow.

For the clock, draw a small circle and a straight line pointing up. Add two tiny triangles on the line, one at the top and one just below it, to show the clock striking midnight.

Then sketch the long banner that starts on the left and curves behind the penguin's body. Keep your pencil lines light and simple.

If you're using the tear-out card, skip any sketching or shaping steps and begin painting where appropriate.

Step 2: Paint the Black Parts

Use black to fill in the dark parts of the penguin, leaving the belly and front of the face white. Work slowly around the curves and use a smaller round brush if you want more control.

As you paint, turn your paper. Rotating the page makes it easier to follow the curves and keeps your hand comfortable, which helps you get cleaner lines.

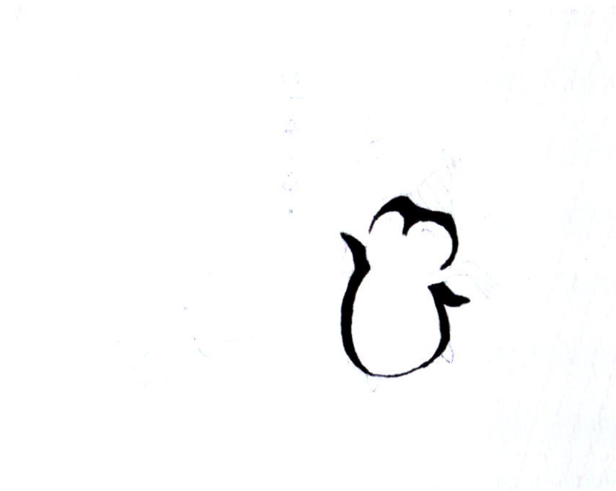

Step 3: Add the Red Stripes

Paint a light wash of cadmium red on the hat, scarf, and the little fluff ball on top by adding more water to the paint. (see Color Mixing, page 12).

To paint the fluff ball, hold your brush upright and make quick, light dashes starting in the center and moving outward. Let this layer dry completely. Then use the same cadmium red, with less water, to add the stripes on the hat and scarf so the color stands out. Add a few quick dashes of the stronger red to the fluff ball, leaving some of the lighter strokes underneath so it stays soft and fuzzy.

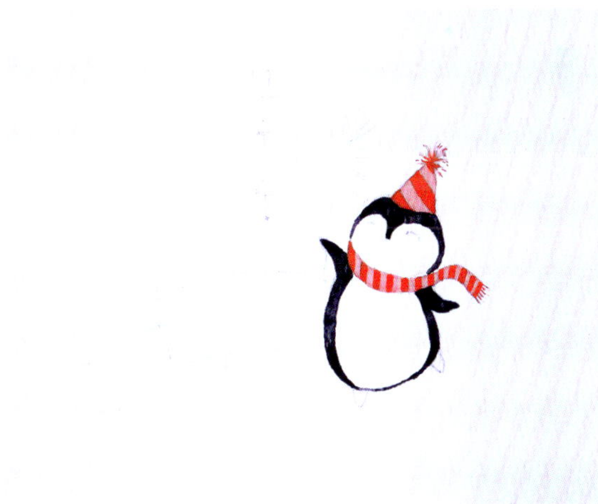

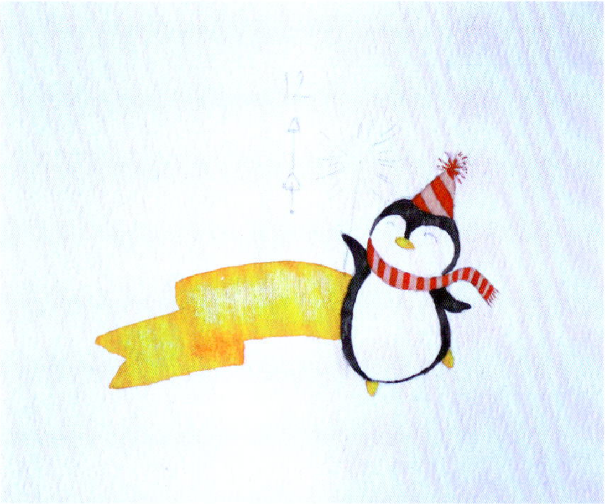

Step 4: Paint the Banner, Beak, and Feet

Paint the whole banner with a light wash of cadmium yellow. While it is still damp, add a little cadmium orange along the edges and blend it with a damp brush so the colors soften together (see Soft Center Glow, page 13). To keep the center lighter, tap the middle with a clean Q-tip while the paint is still damp.

Use the same cadmium yellow to paint the beak and feet. Work slowly with a small brush so the paint stays inside the shapes. While the yellow is still damp, touch a bit of cadmium orange along the edges and soften it with a clean Q-tip so the color blends smoothly.

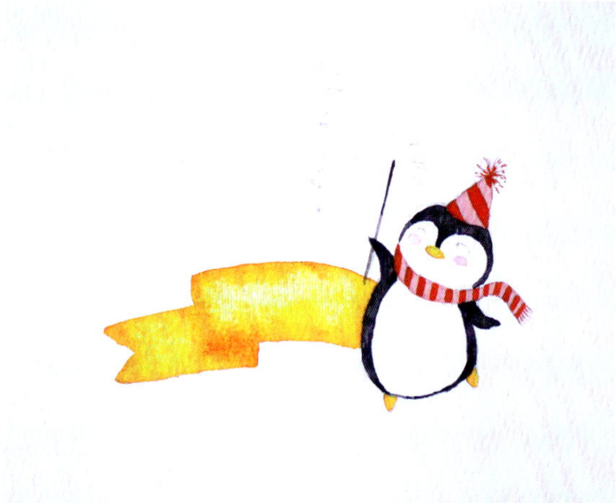

Step 5: Add Cheeks and Stick

Mix a light wash of cherry blossom pink by adding plenty of water to your paint. Paint two small ovals for the cheeks. If the color looks too strong or too wet, gently tap the area with a clean Q-tip to lift a little paint.

For the sparkler stick, use a small detail brush and hold the brush more upright as you paint. Start with a watered down black or gray and paint a thin line in the raised wing. Let it dry. Then use a darker, more concentrated black to paint the upper half of the stick. This gives the stick a clear contrast while keeping the lower part softer.

Step 6: Add Shading to Create a 3D Look

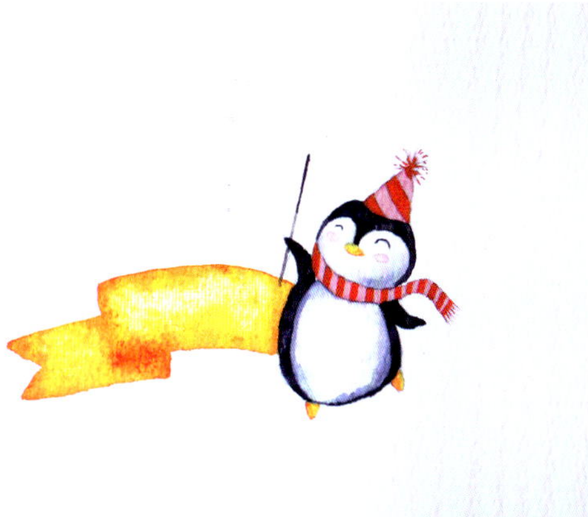

Use gray to add a thin line of shadow along the outer edge of the penguin's body and face. Work in small sections so the paint stays damp and easy to blend. After placing the gray, rinse your brush, blot it on a paper towel, and use the damp brush to gently pull the color inward to soften the edge (see Blending, page 15).

Keep the shading a little darker on the right side of the face and body, since the light is coming from the left. Add a small shadow on the right cheek above the scarf and another under the scarf on the left where it blocks the light. Leave the center of the belly and the front of the face the lightest so the penguin looks round and lifted.

Step 7: Paint the Glow

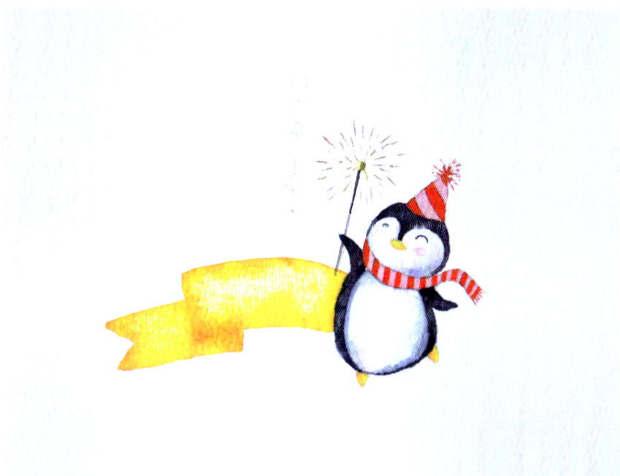

Place a small dot of concentrated cadmium yellow at the tip of the sparkler. While it is still damp, use a clean damp brush to gently spread the color outward in a soft circle (see Radiating Glow, page 19). Keep your touch light so the center stays the brightest.

Once the yellow glow is dry, use gold paint to add short dashes all around it. Space the dashes evenly and point them outward like little rays. Make some longer and some shorter so the burst looks natural and lively.

You do not need to follow your sketch exactly. Add more rays or shift their placement if you like. Watercolor often looks more charming when the lines and shapes slightly.

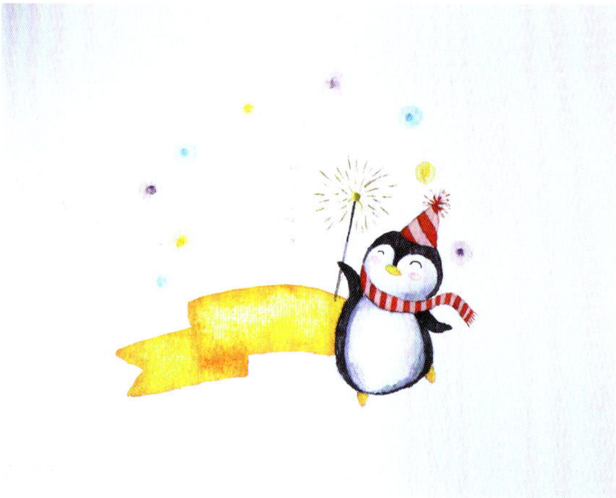

Step 8: Paint the Dots

We will paint some soft, fireworks-inspired dots to fill the background. Start by placing a small dot of concentrated color on the paper. Use yellow, blue, and purple. While the dot is still wet, use a clean, damp brush to gently pull the color outward. Work little by little, moving your brush around the dot in a circular motion so the color spreads into a soft, round glow (see Soft Center Glow, page 13). Keep your touch light so the outer edge stays airy.

Work one dot at a time so the paint stays damp while you blend it. Place the dots around the penguin in a loose curve, like the shape of a clock. They do not need to be the same size. A little variation makes the background feel natural and lively.

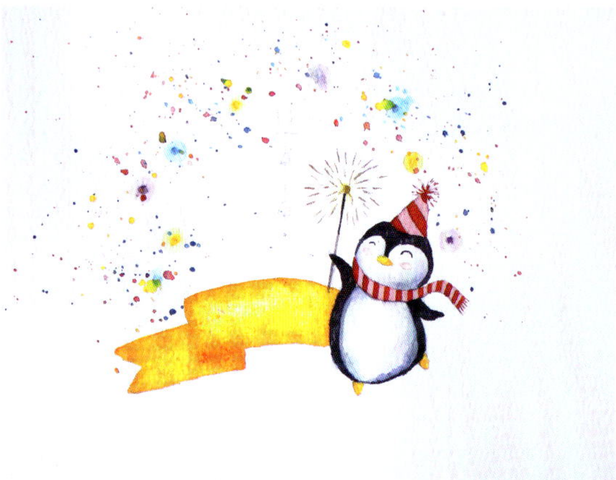

Step 9: Splatter

Let's add splatters to create a festive New Year background. Load your brush with watery paint using the same colors you used for the dots so everything stays consistent. Your brush should be wet enough for the paint to flick off easily. Hold the brush about 4 to 6 inches above the paper and gently tap the bristles with your finger so tiny drops fall onto the page (see Splattering, page 17).

Cover the penguin and the banner with a paper towel so the splatters stay only in the background. You can tear the paper towel into smaller pieces to fit around the shapes. Work one color at a time and add a few splatters, then pause to see how it looks. This helps keep the colors clean and prevents muddy spots. Keep the splatters light and scattered so the background feels lively without taking over the painting.

Step 10: Add the Clock Hands

Use a 005 fineliner to draw one long line pointing straight up for the clock. Add two small triangles on the line, one at the top and one about a third of the way down. Both triangles should point upward to show the clock striking midnight.

If your pen is waterproof, you can fill in the triangles with a light wash of watered-down black without smudging the ink. If your pen is not waterproof, paint the triangles first and outline them after the paint dries. Write "12" above the line to mark the moment of the New Year countdown.

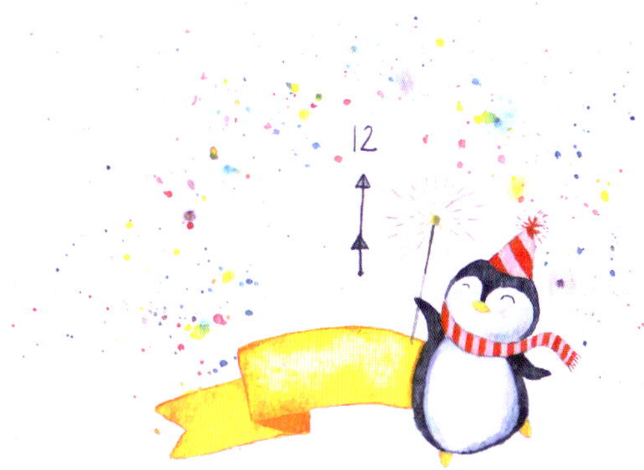

Step 11: Lettering

Start by lightly writing "HAPPY NEW YEAR" in pencil on the banner. This gives you a chance to adjust the size and spacing before you switch to pen. Keep the letters a little long and stretched so they fill the banner. You can place the crossbars and connecting points a bit lower, like the bar in A or where the lines meet in Y, to create a playful look that follows the curve of the banner.

Once the pencil looks right, trace over the letters with your 005 fineliner. Go slowly and keep your hand relaxed so the spacing stays even. When the outline is done, thicken the downstrokes (the left side of each letter). A small amount of extra thickness is all you need to give the letters a clean faux calligraphy look (see Faux Calligraphy, page 30).

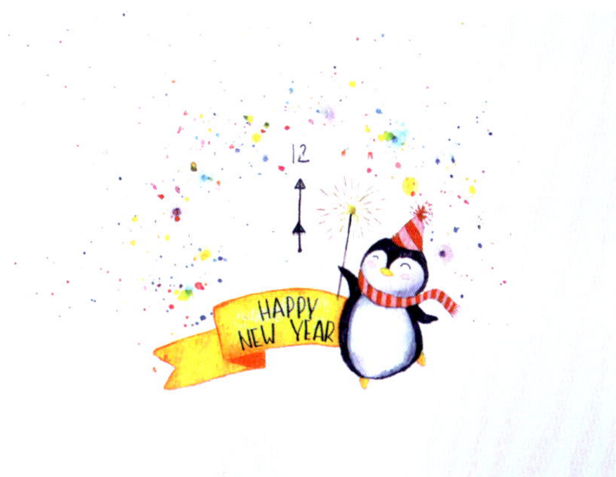

Try This!

Want to make your New Year card feel even more personal and fun? Here are a few ideas to try:

- Change the patterns on the scarf and hat for a new look.
- Add the year to the banner or the hat for a simple personalized touch.
- Add simple firework bursts behind the penguin using small dashes.
- Add a gold border around the whole card for a polished New Year feel.
- Add a second glow around the sparkler in a different color to make it shine even brighter.

What to Write

Simple words for your handmade card. Here are a few ideas to get you started:

- Shine in the New Year
- Let the countdown begin
- A year full of joy ahead
- Bring on the sparkle
- New Year, new joy
- Hope and happiness to you
- A little wish for the New Year
- You made it to midnight
- Happy 20XX
- May this year sparkle

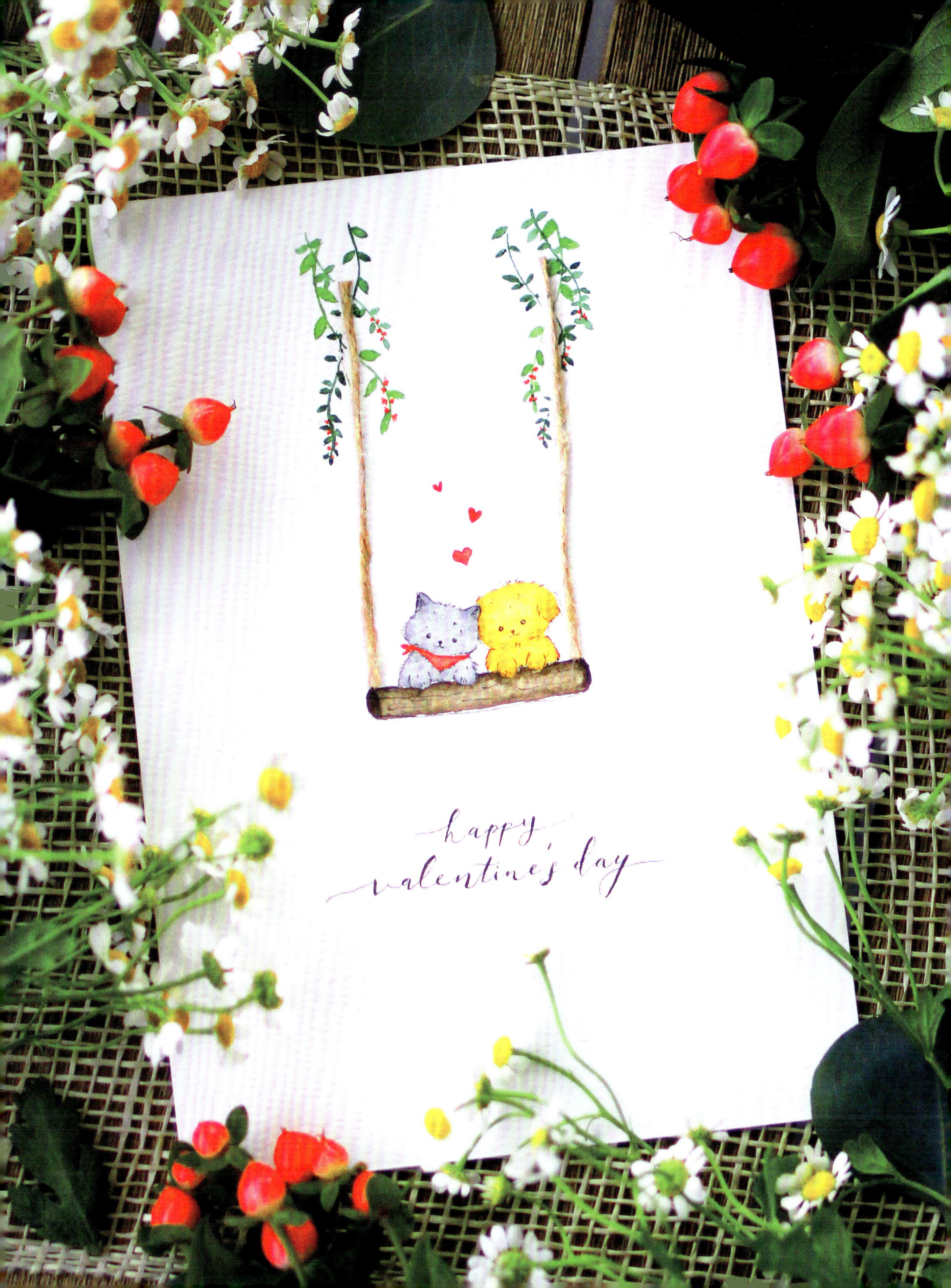
happy
valentine's day

Valentine Card: Swinging Into Love

Paint Colors

(Feel free to substitute similar shades; you don't need to match the exact names.)

- Gray
- Yellow Ochre
- Raw Umber
- Cadmium Red
- Sap Green
- Forest Green

Tools Used

(Feel free to use similar supplies; these are just suggestions!)

- Pencil
- Medium round brush (size 6-8)
- Small round brush (size 2–4)
- Detail brush (size 0 or smaller)
- 005 black fineliner
- Twine or string
- Glue

If you have ever wanted to paint a card that feels cozy and full of love, this is the one. There is something so simple and tender about a cat and dog sitting quietly on a swing together. It reminds me of those everyday moments of connection, being there for someone you care about. Valentine's Day is not just for couples. It is about celebrating the people who make your heart feel full. This card can be for a partner, a friend, a parent, a child, or anyone who makes life a little sweeter.

You do not need any experience to paint this. The sketch is simple, the shapes are soft, and the heart of it is in the feeling. You really cannot mess it up, and sometimes the little imperfections make it even more special. I used twine for the swing, but you can use yarn, embroidery thread, or any pretty string you have. You can even make the swing seat from a tiny piece of cardboard or scrap wood for extra charm. As you paint, think of someone you love and let it be a quiet moment of joy and gratitude. Take your time, enjoy the process, and most of all, have fun. You are making something by hand, and that already makes it meaningful.

Step 1: Light Pencil Sketch

Start by drawing two small animals sitting close together on a swing. Use a round shape for each head, then add simple ears. Give the cat pointy ears and the dog floppy ones. Sketch soft curves for their bodies and tiny arms resting on the swing. Let their heads lean in just a little, like best friends enjoying the view. Keep your pencil lines light so they are easy to paint over or erase later. Try using simple shapes like circles and ovals to place the heads and bodies. If you are unsure about the size or spacing, draw one animal first, then add the other right beside it.

If you're using the tear-out card, skip any sketching or shaping steps and begin painting where appropriate.

Step 2: Paint the Cat

Use gray to paint the cat and add more water to soften the color as needed. Start with a light layer to gently fill in the shape. Leave the small triangle under the face white, since that will be the bandana.

While the paint is still wet, use a clean Q-tip to lift some of the color from the center of the face and body. Add a little more gray to the edges while the paper is still damp to give the shape more depth (see Soft Center Glow, page 13). Keeping the edges darker helps the cat stand out and look rounder and more dimensional.

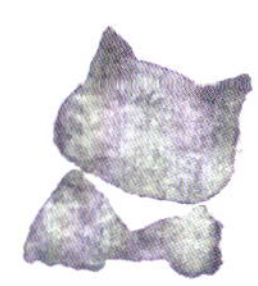

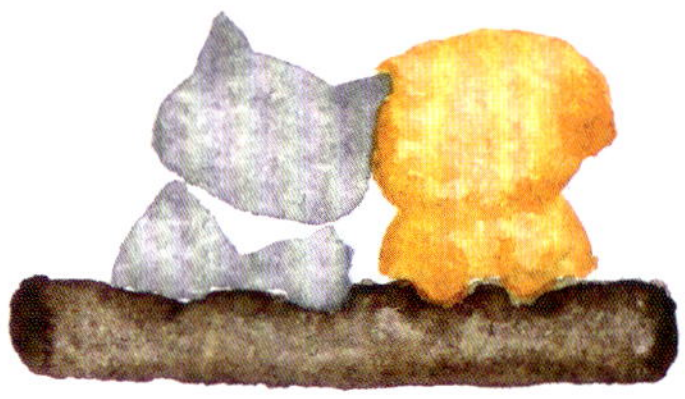

Step 3: Dog and Swing

Use yellow ochre to paint the dog, starting with a light, even layer. While the paint is still wet, use a clean Q-tip to lift a little color from the center of the face and body, just like you did in Step 2. This creates soft highlights and helps the shape feel warm and rounded. Then gently add more yellow ochre around the edges while the paper is still damp to deepen the color.

If the paint dries too quickly, rewet it with a clean damp brush or add another light layer once it is dry.

Let the dog dry completely before painting the swing so the colors do not mix.

For the swing, use raw umber or a soft brown from your palette. Paint the seat with smooth horizontal strokes, and while it is still damp, add a slightly darker brown to the bottom edge or corners. You can lightly drag your brush across the surface to mimic the look of wood grain. It is perfectly fine if the strokes are a little uneven. That soft texture makes it feel more natural and handmade.

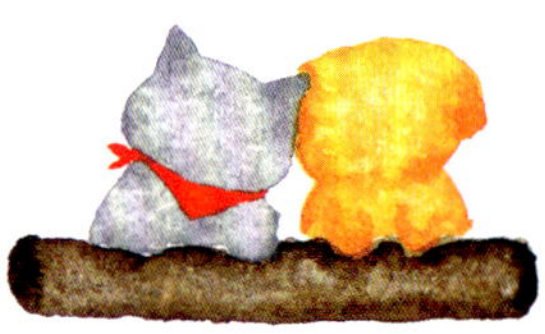

Step 4: Bandana

Use cadmium red to paint the cat's bandana. With a small round brush, gently fill in the small triangle you left white earlier.

Step 5: Add Hearts

Use cadmium red to paint a few small hearts floating up between the animals. Start with slightly larger hearts near them, then make the hearts smaller as they float upward. Keep the shapes simple and let the spacing feel light and natural.

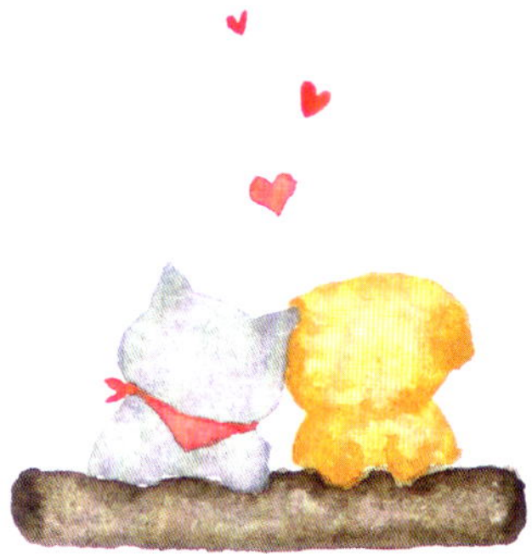

Step 6: Outline the Animals

When the paint is completely dry, use a 005 black fineliner to lightly outline the animals. Trace the outer edges of the heads, bodies, ears, and paws to define the shapes without outlining every detail.

Add a few short, uneven strokes along the edges to suggest fur, especially on the top of the head, around the ears, and along the back. Keep your hand relaxed and your lines playful so the animals feel soft and whimsical.

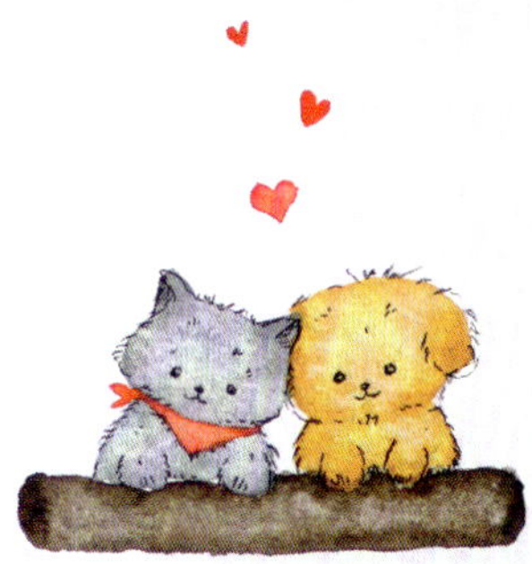

Step 7: Add the Swing Ropes

Cut two pieces of twine and attach them to the top of the swing seat, extending upward. Press them down gently so they stay in place. A good length is about two thirds to three quarters of the height of your paper. This helps the swing feel like it is truly hanging while still leaving space at the top for any extra details.

For a softer and more playful look, you can let the twine curve slightly instead of keeping it perfectly straight. You do not need to press down the entire length. Just a few spots will keep it in place and still feel light.

If you do not have twine, use whatever you have on hand, such as string or yarn. You can also draw the ropes if you prefer.

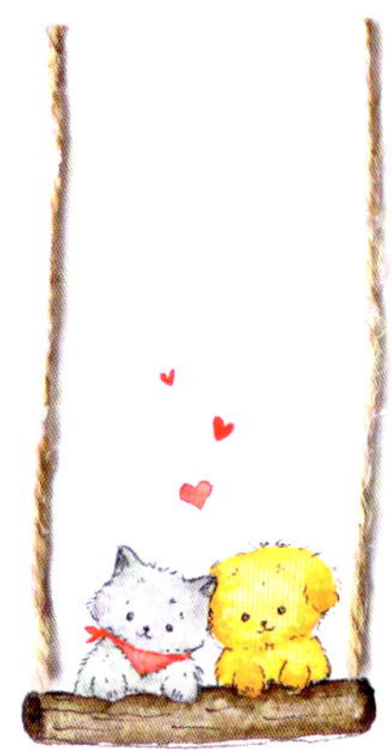

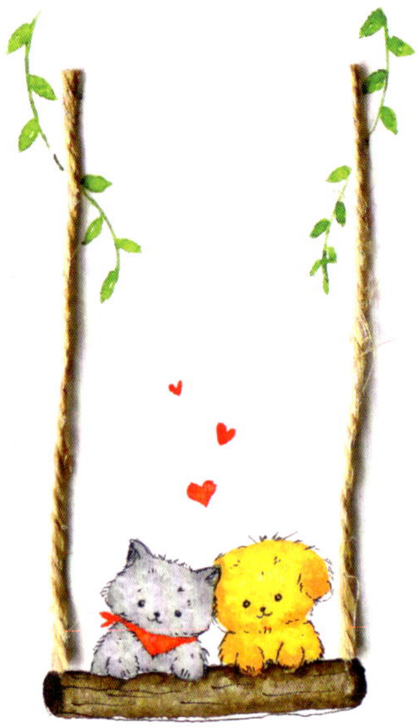

Step 8: Paint the Light Green Leaves

Start by adding the first layer of greenery near the tops of the ropes. Load a small round brush with sap green and add more water to create a light, diluted wash. The color should look soft and airy rather than bold.

Use this light green to paint thin stems, then add small leaves along them. Touch the tip of your brush, press gently, then lift to form each leaf. Let the leaves angle in different directions so they look natural and relaxed.

Keep this first layer light and simple. Let it dry completely before moving on.

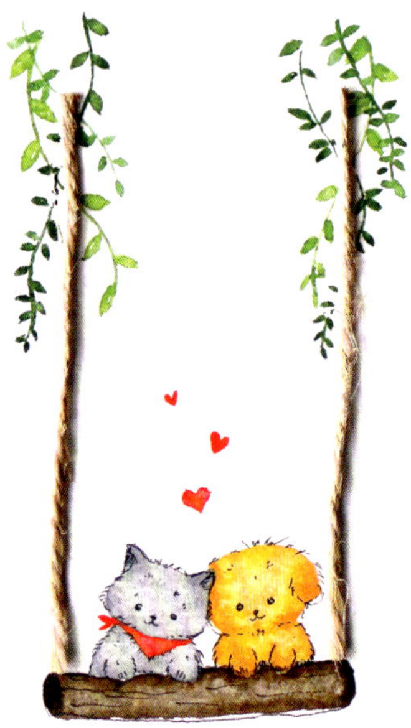

Step 9: Paint the Darker Green Leaves

When the light green leaves are dry, switch to forest green for the second layer. This deeper color will add contrast and dimension to the vines.

Add darker leaves intertwined with the lighter ones, letting them weave naturally through the greenery. Tuck a few closer to the ropes to create depth. Vary the size and direction so the vines feel fuller and more layered.

Keep your strokes loose and relaxed. A little variation makes the greenery look natural and soft.

Step 10: Lettering

Lightly sketch your message under the swing. You can write "happy valentine's day" in simple lowercase letters or choose any short phrase you like. I chose lowercase letters because they are easier for beginners to write neatly, and they give the card a quiet, friendly feel. To center the words, find the middle of your card and place the middle of your phrase on that point. Draw a faint pencil line to guide the height and spacing of your letters.

Once you are happy with the placement, trace over the letters slowly with a fine black pen. If you want your words to look a little more styled, thicken only the downward strokes to create a faux calligraphy look (see Faux Calligraphy, page 30). Keep your hand relaxed and take your time. Simple lettering looks beautiful and gives your card a warm handmade feel.

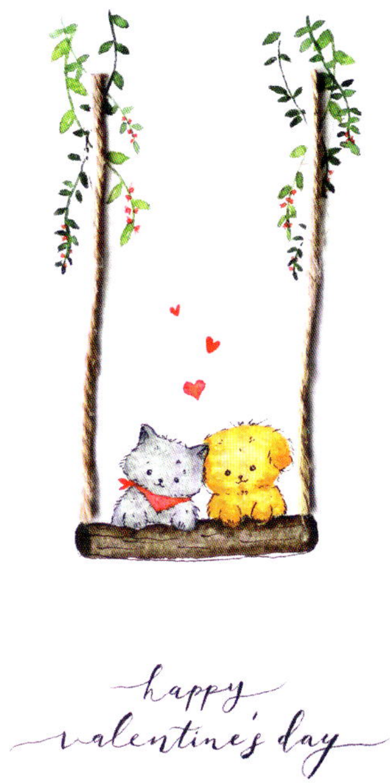

Try This!

Here are some fun and easy ways to change it up:

- Add a little metallic splatter for some sparkle.
- Try just one color for a clean, simple look.
- Swap the greenery for tiny flowers, stars, or other shapes.
- Use the design on a tag, postcard, or gift bag.
- Add someone's name to make it extra personal.

What to Write

Simple words for your handmade card. Here are a few ideas to get you started:

- You make my heart smile
- Love you always
- Swinging through life with you
- Thanks for being you
- You + Me
- Sending love your way
- So glad we're friends
- Better together
- Love and hugs
- You make life sweeter

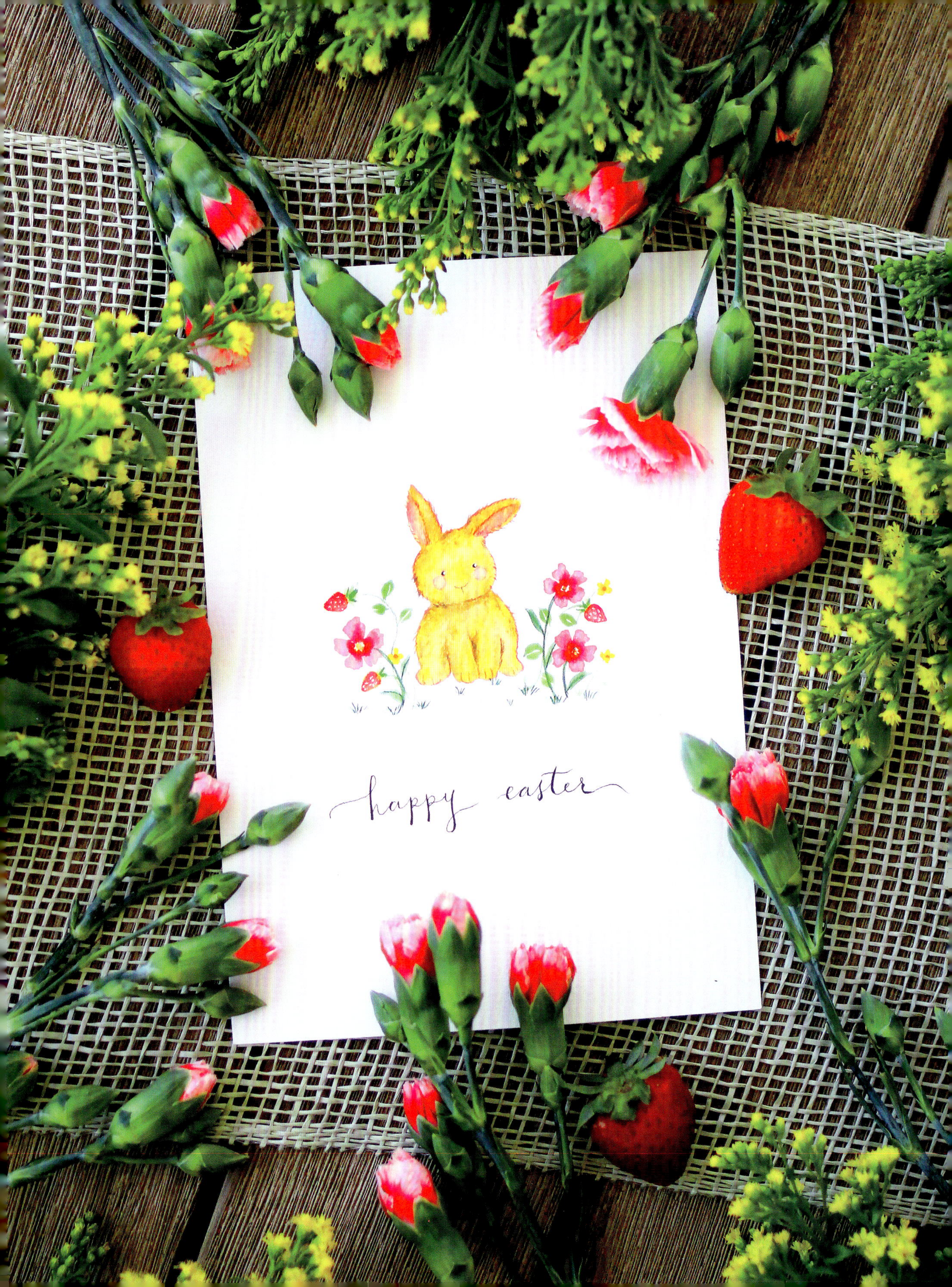
happy easter

Easter Card: Spring Bunny

Paint Colors

(Feel free to substitute similar shades; you don't need to match the exact names.)

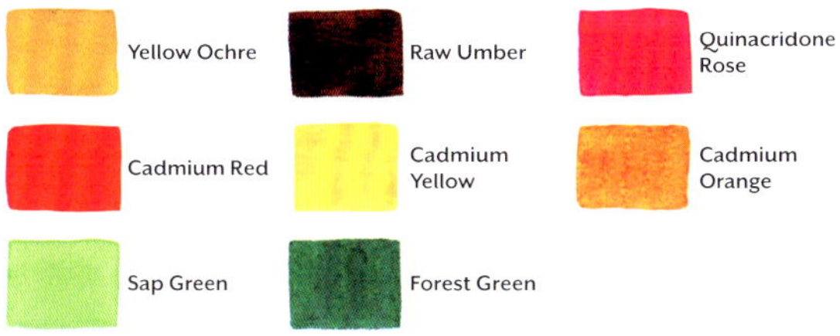

Tools Used

(Feel free to use similar supplies; these are just suggestions!)

- Pencil
- Medium round brush (size 6-8)
- Small round brush (size 2–4)
- Detail brush (size 0 or smaller)
- 005 black fineliner
- White gel pen or white acrylic paint

Bunnies and flowers remind me of spring, and they also show up a lot around Easter. Whether you celebrate Easter or not, this makes a charming spring card. In this project, we will paint a sweet little bunny surrounded by loose spring flowers and a few playful strawberries. It feels light and cheerful, and it's easy to follow, even if you are new to watercolor.

You might wonder why there are strawberries. They are not really an Easter thing, but I love the pop of red they bring. They feel like tiny surprises in a garden, and they balance so nicely with the pinks and greens.

As you paint, try to keep everything loose and gentle. Your bunny does not need to be perfect. Crooked ears are adorable and uneven petals look sweet. Those little imperfections give the card a soft, handmade feel.

Step 1: Light Sketch

Start by lightly sketching a small bunny in the center of your card. Draw a rounded head and an oval body, then add two long ears. Let one ear tilt a little to give the bunny a sweet and relaxed look. Add a tiny nose, a small curved mouth, and two dots for the eyes. Sketch the front paws and the soft lines for the legs. Keep your pencil marks light since we will add the flowers and greenery later with watercolor. The surrounding flowers and strawberries are already in place on the tear-out card.

If you're using the tear-out card, skip any sketching or shaping steps and begin painting where appropriate.

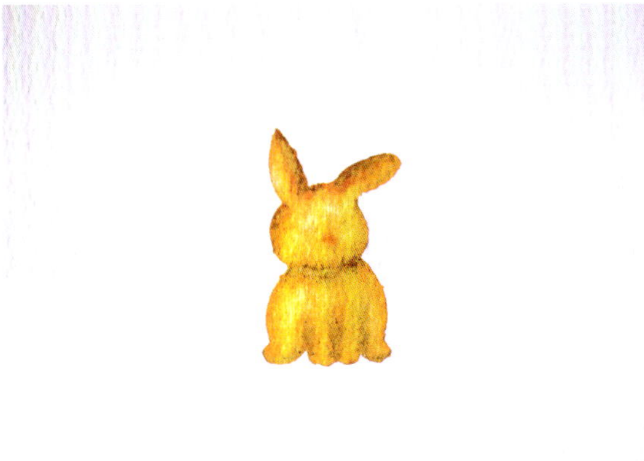

Step 2: Paint the Bunny

Mix yellow ochre with a touch of raw umber to make a soft, warm brown. Add enough water so the color stays light and gentle. Use a medium round brush to fill in the entire bunny with an even wash.

While the paint is still damp, add more of the same mix around the edges, ears, and neck so the outer areas stay slightly darker. Then gently tap the center of the bunny with a Q-tip to lift a bit of color and keep the middle lighter (see Soft Center Glow, page 13).

If any edges dry too quickly or feel a bit harsh, use a clean damp brush to soften them so the shape stays smooth and fluffy.

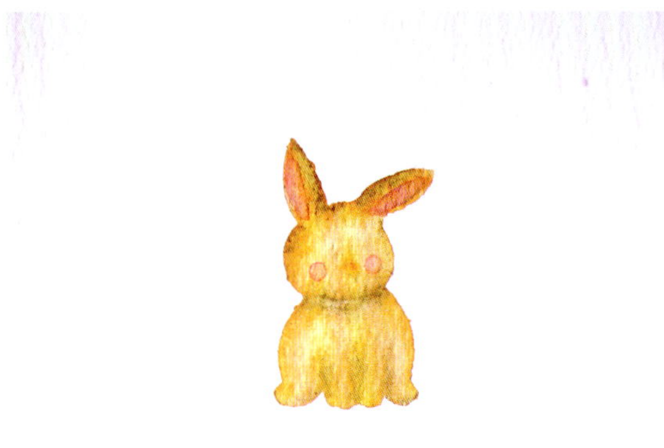

Step 3: Ears and Cheeks

Once your bunny is completely dry, mix quinacridone rose with plenty of water until the color looks soft and light. Use a small round brush to paint the inside of both ears. Then add two tiny circles on the cheeks for a gentle blush.

While the pink is still damp, lightly dab the centers with a clean Q-tip to soften the color and create a natural highlight. This little step keeps the ears and cheeks looking light, soft, and sweet.

Step 4: Face and Fur

When everything is completely dry, use your 005 fineliner to draw two tiny dots for the eyes. Place them just below the center of the face to keep the bunny looking extra sweet.

With a detail brush, use a slightly darker mix of yellow ochre and raw umber to paint the nose. Make a soft curved line across the top and a short line going down the center, almost like a curved "T."

To add fur texture, load your detail brush with the same darker brown mix. Use light pressure and flick tiny strokes around the ears, along the head, and down the sides of the body. A few delicate strokes are enough.

If any line looks too strong, gently dab it with a Q-tip to soften it.

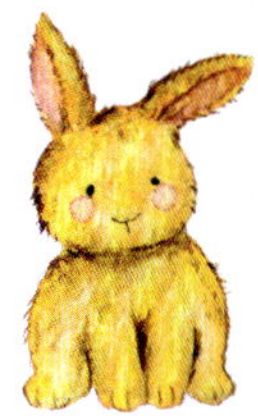

Step 5: Paint the Flowers

Now let's add a few flowers around your bunny. Load the tip of your round brush with a light wash of quinacridone rose. To make one flower, paint five loose petals in a soft circle. Press your brush down lightly, give it a tiny wiggle, and then lift. Repeat for each petal. The little wiggle helps create natural, imperfect shapes.

While the quinacridone rose is still damp, touch the center with a tiny bit of cadmium red and let it blend outward on its own. Leave a small spot in the middle untouched so the flower has a soft highlight. Continue painting the rest of the flowers the same way.

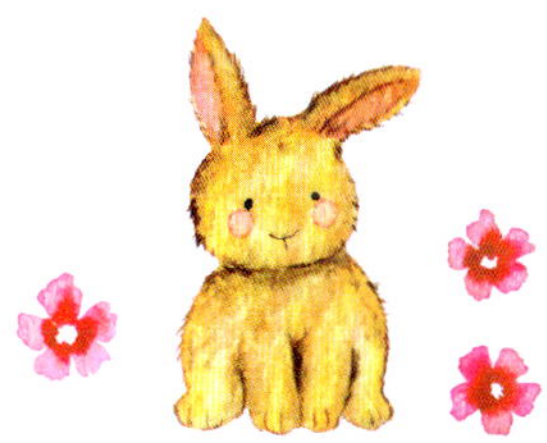

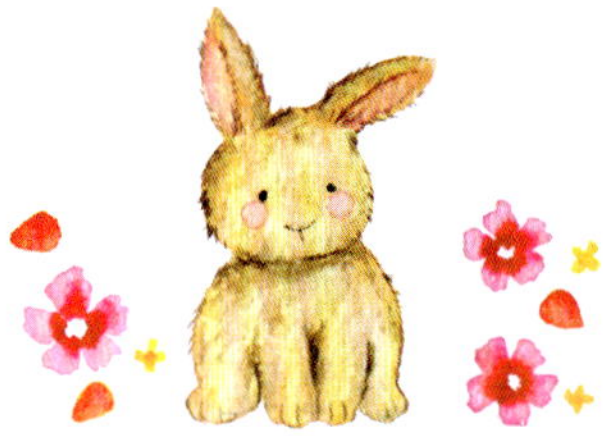

Step 6: Strawberries and Yellow Flowers

Let's add a few small accents around the bunny. For the strawberries, start with cadmium yellow and paint a tiny teardrop shape with the point facing outward. The yellow base warms up the red and gives the strawberry a soft glow. While the yellow is still damp, add cadmium red and let the colors blend on the paper. Before it dries, dab one small spot with a Q-tip to lift a little color and create a soft highlight.

For the tiny yellow flowers, load your detail brush with cadmium yellow. Lightly dab four tiny petals in a simple cross shape to form each flower. Keep these more delicate than the pink ones so they add variety. While the yellow is still damp, drop a hint of cadmium orange into the center and let it blend softly. If the center looks too strong, touch it lightly with a Q-tip to soften it.

Scatter the flowers around the bunny in a way that feels balanced. A simple guide is to place one on each side and one near the bottom to frame the bunny gently.

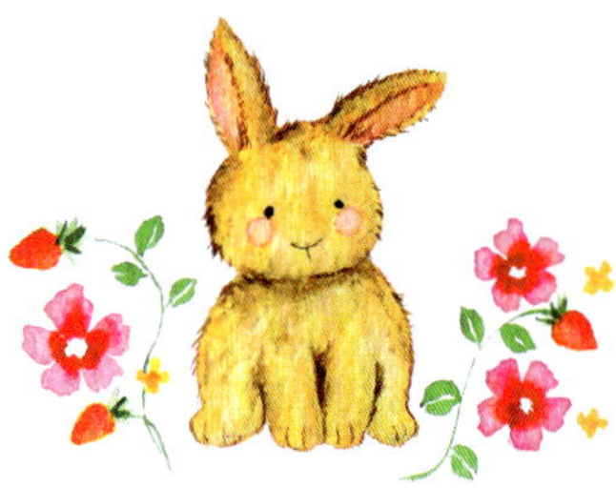

Step 7: Stems and Leaves

Use a light wash of sap green to paint the strawberry tops. Make a few short flicks that curve outward to form the leafy shape. Leave a small white gap in the center so the leaves look fresh. Use the same light green to paint the curved stems that connect the strawberries to the flowers.

Next, paint the strawberry leaves. Press your brush down and pull in a curved stroke, then repeat on the other side so a thin white gap stays in the middle. This white line becomes the center vein (see Two-Stroke Vein Leaf, page 24). Keep your strokes simple and relaxed.

When this layer is completely dry, use forest green to add a few more short flicks to the strawberry tops for contrast and extra depth. Use just a little of the darker color so everything stays soft.

Step 8: Paint the Pink Flower Stems and Leaves

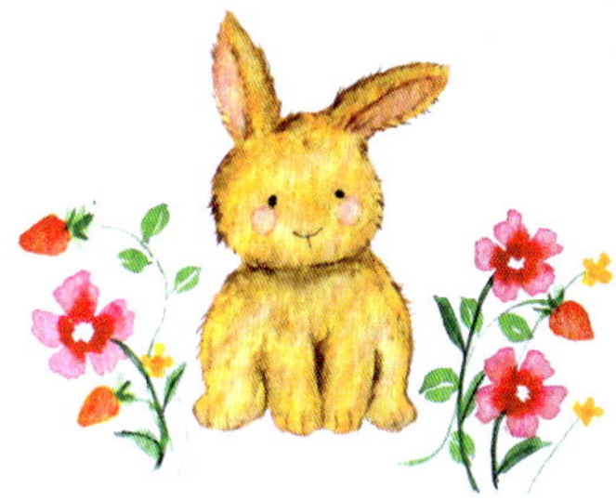

Load your brush with a light wash of sap green and paint the stems of the pink flowers using soft, gentle curves. Then add the leaves. These leaves are longer and slightly curved, almost like small banana shapes. Press your brush down to form the rounded base, then lift to create the tip (see One-Stroke Leaf, page 23). Angle the leaves in different directions so they feel natural and relaxed.

When this layer is dry, switch to forest green. Use your detail brush and light pressure to deepen parts of the stems and add simple lines as veins to the pink flower leaves.

Step 9: Add the Grass

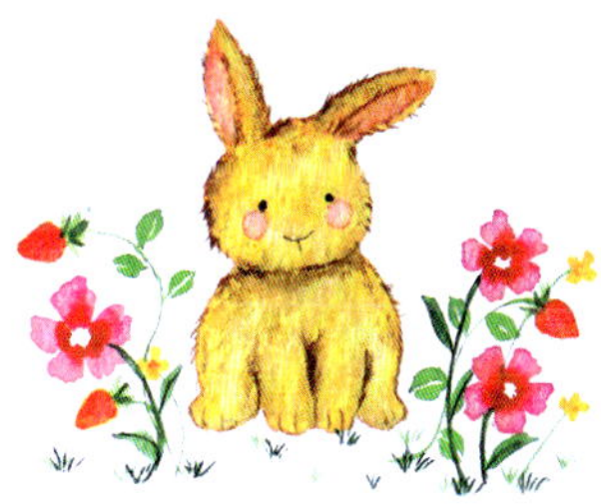

Load your brush with sap green and use quick upward flicks to paint small blades of grass (see Flicks, page 21). Start each stroke with a little pressure at the base, then lift your brush quickly so the top ends in a fine point. Keep your strokes short and light so the grass looks soft and natural.

When the first layer is dry, switch to forest green and add a few more flicks for depth. Place some blades close together and vary the length and angle so the grass patches look full and lively. Just a few extra strokes will make the whole scene feel grounded and complete.

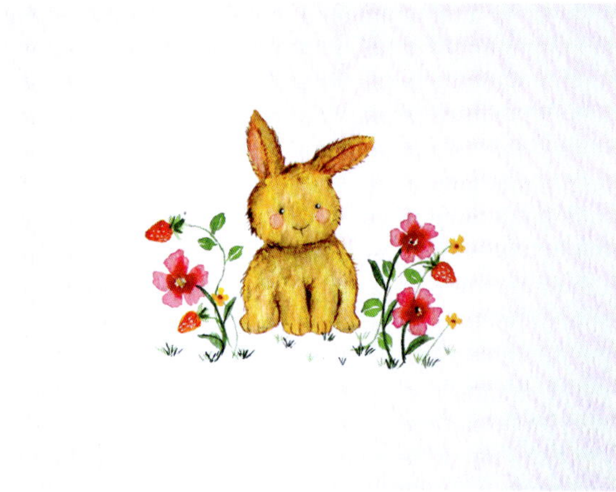

Step 10: Centers and Highlights

Use yellow ochre to dot the centers of the pink flowers (see Dotting, page 21). Let this dry, then tap a tiny touch of raw umber or another darker color into the center for added depth. Use only a small amount so the centers stay soft.

For the little yellow flowers, place another tiny dot of yellow ochre in the center to finish them.

Once everything is completely dry, use a white gel pen or white opaque paint, such as acrylic or gouache to add a few tiny seed dots on each strawberry. Keep the dots light and spaced apart so they don't overpower the red. Add one tiny white dot to each eye as well. Tap gently with very soft pressure so the dots stay neat and clean.

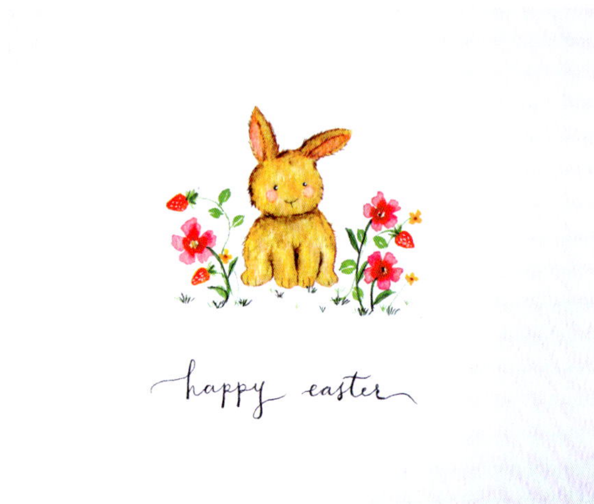

Step 11: Lettering

Lightly write "happy easter" in pencil below the bunny. Use the center of the bunny to help guide your spacing. If it helps, draw a soft guideline with a ruler to keep the letters even. Keep the letters rounded and simple. You can write in lowercase or any style you like.

Once you are happy with the placement, trace over the pencil with a 005 black fineliner. Think of it as drawing each stroke rather than writing quickly. To create a faux calligraphy look, thicken only the downward strokes of each letter (see Faux Calligraphy, page 30). Work slowly and keep your hand relaxed.

Try This!

Looking for simple ways to change your design? Here are a few ideas to try:

- Use carrots, painted eggs, or tulips instead of strawberries.
- Add extra flowers or play with different color palettes.
- Turn it into a spring-themed art print by leaving off the words.
- Make a matching tag, bookmark, or gift bag using just the bunny.
- Try a patterned background with soft dots or sky washes.

What to Write

Simple words for your handmade card. Here are a few ideas to get you started:

- Some bunny loves you
- Wishing you a hoppy day
- Sending Easter smiles
- Wishing you sunshine and blooms
- Hello spring, hello joy
- He is risen, hallelujah
- Blessed Easter to you
- Happy spring
- Bloom where you are planted
- May your day bloom

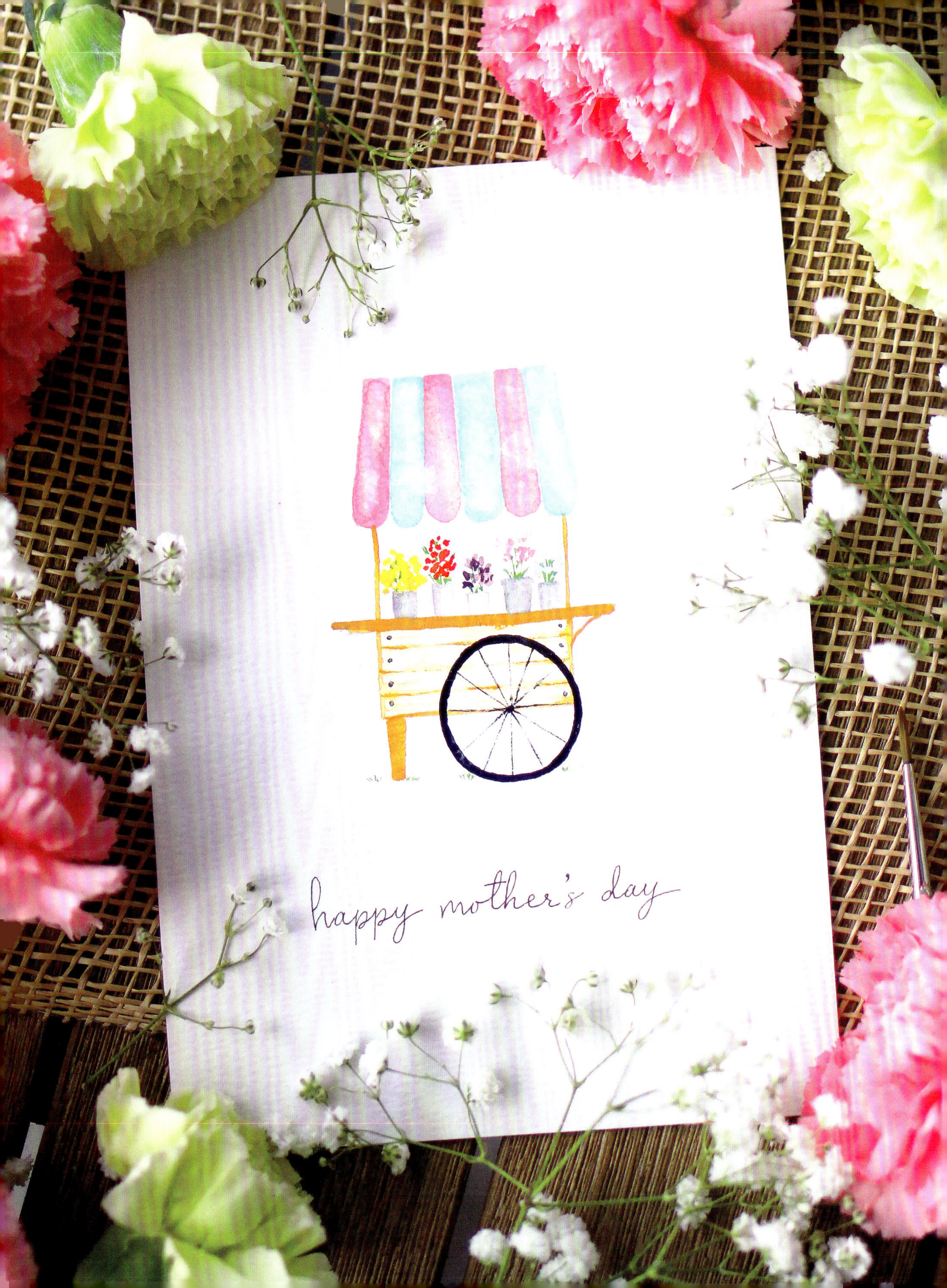
happy mother's day

Mother's Day Card: Flower Cart

Paint Colors

(Feel free to substitute similar shades; you don't need to match the exact names.)

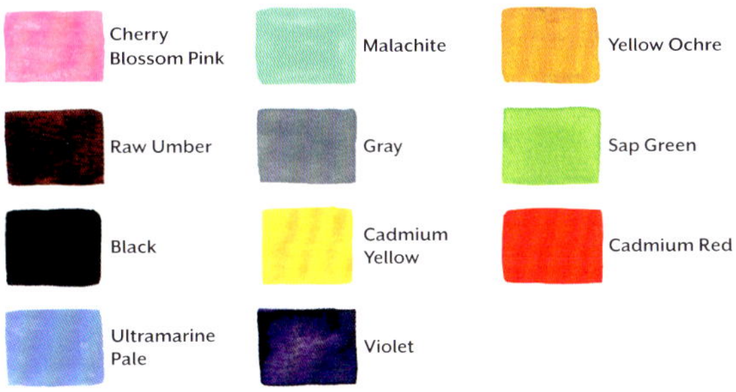

Tools Used

(Feel free to use similar supplies; these are just suggestions!)

- Pencil
- Ruler
- Medium round brush (size 6-8)
- Small round brush (size 2–4)
- Detail brush (size 0 or smaller)
- Small flat brush (size 2)
- 005 black fineliner

Flowers have always been a symbol of love, care, and gratitude, which makes them just right for Mother's Day. A little flower cart feels like a tiny garden on wheels, filled with color and joy. The flowers here are painted in the simplest way, just loose little blobs of color that turn into a cheerful bouquet once they are all together. We will also use the lifting technique in this card to create soft highlights and depth, making everything look lighter, brighter, and fuller of life.

Each flower can feel like a small thank you gathered in the cart to celebrate love. Every brushstroke adds to the charm, and the handmade touches are what make this card so special. This project is light and beginner friendly, a lovely way to paint from the heart for Mother's Day.

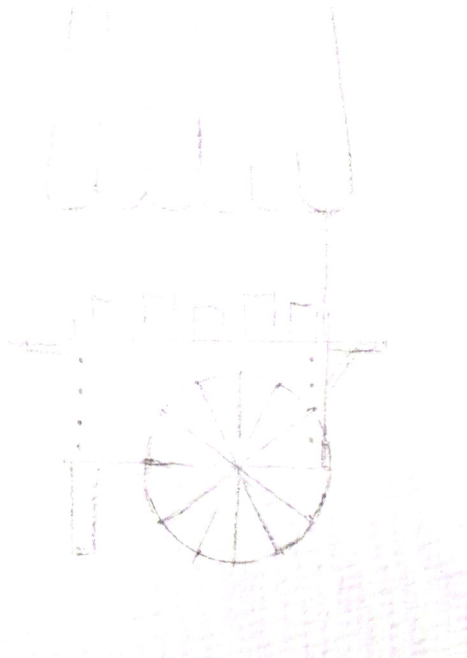

Step 1: Light Sketch

Lightly sketch the cart. Use a ruler to keep the base and shelf lines straight. Add two posts and a scalloped canopy on top. Inside the cart, draw a few flowerpots in slightly different sizes to give it a playful feel.

For the wheel, trace around a small cup or lid to create a circle. Mark the top, bottom, left, and right, then add a few marks in between. Place a small dot in the center and draw light lines out to each mark, like slices of a pie.

Keep your pencil lines light so they blend into the paint later. A little unevenness adds charm.

If you're using the tear-out card, skip any sketching or shaping steps and begin painting where appropriate.

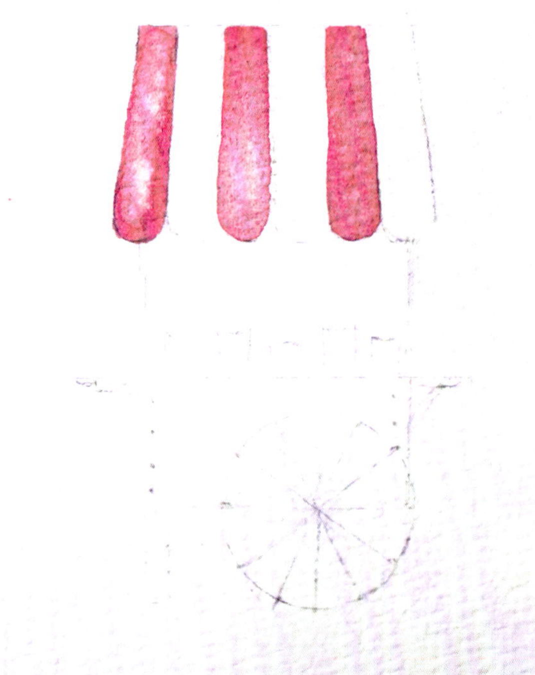

Step 2: Paint the Pink Stripes

Load your medium round brush with cherry blossom pink and paint every other canopy stripe. Start at the top of each stripe and pull your brush downward in smooth, even strokes (see Flat Wash Stroke, page 22).

While the paint is still damp, gently tap the center of the stripe with a Q-tip to lift a little color. This creates a soft highlight that makes the stripes look fuller and more rounded (see Lifting, page 13).

Step 3: Paint the Malachite Stripes

Load your medium round brush with malachite. Paint the remaining canopy stripes using the Flat Wash Stroke, just as you did in Step 2. Start at the top of each stripe and pull your brush downward in smooth, even strokes.

While the paint is still damp, gently touch the center of each stripe with a Q-tip to lift a little color. Follow the same lifting you used in Step 2 so the highlights stay soft and consistent.

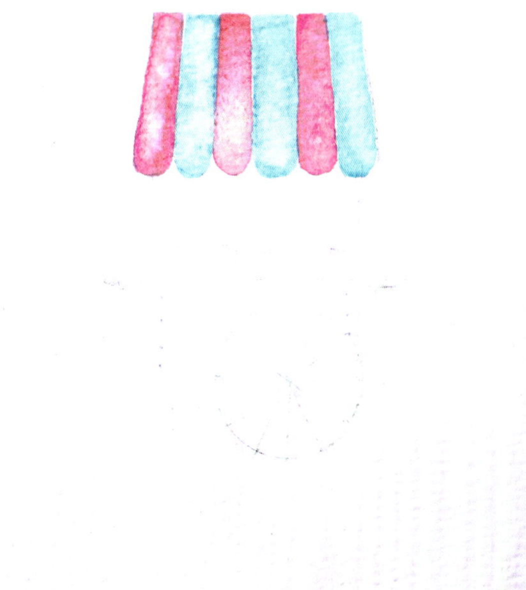

Step 4: Paint the Cart Base

Use a medium round brush and load it with a light mix of yellow ochre. Create a flat wash, an even layer of color, by using the Flat Wash Stroke you used in the last steps. Start on one side of the rectangle and pull your brush across in smooth horizontal strokes. Continue in the same direction stroke until the entire base is filled.

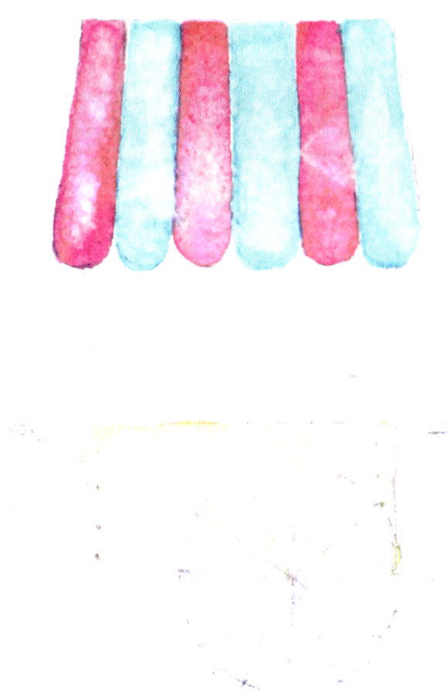

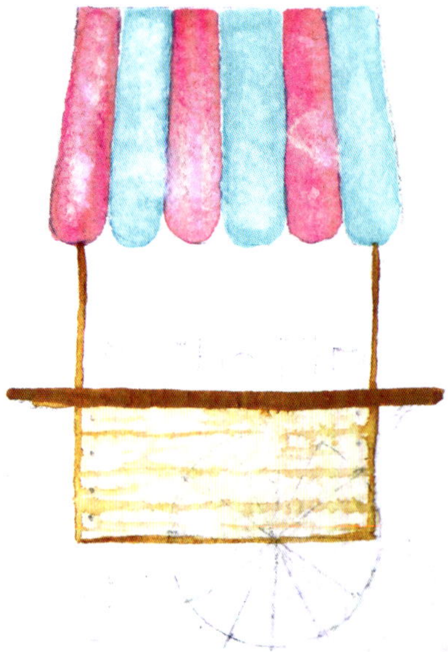

Step 5: Add the Wood Lines and Paint the Posts

While the yellow ochre wash is still a little damp, load your detail brush with a more concentrated yellow ochre (more paint and less water). Paint light horizontal lines across the cart base to show the wood markings and to define the planks. Because the first layer is still damp, the lines will soften and blend in gently.

After the cart base dries a bit more, load your small round brush with raw umber. Paint the two posts with one steady downward stroke for each post. Then paint the long table plank across the top of the cart with the same raw umber.

While the raw umber on the posts is still damp, gently touch a Q-tip to the center of each post to lift a little color and add a soft highlight.

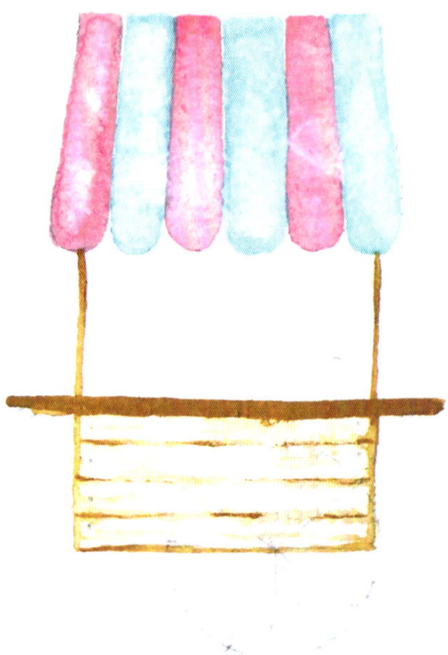

Step 6: Add the Darker Wood Lines

Once the cart base is completely dry, load your detail brush with a richer raw umber (less water and more paint). Add a few darker horizontal lines across the planks to give the wood extra depth. Keep these lines light and spaced out so they do not cover the softer yellow ochre markings underneath.

Step 7: Paint the Foot of the Cart

Mix a touch of yellow ochre into your raw umber to create a lighter brown (see Color Mixing, page 12). Use your small round brush to paint the foot at the bottom of the cart with one smooth stroke. Keeping this foot a lighter brown helps balance the design so the focus stays on the cart and the flowers above.

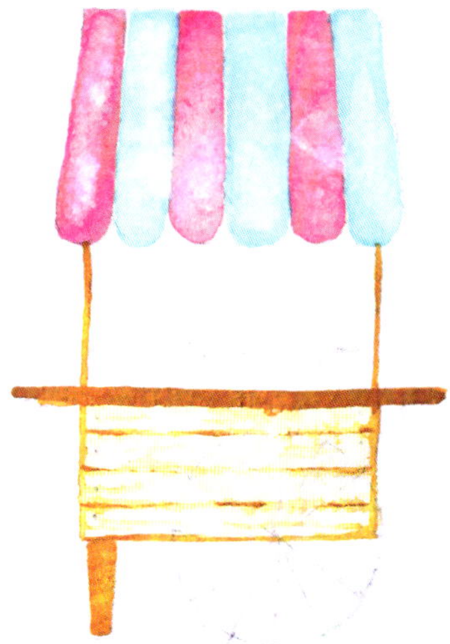

Step 8: Paint the Wheel

Use a detail brush and black paint to outline the wheel and spokes. After loading your brush, gently blot it on a paper towel to make sure it is not too wet. Start by painting the outer circle, then add the lines from the center outward, like slices of a pie. Keep your brush pressure light so the lines stay thin (see Thin Lines, page 20).

You can practice a few thin strokes on scrap paper first if you like. It is perfectly fine if the lines are not exact. Small variations give the wheel character.

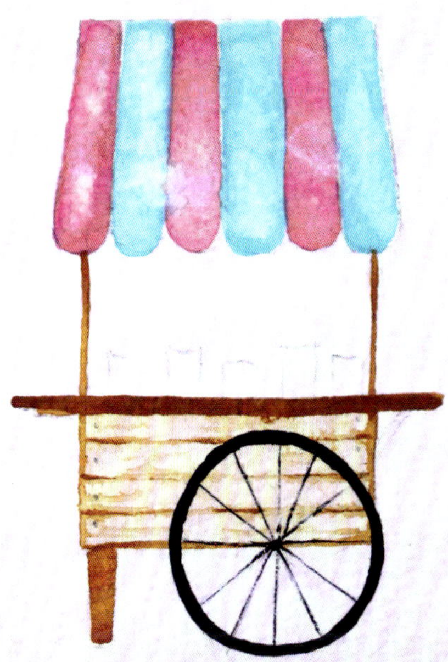

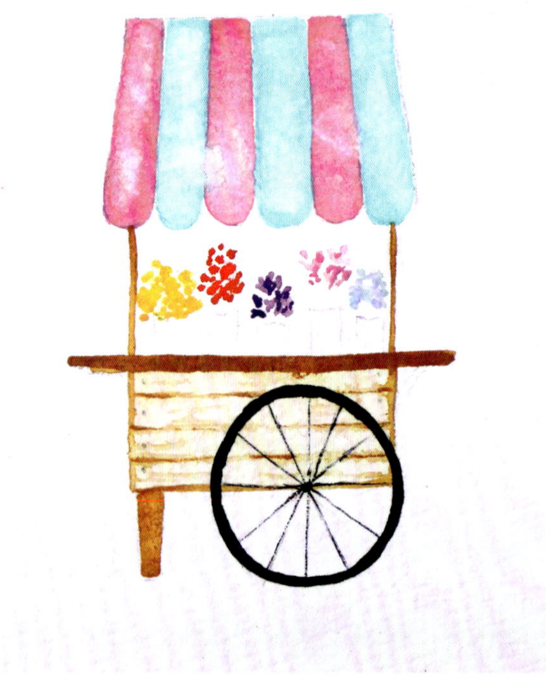

Step 9: Paint the Flowers

Use a small round brush to dab little blobs of color across the top of the cart (see Dabbed Dots Flower, page 27). I used cadmium yellow, cadmium red, violet, cherry blossom pink, and ultramarine pale in that order, but you can choose any colors you like.

For the first layer, use a watered-down version of each color. Lightly dab small dots to form loose flower shapes. Keep your brush pressure light so the dots stay soft.

Once the first layer is dry, add a slightly darker value of the same color on top. Dab a few darker dots into each flower cluster, but do not cover the lighter layer. Leaving some of the softer dots showing gives the flowers natural highlights and makes them look fuller and livelier.

Keep the shapes loose. The mix of light and dark dots creates the look of tiny overlapping petals.

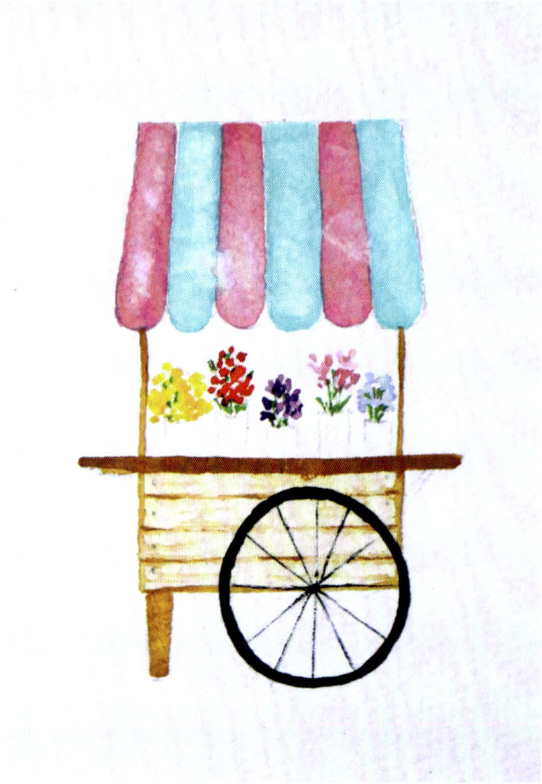

Step 10: Paint the Stems and Leaves

Load a small round brush with sap green. Using just the tip of your brush, paint thin lines coming down from each flower cluster to create the stems. Keep the strokes loose and natural.

Add a few quick, light strokes along the stems to suggest leaves. These can be small, simple dashes rather than detailed shapes. Keep everything soft and loose.

Step 11: Paint the Pots

Mix a light gray by adding plenty of water to your paint. Use a small round brush to fill in each flowerpot with this light gray wash. While the paint is still damp, add a few darker gray strokes along the sides so the colors blend softly. Keep the center of each pot lighter to show where the light hits.

If you want the highlights even softer, gently lift a little paint from the center with a Q-tip, just like you did earlier. These small light areas help the pots look more rounded and dimensional. Let everything dry completely before moving on.

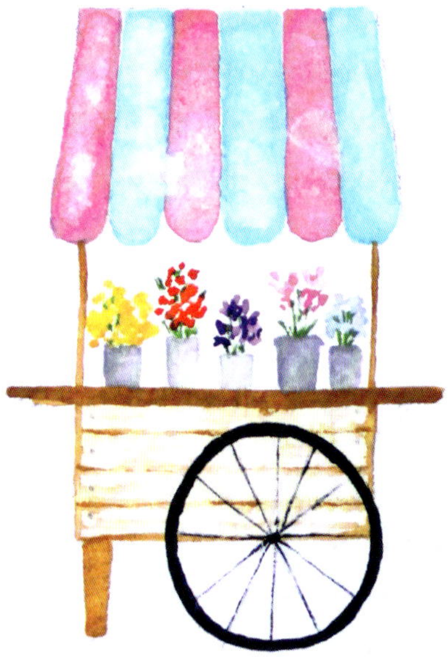

Step 12: Add the Nails

Dip a detail brush into black paint. Hold the brush straight up and gently touch the tip to the paper to create small dots. Place the dots along the edges of the cart. They do not need to be perfectly spaced. Because the cart is dry, the dots will stay crisp. These tiny marks are quick to add but make the cart look more complete.

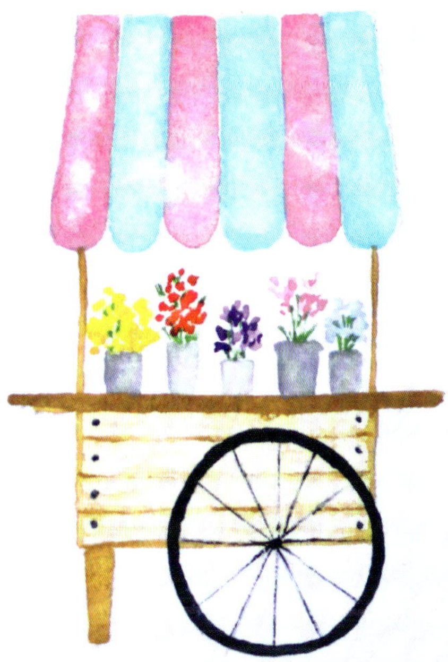

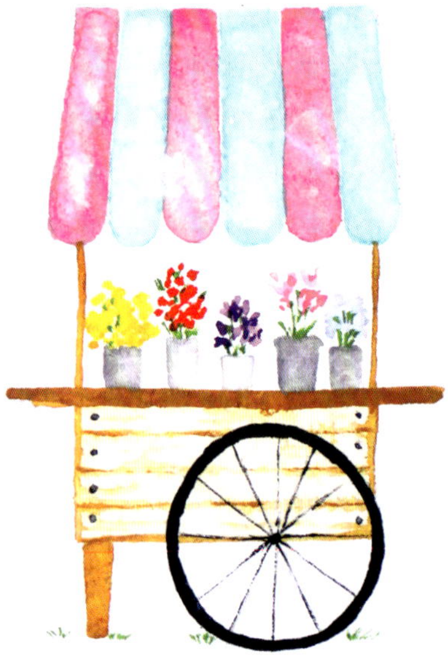

Step 13: Add the Grass

Load a small round brush with sap green. Using just the tip of your brush, paint quick dashes at the bottom of the cart and wheel to suggest blades of grass. Keep the strokes light and leave space between them so the grass does not turn into a solid block of color.

Use different amounts of water in a few strokes so some blades look lighter and some look a little darker. This small variation helps the grass look soft and natural.

Do not try to make every blade the same length or pointing in the same direction. A little unevenness helps the grass look more real.

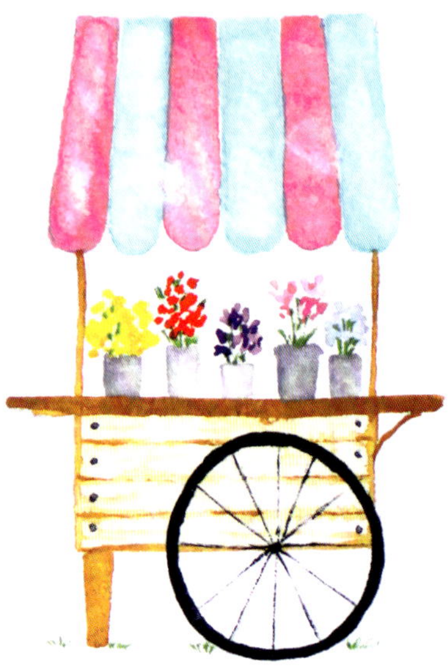

Step 14: Lettering

Lightly sketch your words in pencil first so you can adjust the size and spacing before committing to ink. To help keep the letters straight, draw a faint guideline and erase it after the ink dries. If centering feels tricky, find the middle of your card and align your phrase from that point.

Practice your lettering on scrap paper until you feel comfortable. A simple, loose script works well with the soft watercolor style, but you can write in any style you like.

When you are ready, trace over your pencil lines with a 005 black fineliner. Write slowly and keep your hand relaxed so your lines stay smooth and steady. Let the ink dry completely before erasing the pencil.

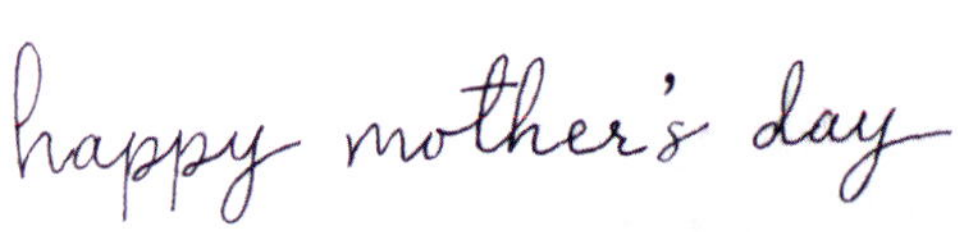

Try This!

Want to give your Mother's Day card a new twist? Here are some fun ways to change it up:

- Use soft pastels or brighter colors for a fresh new look.
- Add butterflies, hearts, or extra flowers around the cart.
- Paint different kinds of flowers, like tulips, daisies, or roses.
- Paint a little pathway under the cart with light brown or gray.
- Add more grass or small flowers at the bottom for extra detail.

What to Write

Simple words for your handmade card. Here are a few ideas to get you started:

- To the best mom
- Thank you, Mom
- Love you, Mom
- Best mom ever
- Love you always
- For someone special
- Sending love today
- So thankful for you
- With all my love
- You fill my heart

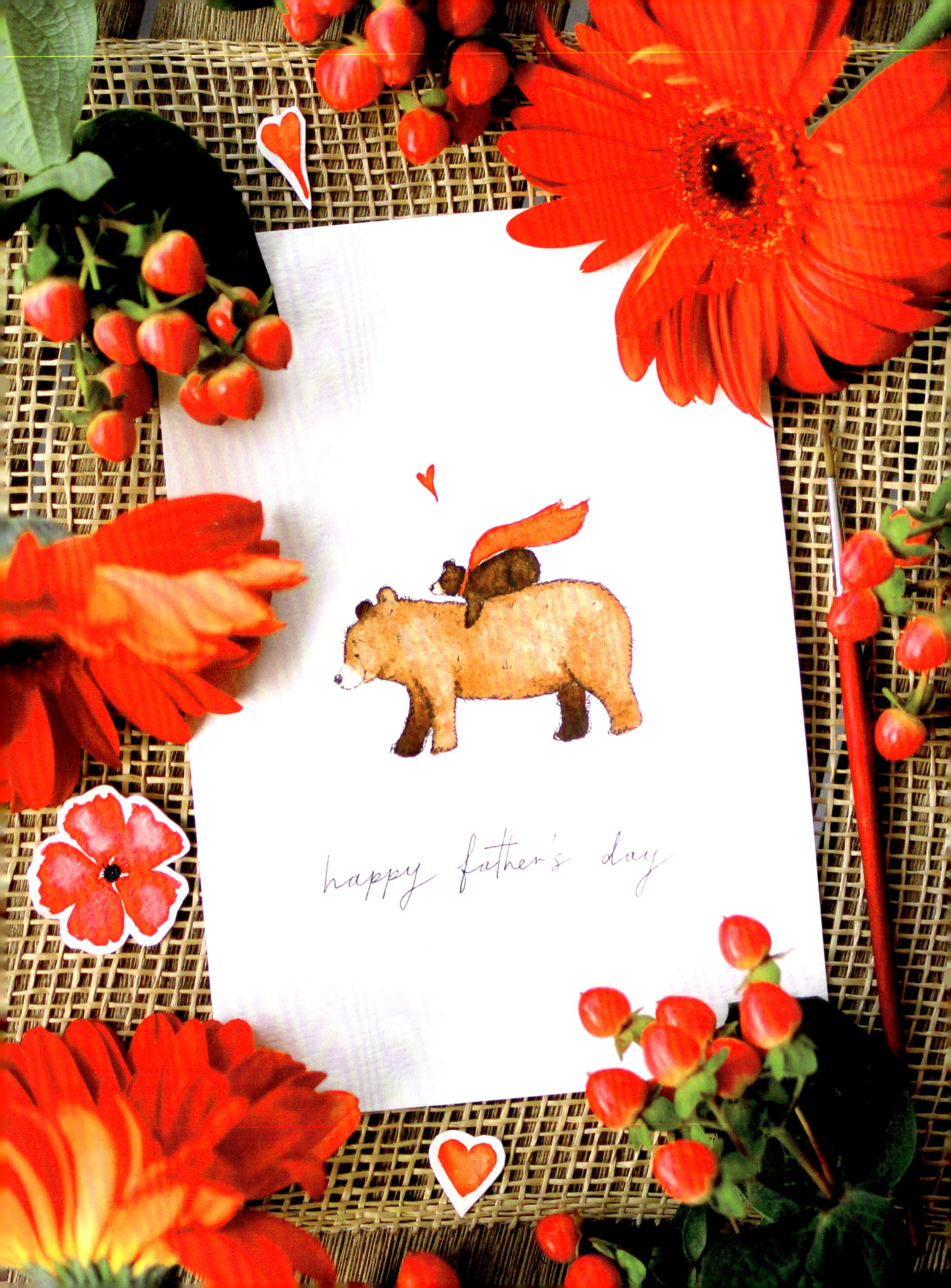
happy father's day

Father's Day Card: Big Bear, Little Bear

Paint Colors

(Feel free to substitute similar shades; you don't need to match the exact names.)

Yellow Ochre

Raw Umber

Natural Beige

Cadmium Red

Tools Used

(Feel free to use similar supplies; these are just suggestions!)

- Pencil
- Medium round brush (size 6-8)
- Detail brush (size 0 or smaller)
- 005 black fineliner

Father's Day makes me think about the steady love that dads give. It is not loud or showy. It is the small moments, the patient help, and the calm presence that makes you feel safe without even realizing it. I wanted this card to reflect that gentle kind of love, just a big bear carrying a tiny cub who trusts him completely. The bright red cape adds a playful touch because kids often see their dads as real-life superheroes.

As you paint, keep the shapes loose and relaxed. The bears do not need perfect lines. A slightly crooked ear or uneven paw will still look cute. Soft edges and small wobbles are part of watercolor, and they give your card that warm handmade feel.

This card works for anyone who has lifted you up, whether that is a dad, a grandpa, a brother, or someone steady and caring in your life. It is a thoughtful way to say thank you and a sweet project to paint at any level.

Step 1: Light Sketch

Use a pencil to draw a big jellybean shape for the bear's body. Add short legs, a round head, two small ears, and a soft curve for the nose.

On top of the big bear, sketch the cub using a small oval for the body and a circle for the head. Let one arm drape forward so it looks like the cub is holding on.

Keep your pencil lines loose and light.

If you're using the tear-out card, skip any sketching or shaping steps and begin painting where appropriate.

Step 2: Paint the Bear

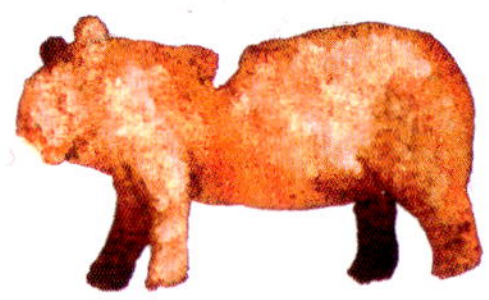

Mix a soft warm brown by starting with yellow ochre and adding a little raw umber until you like the color. Test it on scrap paper first. (see Color Mixing, page 12).

Fill in the big bear with this warm brown, leaving the snout unpainted. Keep your brush wet so the wash goes on smoothly.

Lightly dab the inner body and face with a Q-tip to lift some color. This will make the edges appear darker and create depth (see Soft Center Glow, page 13).

If you want deeper color on the legs or ears, add a little more raw umber while the paint is still wet.

Let everything dry, then paint the snout with a light wash of natural beige.

Step 3: Paint the Cub

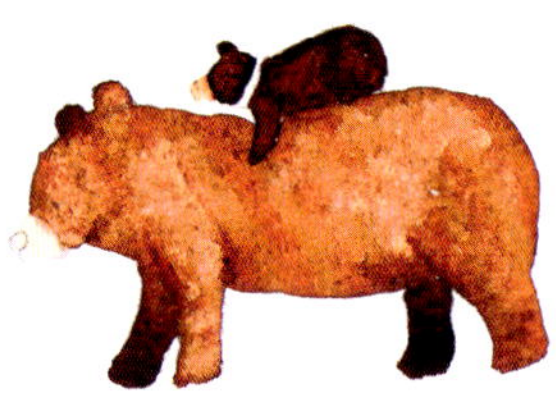

Fill in the cub with raw umber, leaving the snout area unpainted at first. Add more water to make the cub lighter or more paint to make it darker. Because the space is small, the color can become strong quickly. If it feels too dark, lightly tap the center with a clean Q-tip to lift some color.

When the body is dry, paint the snout with a light wash of natural beige.

Step 4: Paint the Cape

Paint the cub's cape with cadmium red. Keep your brush slightly wet so the color goes on smoothly. While the paint is still damp, gently dab one small spot with a clean Q-tip to lift a little color and create a soft highlight.

As you paint, it does not need to match the sketch exactly. Small changes often make the cape look even more natural and expressive.

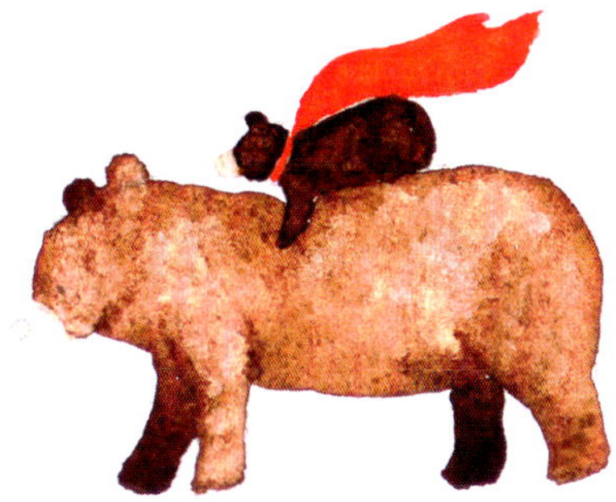

Step 5: Final Details

Paint a tiny heart above the bears using cadmium red. Let it dry completely.

Use a 005 black fineliner to add fur. Flick your pen outward in short, light strokes along the back, legs, and belly. Add a few tiny strokes inside the body to break up the larger brown areas. Draw a couple of small dashes inside the front ear for shadow. When you draw the noses, leave a tiny gap or break in the line to create a soft highlight. Finish with simple dots for the eyes and a small, curved line for the smile.

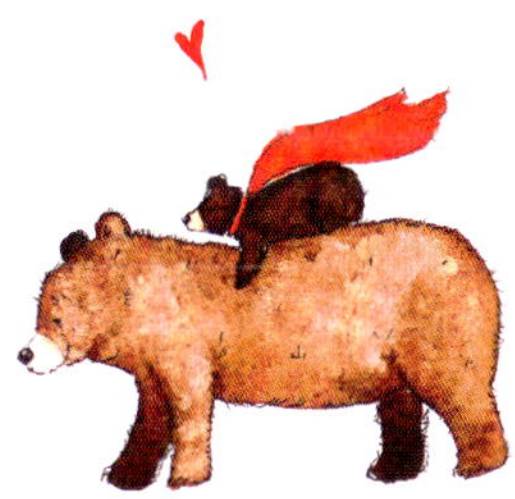

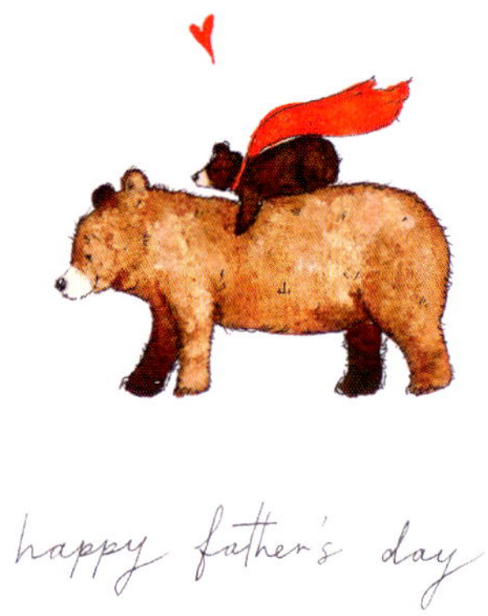

Step 6: Lettering

Now add your message. A little wobble makes it feel more handmade. I wrote my words under the bears in simple lowercase letters, but you can place your message wherever it looks best.

Lightly sketch your words in pencil first. To help with spacing, start with the middle word. For example, if you are writing "happy father's day," begin with "father's," then add "happy" and "day." Keep the letters small and simple, then trace over them with a 005 fineliner. Go slowly and remember, tiny imperfections are part of the charm.

Try This!

Here are some fun and easy ways to make this card your own:

- Try different bear colors like gray, golden brown, or even a black and white panda.
- Paint the cape a fun color like blue, green, or rainbow.
- Add tiny hearts, butterflies, or little stars around the bears.
- Paint tiny footprints leading up to the bears.
- Add a name to personalize it and make it extra special.

What to Write

Simple words for your handmade card. Here are a few ideas to get you started:

- Love you, Dad
- Thanks for carrying me
- You're my hero
- To the best Dad
- Thank you for always being there
- You lift me up
- You mean the world to me
- Thanks for all the little things
- My forever hero
- Superdad in disguise

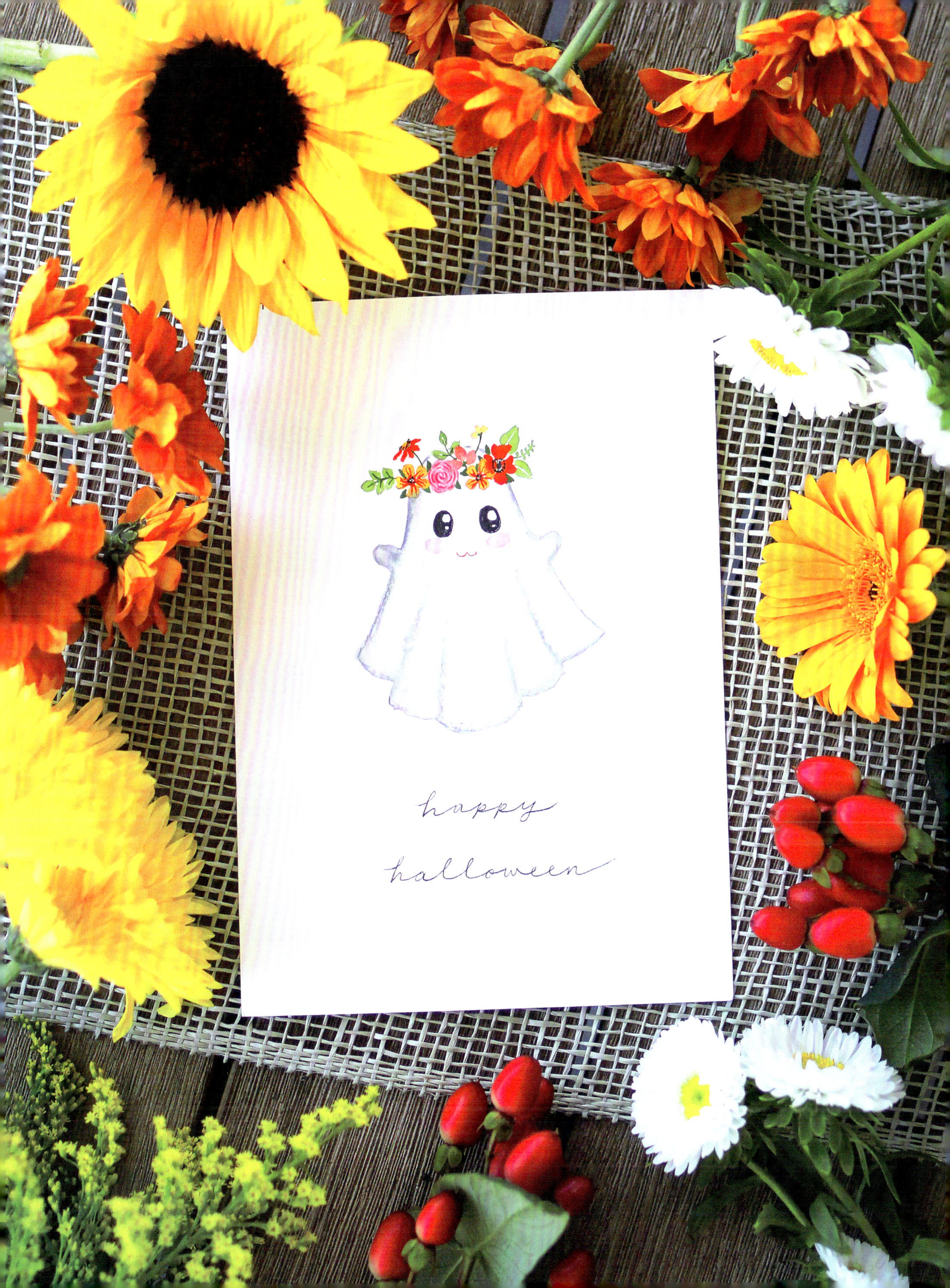
happy
halloween

Halloween Card: Ghost

Paint Colors

(Feel free to substitute similar shades; you don't need to match the exact names.)

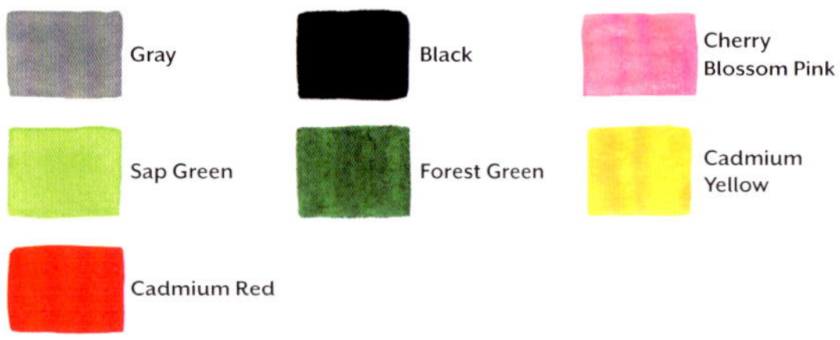

Tools Used

(Feel free to use similar supplies; these are just suggestions!)

- Pencil
- Medium round brush (size 6-8)
- Small round brush (size 2–4)
- Detail brush (size 0 or smaller)
- 005 black fineliner
- White gel pen or white acrylic paint

This card is perfect for both adults and kids. Halloween can feel busy, so I wanted a project that's quick, cute, and easy to paint. The ghost's soft folds, simple shape, and sweet smile make it a fun choice when you want something playful without a lot of steps.

If you want to keep things simple, you can paint just the ghost and finish your card in minutes. If you have more time, you can add flowers, pumpkins, or even a soft moon glow in the background. Beginners can keep it easy, and more experienced painters can play with extra details.

Painting a ghost is a great way to practice soft blending because you don't need perfect lines. Tiny changes in the eyes or cheeks give your ghost its personality, and every version turns out a little different. That handmade look is what makes these cards feel special and personal.

Step 1: Light Pencil Sketch

Lightly sketch a soft bell shape for the ghost. Let the bottom flare out like a sheet and add a few folds. Keep the folds smaller near the sides and a bit wider toward the middle. Add two small arms that curve out slightly, then draw two round eyes and a tiny, curved mouth.

On top of the head, sketch a simple flower crown. Draw one small rose, then add a few simple flowers around it using simple four or five petal shapes and a few turned sideways for variety. The flowers do not need to match on both sides. In fact, it is best when they do not, because a little unevenness makes the crown look more natural. Keep your pencil lines light so they will not show through the paint. You can always adjust the sketch as you paint.

If you're using the tear-out card, skip any sketching or shaping steps and begin painting where appropriate.

Step 2: Wet the Ghost

Use a clean damp brush to wet the ghost shape. The paper should look slightly shiny but not have puddles. This light layer of water will help the paint spread softly in the next step.

Step 3: Shape the Ghost

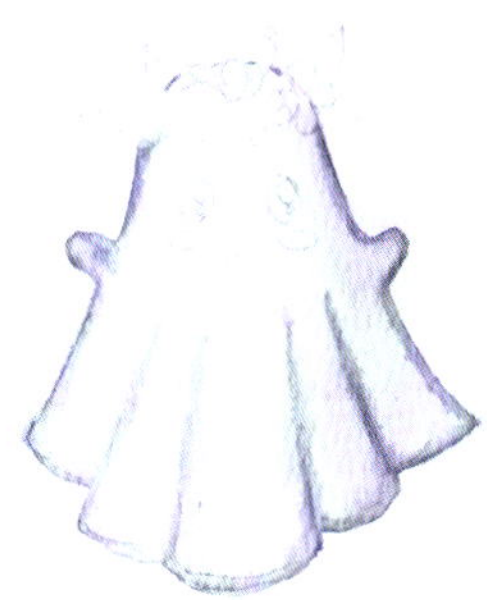

While the paper is wet, use gray paint to softly outline the ghost one section at a time. Rinse your brush, then use the clean damp brush to pull the gray inward toward the center. If you don't rinse your brush, the ghost will turn too dark. Work slowly, blending one section at a time so the edges stay darker and the middle remains very light. Rewet the ghost with a damp brush if the paper starts to dry. Keep the middle of the ghost soft and pale to give it a light, glowing look.

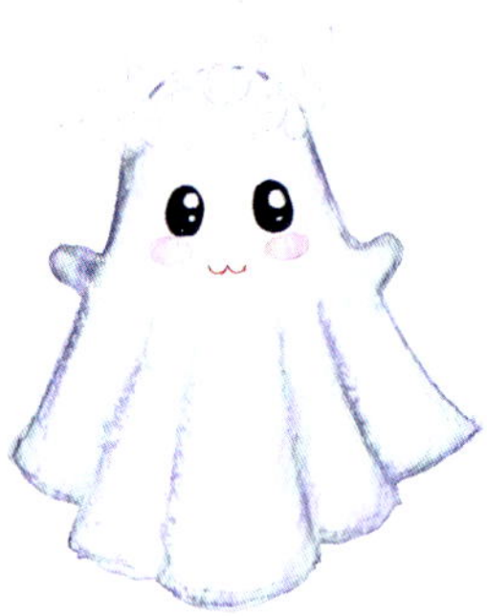

Step 4: Add the Face

Make sure the ghost is completely dry. Use a black pen to draw the eyes, leaving small white areas inside for the highlights. Take your time here because the eyes set the expression.

Next, use a detail brush to paint two soft pink ovals for the cheeks. While the paint is still damp, gently dab each oval once with a Q-tip. Use a thin detail brush to paint a small, curved mouth low on the face.

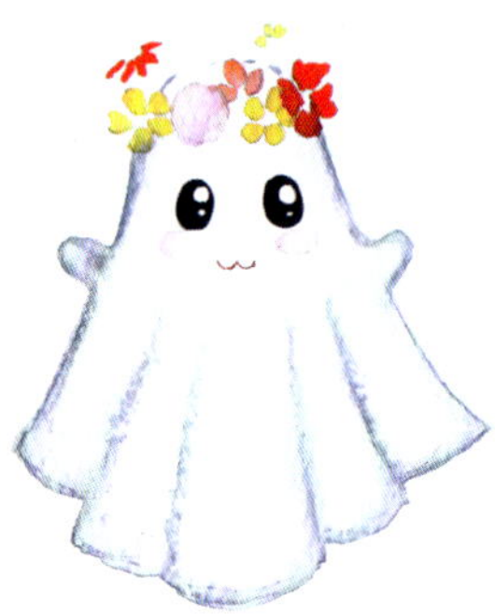

Step 5: Paint the Base Flowers

Use a small round brush to paint the flowers on the ghost's crown. Start by painting a small rose using cherry blossom pink. Keep it simple by painting a circle for the base shape.

Using your sketch as a guide, paint the remaining flowers in cadmium red and cadmium yellow.

While the paint is still damp, lightly dab each flower once with a Q-tip to lift a little color and soften the petals. Leave a small space in the center of a few flowers for details later.

Step 6: Add Flower Details

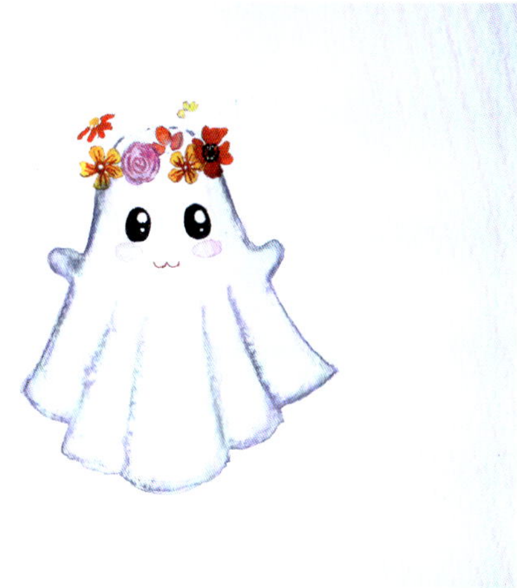

Use a detail brush to add finishing touches to each flower once the base layers are completely dry.

Start with the rose. Using cherry blossom pink, paint tiny C-shaped strokes in the center and work outward to build the petals. Keep these C-shaped strokes slightly darker than the base layer so the rose stays delicate.

For the yellow flowers, paint a small center circle using cadmium red. Add light lines that dash outward from the center. Use gentle pressure so the lines stay delicate.

For the front facing red flower, use black to paint a small center circle. Add tiny dots around the circle, leaving a little space between each one. Connect a few of the dots with short dashes.

Add a small yellow center to the red daisy like flower turned to the side.

Step 7: Paint the Leaves

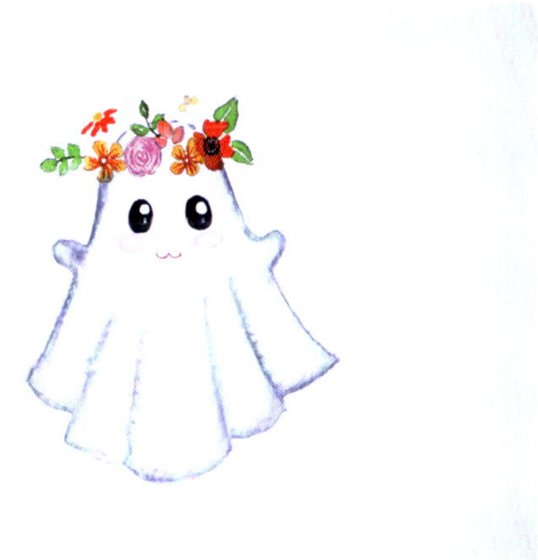

Use a small round brush loaded with sap green to paint the leaves in the flower crown. Add leaves in different sizes and directions to fill the gaps between the flowers. Then add a few darker accents using forest green so the crown has more depth.

To paint each leaf, make two strokes by pressing your brush down and lifting it up on each side, leaving a small gap in the middle for the vein (see Two-Stroke Vein Leaf, page 24). Paint a few leaves without a vein so they do not all look the same.

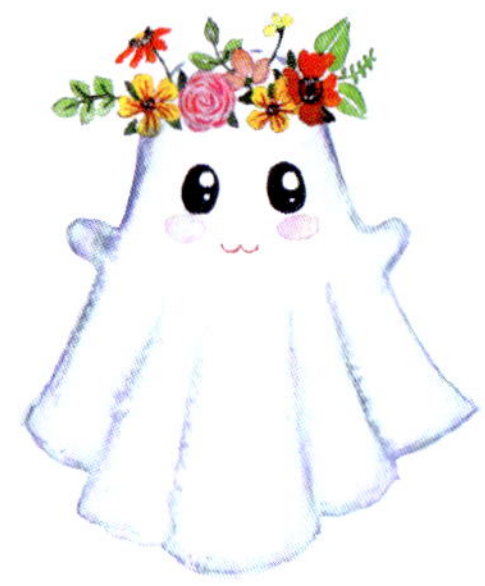

Step 8: Add Final Touches

Use a detail brush and forest green to add a few small leaves behind the flowers. With a light touch, outline a few leaf veins and stems so the details stay soft. Add a thin stem to the sideways flowers so they don't look like they are floating.

Next, use a tiny amount of black on your detail brush to add small dots to deepen the flower centers, including the sideways red flower. If you want the rose to stand out more, add a slightly darker pink to a few of the tiny C shapes. Keep this subtle so the rose stays delicate.

This is a good time to step back and look at your work. If any areas feel empty, add a small touch such as a simple fern like stem.

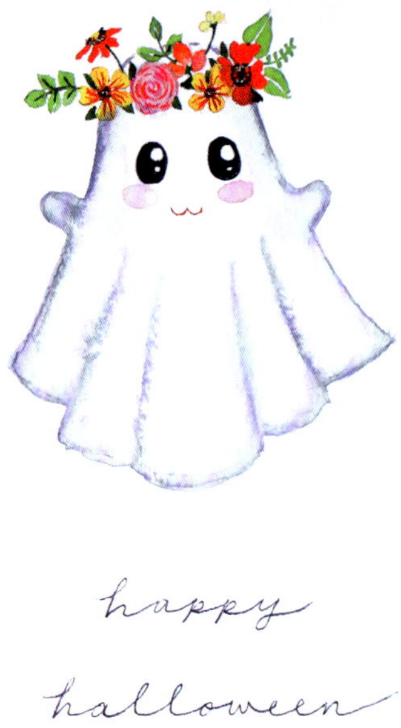

Step 9: Lettering

Lightly draw two pencil lines to guide where your words will sit. Find the center of your card and place the middle of your phrase there so the words feel balanced.

Practice the lettering on scrap paper first until the spacing feels natural. A simple cursive works well with the soft look of the ghost, but clean print letters look just as nice.

When you are ready, use a 005 black fineliner to trace over your pencil lines. Write slowly and keep your hand relaxed. If your letters wobble a little, that is perfectly fine. Small variations give your card a handmade charm.

Let the ink dry fully before erasing the pencil lines so the words stay crisp.

Try This!

Want to make your ghost card even more fun? Here are a few ideas to try:

- Paint the ghost holding a tiny pumpkin or candy bucket.
- Add a second smaller ghost beside it for a cute friend version.
- Replace the flower crown with autumn leaves and acorns for a cozy fall look.
- Add a soft shimmer along the ghost's edges using glitter ink or metallic watercolor.
- Turn it into a friendship card by writing "You're Bootiful!" at the bottom.

What to Write

Simple words for your handmade card. Here are a few ideas to get you started:

- Hey boo
- Trick or treat
- You're such a treat
- Boo to brighten your day
- You're my favorite treat
- You're my favorite little ghost
- Just boo cause
- You make spooky season sweet
- A little boo to make you smile
- Have a sweet and spooky day

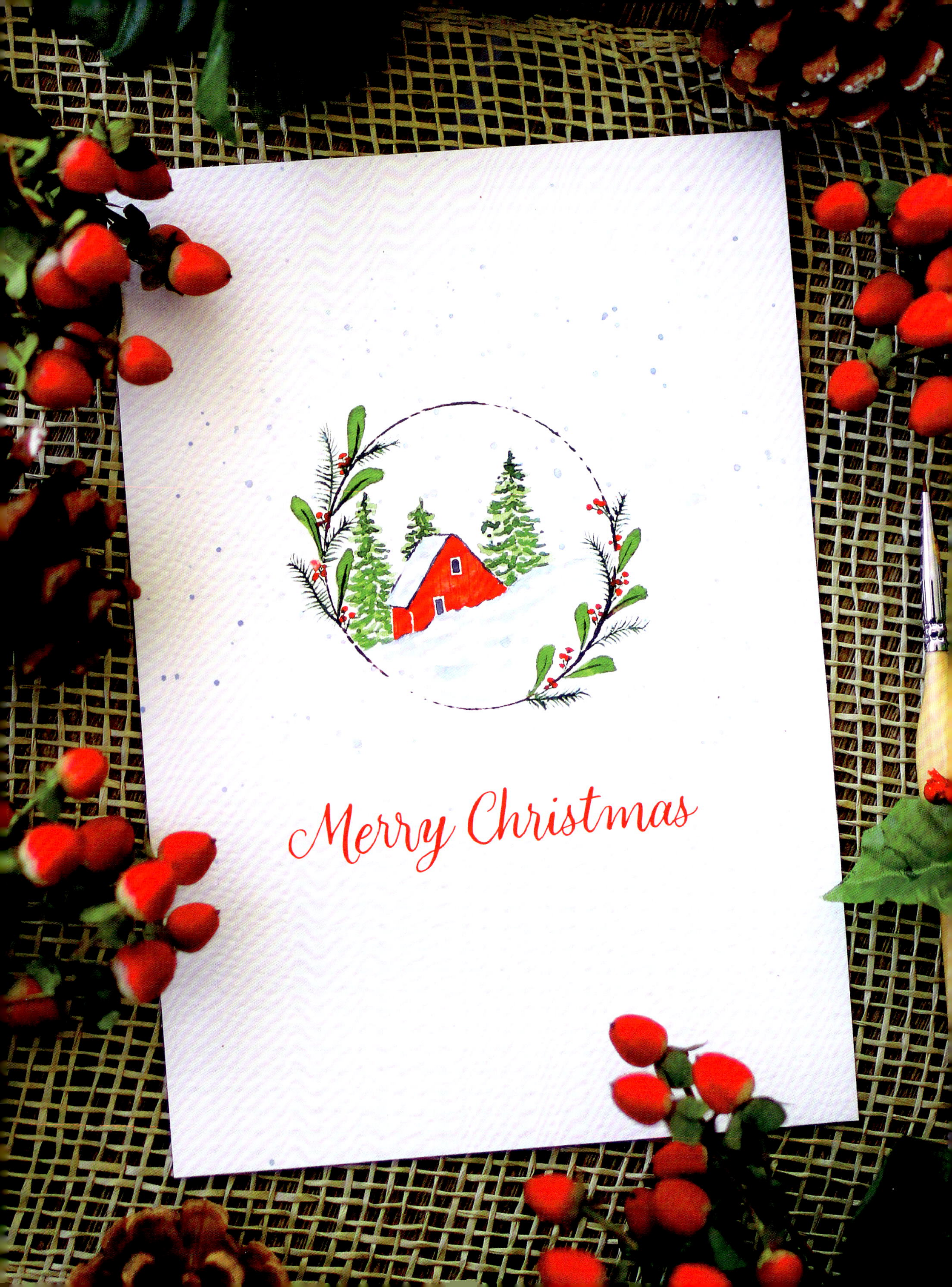
Merry Christmas

Christmas Card: Snowy Red Cabin

Paint Colors

(Feel free to substitute similar shades; you don't need to match the exact names.)

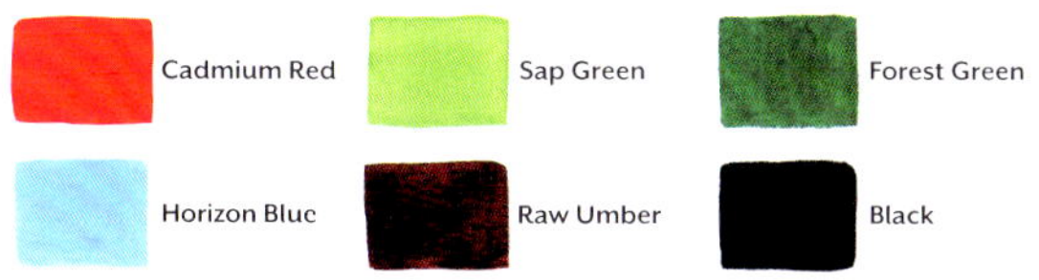

Tools Used

(Feel free to use similar supplies; these are just suggestions!)

- Pencil
- Medium round brush (Size 6–8)
- Small round brush (Size 2–4)
- Detail brush (size 0 or smaller)

There is something calming about a quiet winter day. In this card, the little red cabin rests in the snow with a few evergreens around it and a tiny wreath on the door that feels like a gentle welcome home. The circle frame makes it feel like you are looking through a cold window at a quiet winter moment.

We will build the scene with soft washes, loose trees, and light splatters for falling snow. Around the circle, you will add simple greenery and bright berries for a cozy Christmas touch. The steps are simple and forgiving.

Those soft edges and small color changes are what make the card feel personal, like something only you could paint. Light layers and small details are enough to bring the cabin to life. Take your time and enjoy the process as each part slowly comes together.

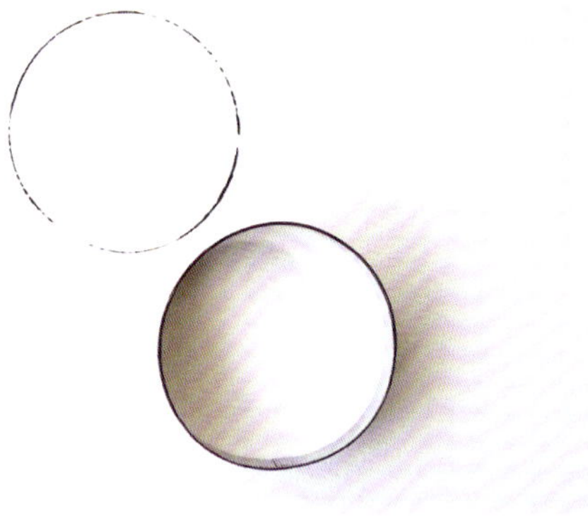

Step 1: Circle Frame

Find something round like a cookie cutter, jar lid, or cup. Brush an even layer of paint onto the rim so it transfers cleanly when pressed onto the paper.

Mix raw umber with a tiny touch of black to make the brown slightly darker (see Color Mixing, page 12).

Press the rim gently onto your paper to make the circle. If the circle print looks light or uneven, that is perfectly fine. Use a detail brush to connect any gaps. The circle is simply a guide for your design.

If you're using the tear-out card, skip any sketching or shaping steps and begin painting where appropriate.

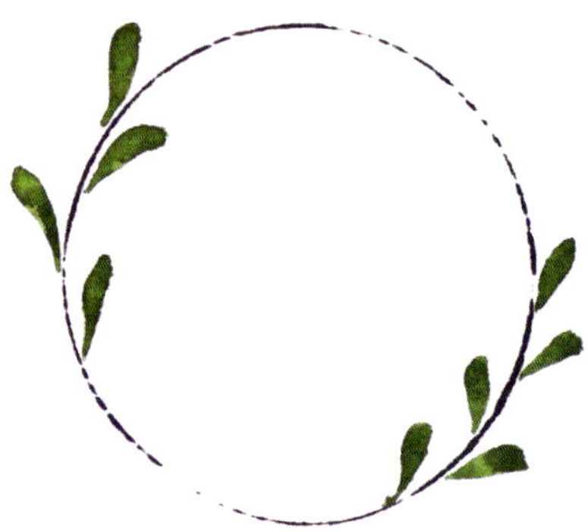

Step 2: Paint the Rounded Leaves

Use a small round brush and sap green to paint the rounded leaves. Press the brush down, then pull it back toward the starting point so the tip of the leaf stays soft and rounded. Place the leaves on two sides of the circle. Avoid placing the leaves directly across from each other. Let them rise gently along the curve of the circle (see Rounded-Base Leaf, page 25).

Step 3: Paint the Pine Needles

Use the tip of your detail brush to paint a thin curved stem using raw umber. Add short dashes along the stem to create the pine needles. Keep the pressure light so the strokes stay thin, and let a few curve slightly for a natural look (see Pine Leaf Branch, page 26).

For the pine, paint a thin brown line that curves loosely outward from the circle. Add the pine on the opposite side from the rounded leaves so the wreath feels balanced.

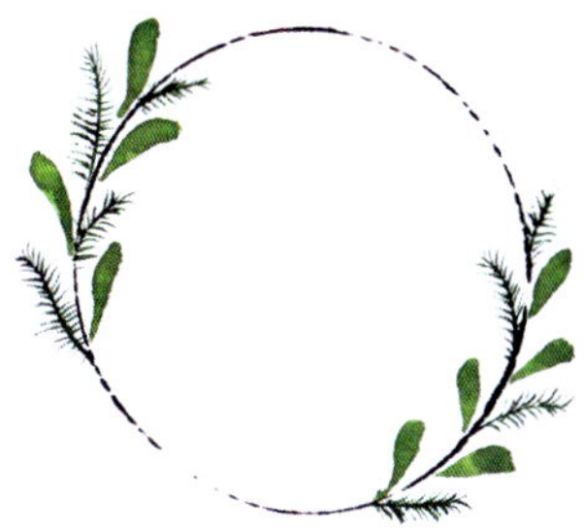

Step 4: Painting Berries

Use the tip of a small round brush to tap in little dots of cadmium red for the berries. Place them near the base of the leaves and pine needles close to the circle, so they look like they are growing from the stems. Paint the berries in small groups of three or four so the circle does not feel too busy.

You can connect the berries with a thin line of sap green if you want, but they also look nice as simple dots.

When the leaves are dry, use a detail brush and the same dark brown mixture from Step 1 (raw umber with a tiny touch of black) to add a soft line inside each rounded leaf. Start at the base of the leaf and paint upward so the line stays thin and stops before the tip.

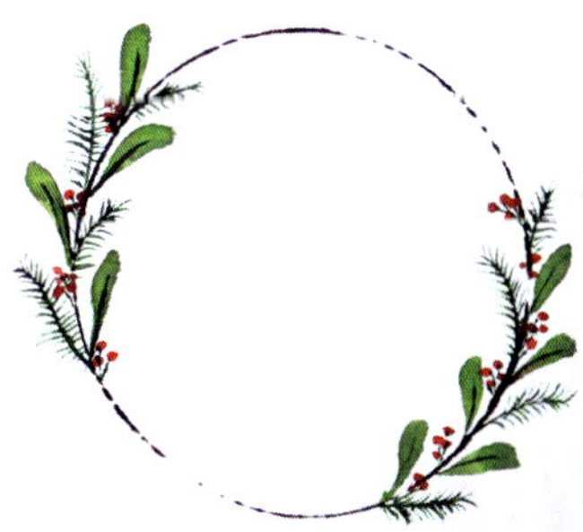

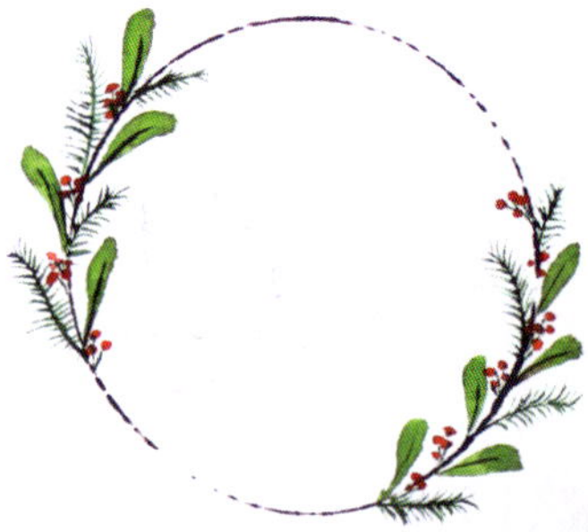

Step 5: Lightly Sketch

Once the circle frame is dry, lightly sketch the scene inside it.

Begin with a soft curved line for the snow. Keep your pencil lines very light so they blend easily under the paint.

Sketch the cabin using simple shapes. Draw a rectangle for the body and a triangle for the roof. Add a small door or window. Try placing the cabin slightly to one side rather than in the center so the scene feels more balanced.

Next, add a few tall trees behind the cabin using light lines. Draw the trunk first, then add short angled lines for the branches. Keep everything simple. The paint will add most of the character later.

Your sketch is only a guide, so adjust shapes and placement as you paint and let the scene develop naturally.

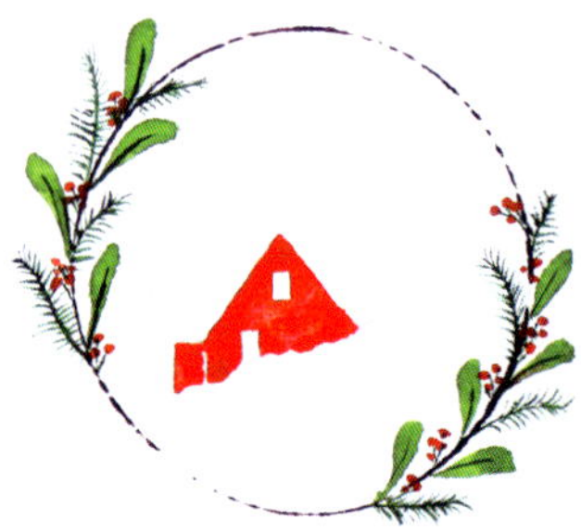

Step 6: Painting the Cabin

Use a small round brush to fill in the cabin with a wash of cadmium red. Take your time around the windows and door so those shapes stay clean. As you paint, leave a thin straight line unpainted where the front wall meets the side wall. This narrow strip acts as a highlight and helps the cabin look more three dimensional.

While the paint is still damp, use a small piece of paper towel to lift a bit of color from the center of each wall. Keep the edges slightly darker. This creates soft shading and adds depth. (see Lifting, page 13).

Step 7: First Layer of Pines

Use a light wash of sap green, with more water than paint, to create the first layer of pine trees behind the cabin. Start at the top of each tree with the tip of your brush.

Build the tree one layer at a time. Begin with small dabs at the top, then gradually make each layer slightly wider as you move downward. Gently tap the brush and add a slight wiggle so the shape spreads softly from side to side.

Leave small touches of white between the layers so the trees look soft and airy. Let each tree be a little different in height and width.

If the paint feels too wet, dab your brush on a paper towel to remove excess water before continuing. Try not to overthink it. Let the shapes stay loose and light.

Step 8: Second Layer of Pines

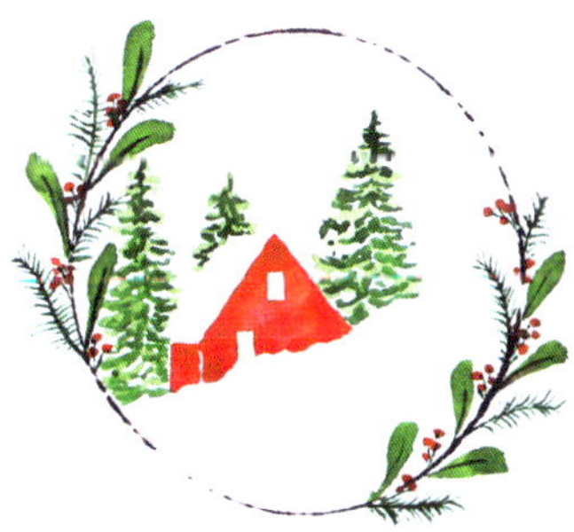

Once the first layer is completely dry, use forest green to add a second layer to the trees.

Build this layer the same way, starting at the top and working your way down. Use small dabs and gentle wiggles to shape the tree, but keep most of the darker green toward the center.

Let the lighter sap green from the first layer show around the edges. This creates contrast and helps the trees look fuller and more defined.

Keep the strokes soft and avoid covering everything. The lighter areas give the trees depth and make them feel more natural.

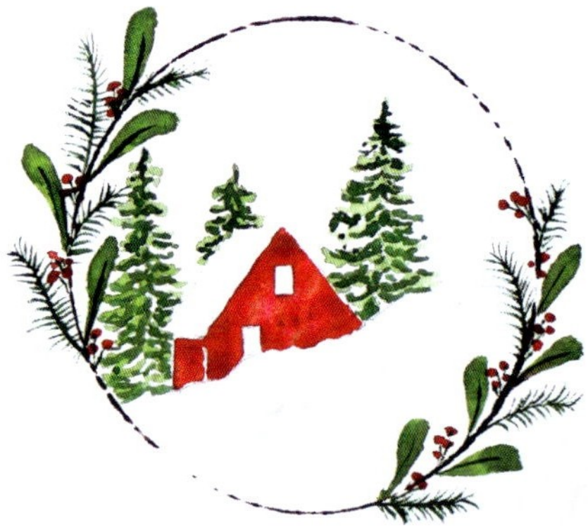

Step 9: Paint the Snow

Mix a light blue using horizon bue (more water than paint) until you get the value you like (see Controlling Values, page 12).

Test it on scrap paper to check the color. Use this light blue to paint gentle strokes across the snow on the ground, leaving some white paper showing. This keeps the snow looking soft and natural.

Use the same light blue on the roof of the cabin so it looks like snow resting on top.

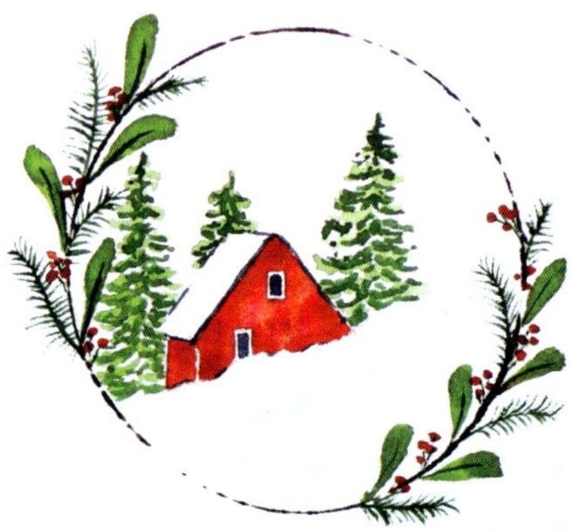

Step 10: Paint the Windows and Add the Roof Line

When the snow is completely dry, use a detail brush and slightly watered down black to paint the window and door. Leave a thin white trim around them so they stay bright and clean.

Use the same slightly watered down black to lightly outline the roof. Then add a few soft lines where the snow meets the cabin and along the ground. Keep these lines gentle and loose. A few touches are all you need to define the edges without making anything look harsh.

Step 11: Add Snow Shadows

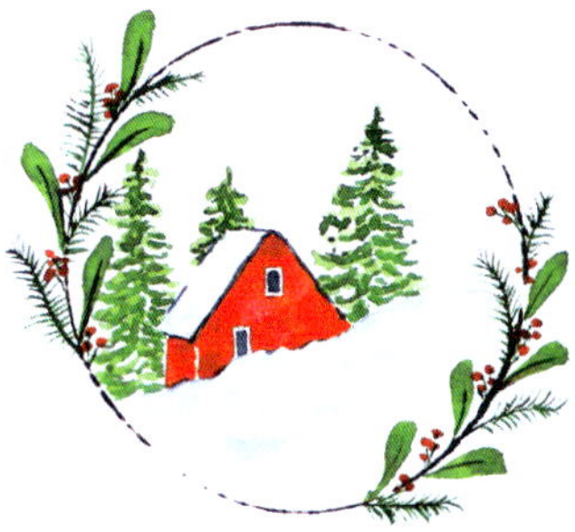

When the outlines are dry, mix a slightly darker blue by using horizon blue with less water than you used for the snow. Use this color to add soft strokes on the ground and on the roof. Place the darker strokes in the dips of the snow or along the roofline so the shapes feel more defined.

As you paint, leave breaks of white paper showing on the ground. The untouched white paper is what makes the snow look bright and clean. The blue is only there to add gentle changes in color so the snow looks soft but still has shape.

If any lines look sharp, use a damp brush to gently soften the edges into the lighter blue (see Softening Hard Lines, page 16).

Step 12: Add Wood Lines to the Cabin

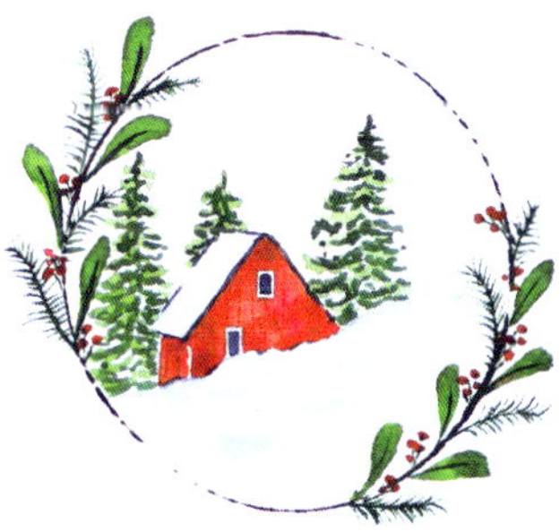

Mix a slightly stronger cadmium red by using less water than your first wash. This creates a slightly richer color that shows as gentle texture on the cabin.

Using a detail brush, paint light vertical lines on the cabin to suggest the wood boards. Keep your pressure soft so the lines stay thin. Space them out so you can still see the main red color between each one. A few simple lines are all you need for the cabin to look textured and finished.

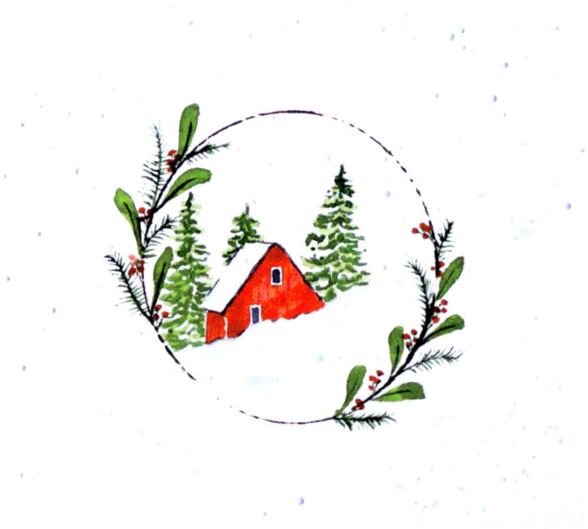

Step 13: Splattering Snow

Load your medium round brush with a watery mix of horizon blue and use the splatter method to add falling snow (see Splattering, page 17).

Hold the brush over your paper and tap it gently with your finger or another brush so small drops scatter across the scene. Try this once on scrap paper to check the size of the splatters. Light splatters work best so the snow looks soft and does not cover too much of the picture.

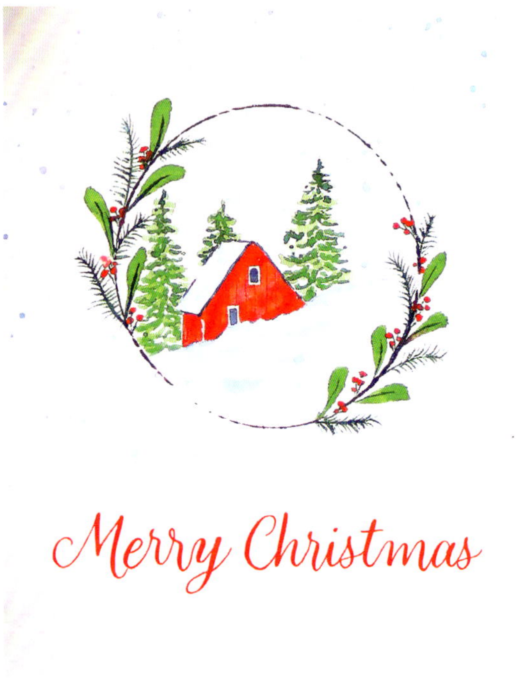

Step 14: Lettering

To finish your card, you can add your holiday message under the circle. In the photo, I added the words digitally to show that there are many different ways to do your lettering. You can write the message by hand, use stamps or stencils, or even leave the front blank and write your note inside. Choose whatever feels easy and comfortable for you.

If you want to letter it yourself, remember that lettering is really just drawing simple lines and shapes. Take your time and go slowly.

Try This!

Want to give your snow scene a new twist? Here are some fun ways to change it up:

- Paint the cabin a different color for a whole new look.
- Add footprints in the snow leading up to the cabin.
- Add a small fence or pathway leading up to the cabin.
- Paint a night version with a dark blue sky and bright stars.
- Add a tiny wreath or bow on the cabin door.

What to Write

Simple words for your handmade card. Here are a few ideas to get you started:

- Season's greetings
- Happy holidays
- Rejoice
- Peace
- Joy
- Warm winter wishes
- From our home to yours
- Christmas blessings
- Noel
- Believe

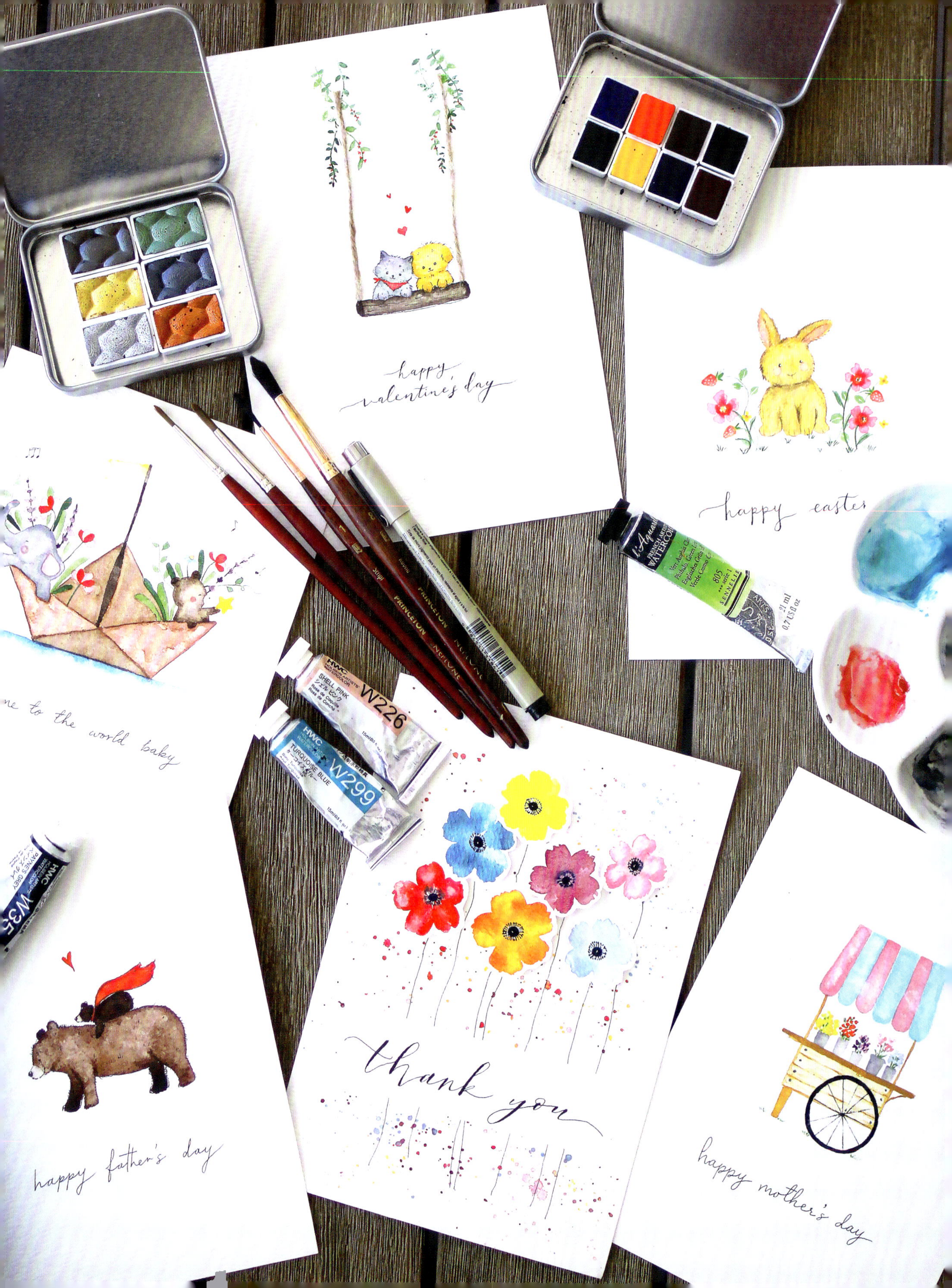
happy valentine's day
happy easter
to the world baby
happy father's day
thank you
happy mother's day
PRINCETON
HWC
SHELL PINK
W226
TURQUOISE BLUE
W299

CHAPTER 5

Bonus Content

More Cards to Paint

Celebrate meaningful traditions through video tutorials for Lunar New Year, Diwali, Hanukkah, Ramadan, and Bar and Bat Mitzvah designs. Scan the QR code at the right to watch each card come to life from beginning to end.

Each design reflects a special moment filled with light, faith, growth, and joy shared with family and community.

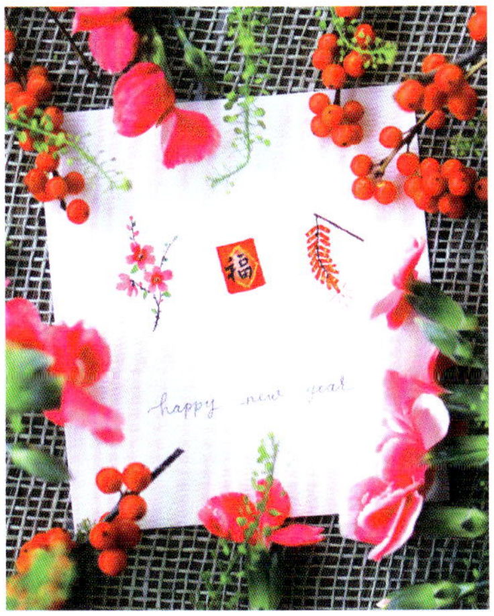

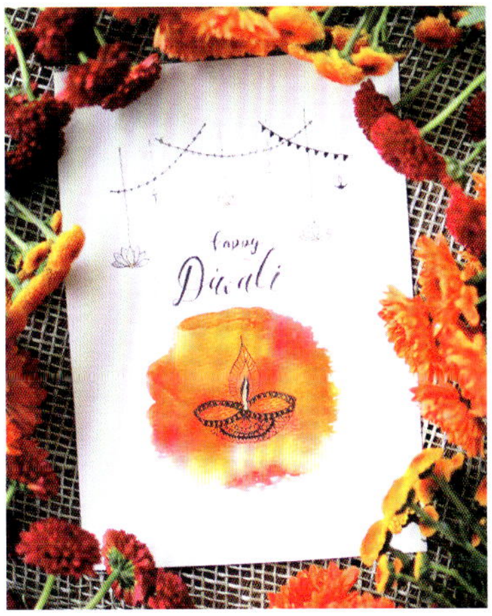

Scan to watch these card painting videos.

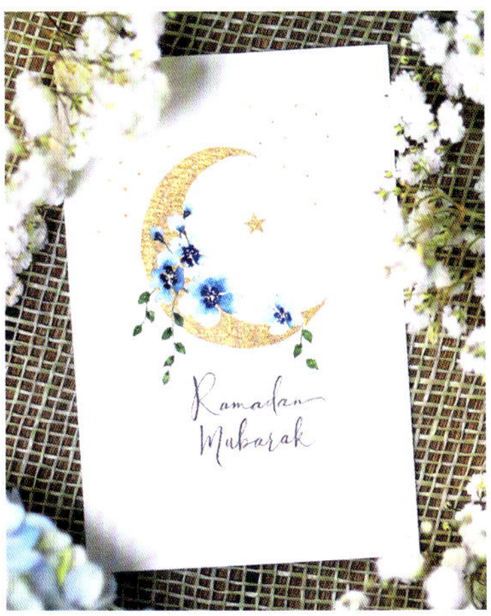

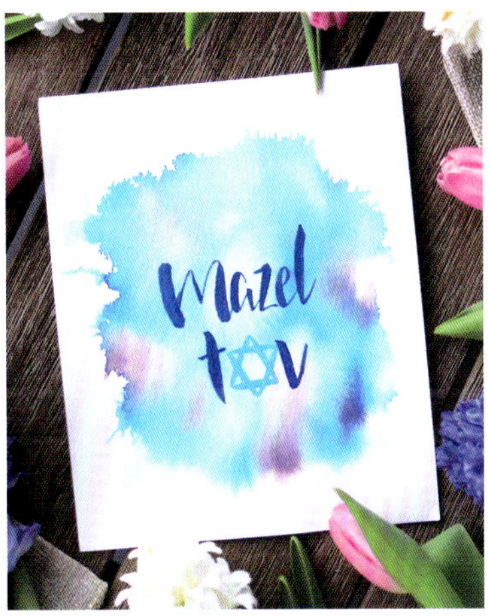

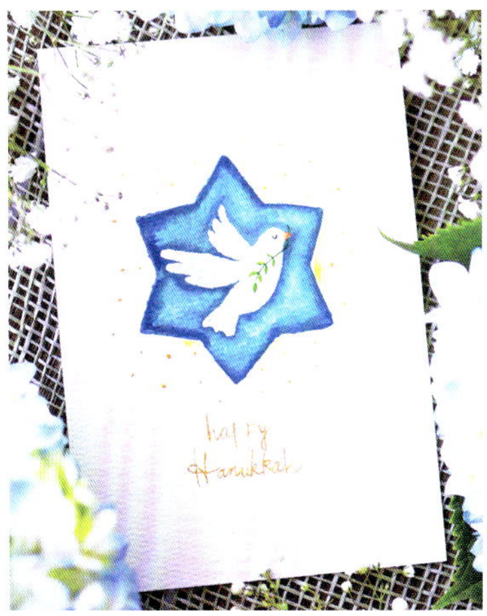

Keep Painting With Me

There is even more to explore.

Through the QR code at the right, you can explore additional video tutorials for seasonal cards, encouragement, birthdays, thank you notes, and everyday moments worth celebrating.

No matter the season or occasion, there is always another moment worth painting and sharing.

Scan for more painting videos.

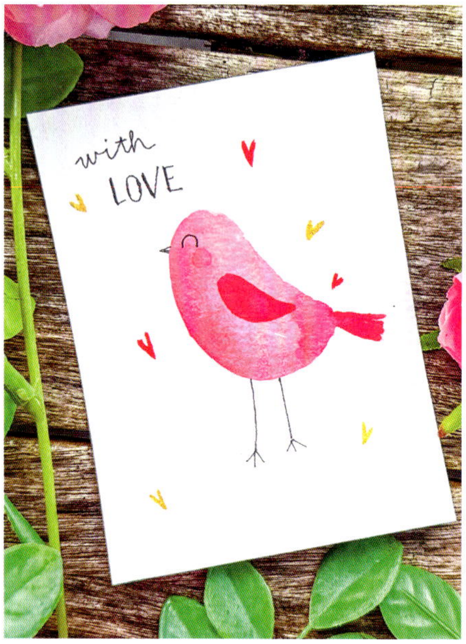

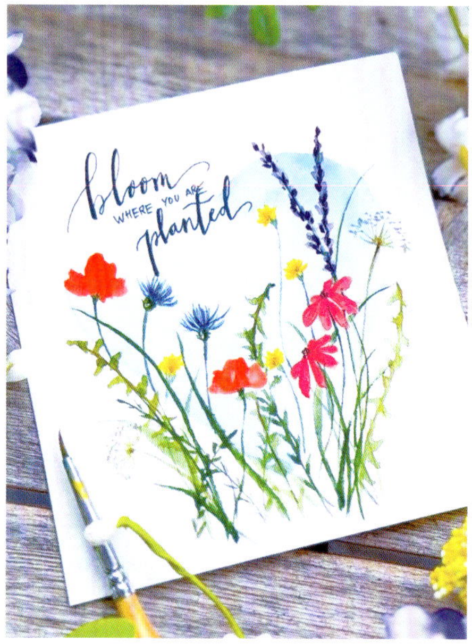

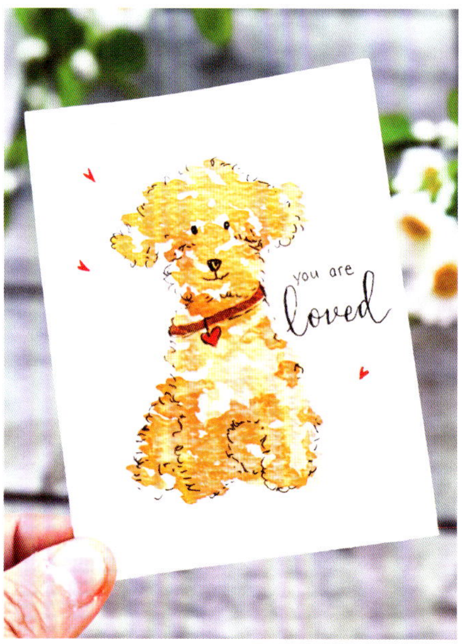

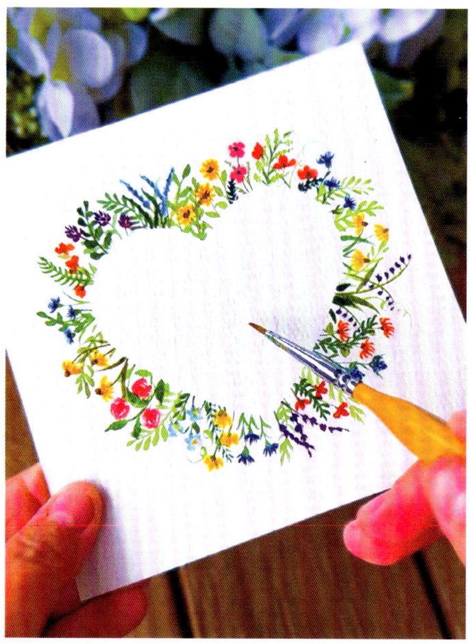

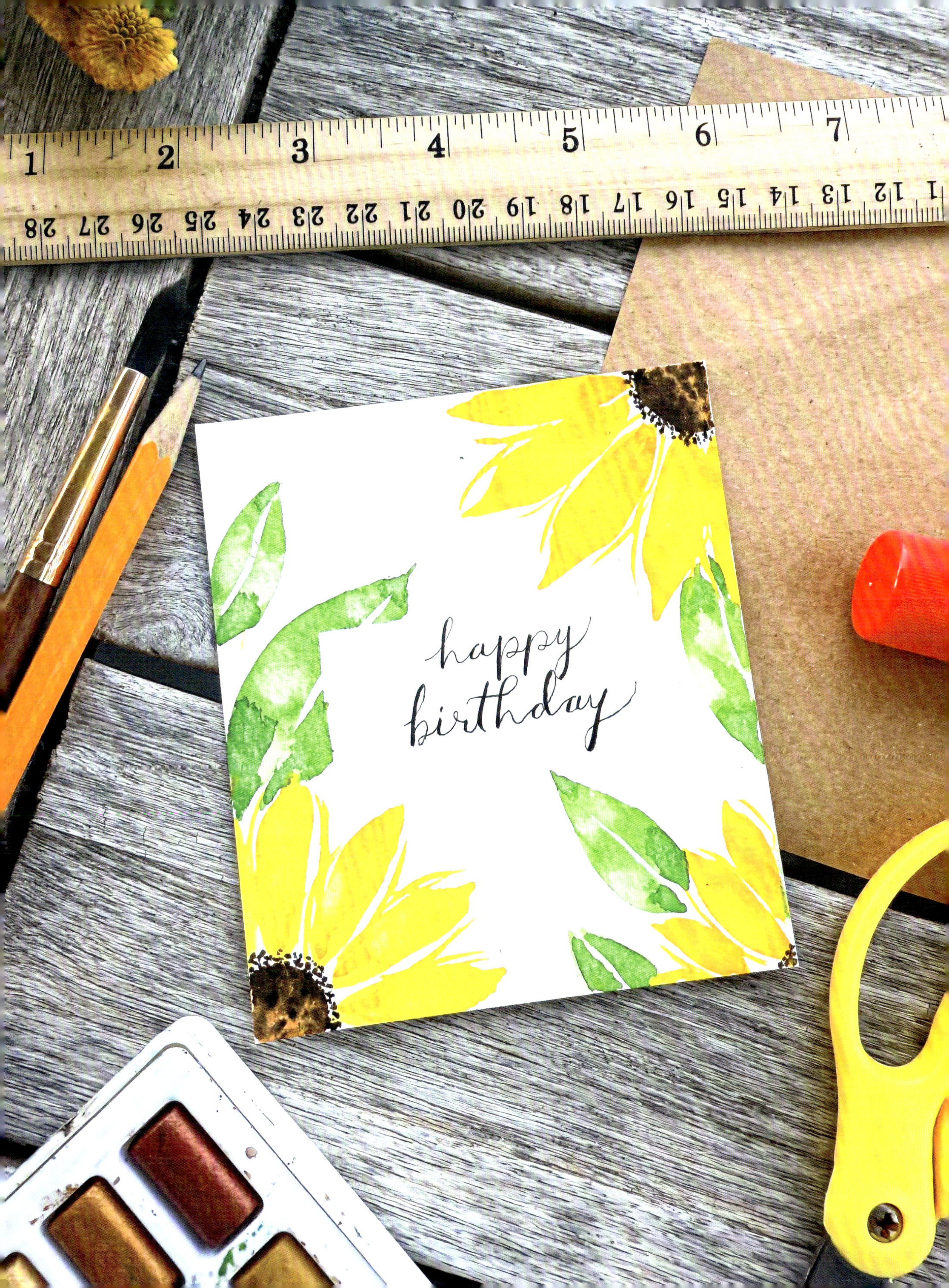
happy
birthday

Make an Envelope for Your Card

My watercolor cards often end up in different sizes. Sometimes I paint on a larger sheet and trim it down, and other times I paint on whatever scrap paper I have nearby. Because of that, I rarely have the "right" envelope ready. This simple method lets you quickly make a custom envelope that fits your card perfectly.

Before You Start: How I Choose My Paper Size

Before I begin folding, I cut my paper to the right size using this simple formula:

- Measure the longest side of your card and add about 3 inches.
- Cut a square using that number.
- Using a square helps all four corners fold evenly around the card.

Examples:

- 4 × 6 card: longest side 6: 6 + 3 = 9
  Cut a 9-inch square
- 5 × 5 card: longest side 5: 5 + 3 = 8
  Cut an 8-inch square

Once your square is ready, you can begin folding the envelope.

Folding the Envelope

Place your card in the center of a square sheet of paper turned like a diamond. Lightly fold the paper corner to corner to create a soft center crease, then open it again. Set the card back in the center with the longer side horizontal. Fold the left and right corners toward the middle so the edges meet neatly. Open the paper and trim the small triangles created by the folds. Fold the bottom flap up and make a small pencil mark on each side where it meets the side flaps. Cut along those marks so the bottom flap fits smoothly inside. Apply glue to the inside edges of the side flaps and fold the bottom flap up to seal the envelope. Slide your card inside to check the fit. If you like, round the corners of the top flap with a corner punch for a softer look.

Step 1

Place your card in the center of the paper, turned like a diamond.

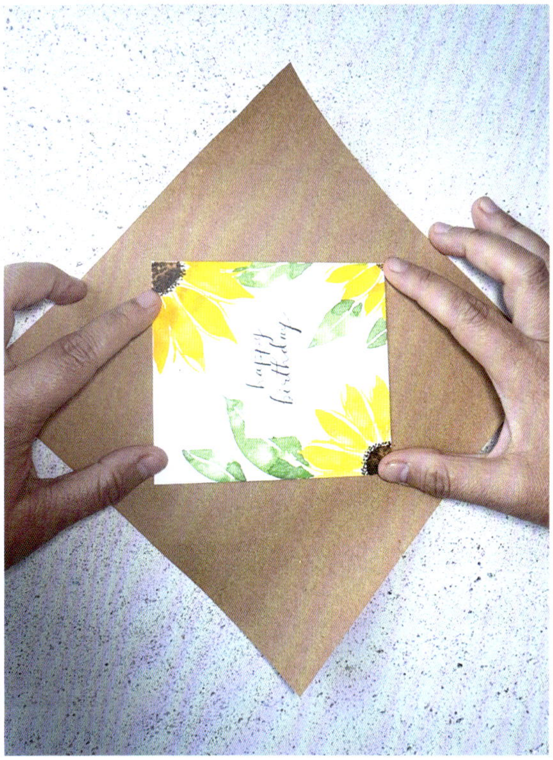

Step 2

Fold one corner to the opposite corner to create a light center crease.

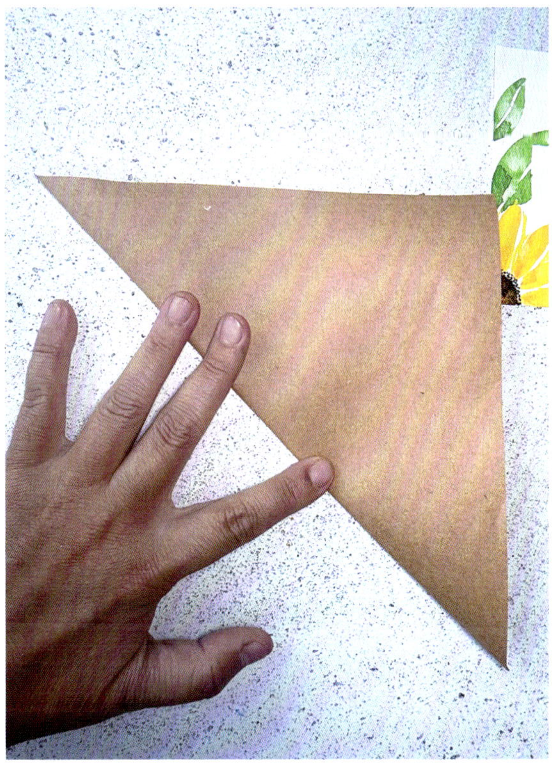

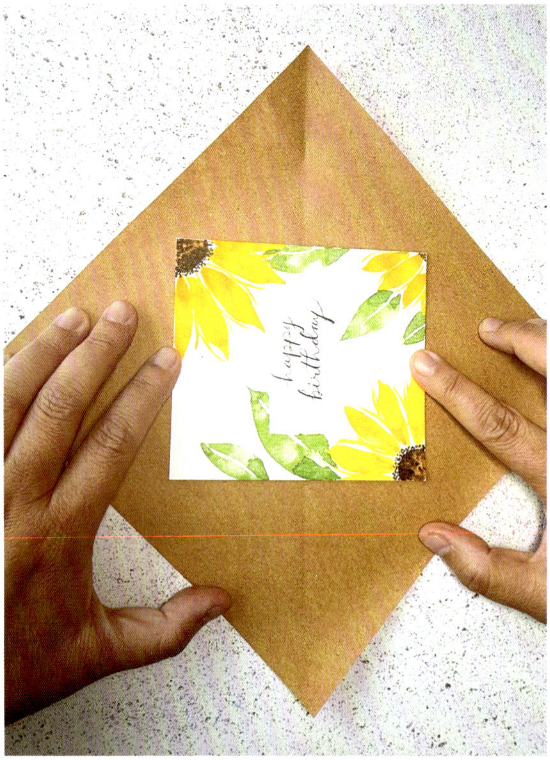

Step 3

Place the card back in the center, aligning it with the crease.

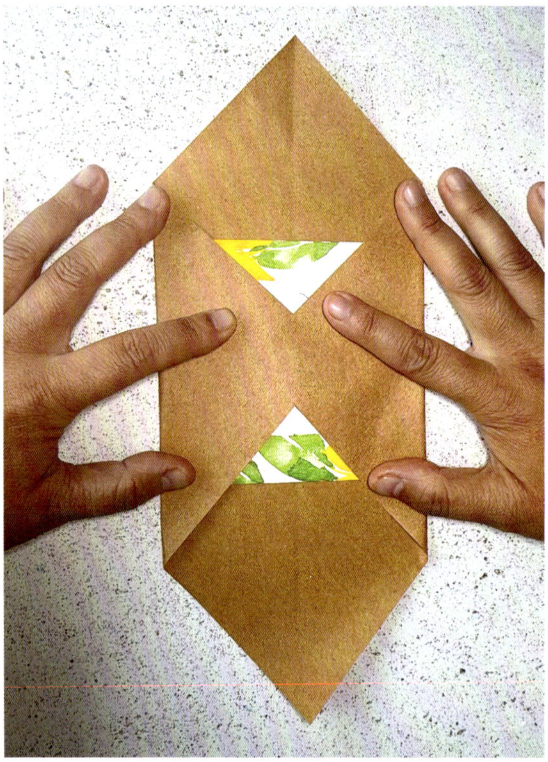

Step 4

Fold the left and right corners inward so the edges meet neatly.

Step 5

Open the paper and trim the small triangles created by the folds.

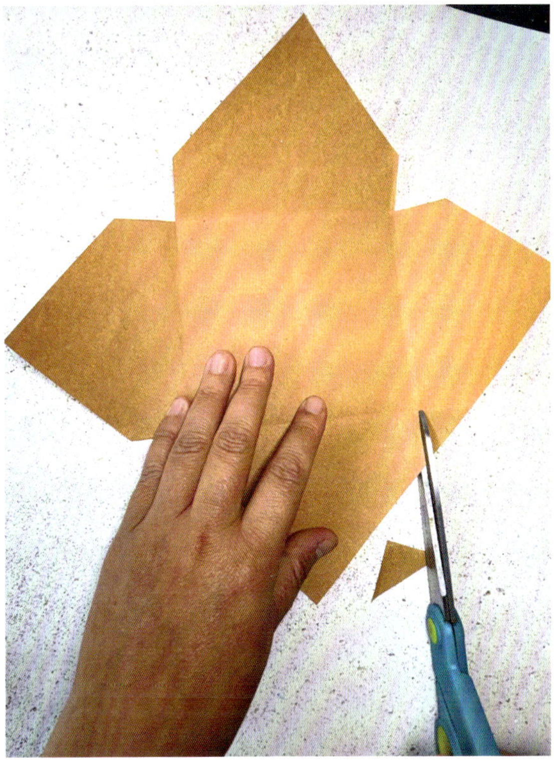

Step 6

Fold the bottom flap up and mark where it meets the side flaps.

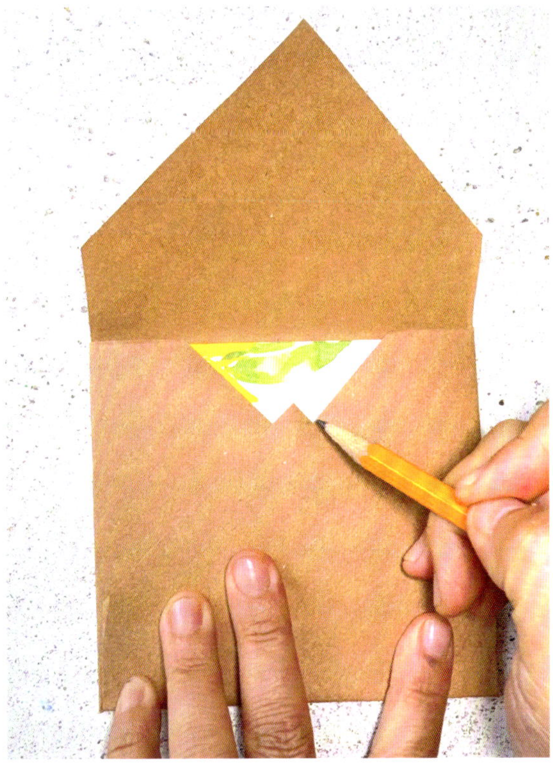

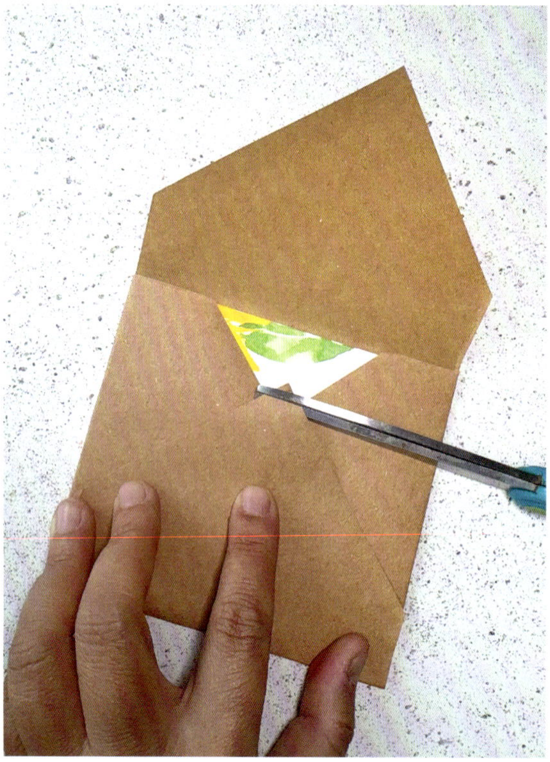

Step 7

Cut along the marks so the bottom flap fits smoothly inside.

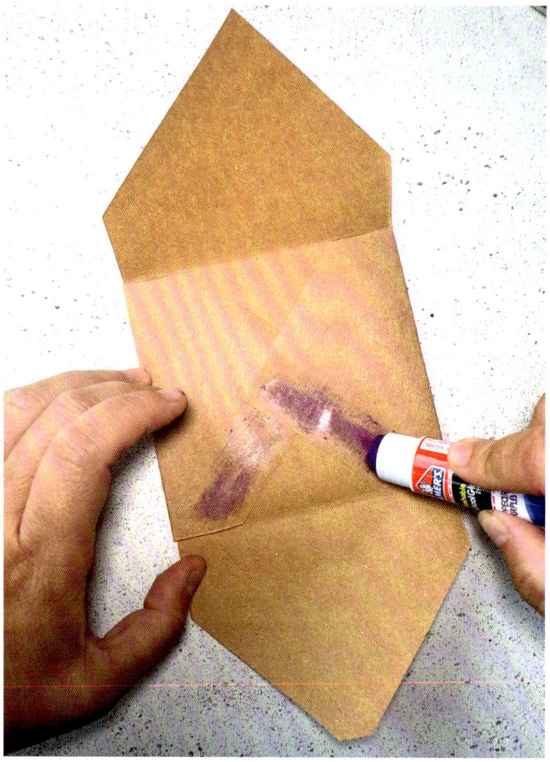

Step 8

Apply glue to the inside edges of the side flaps.

Step 9

Fold the bottom flap up to seal the envelope.

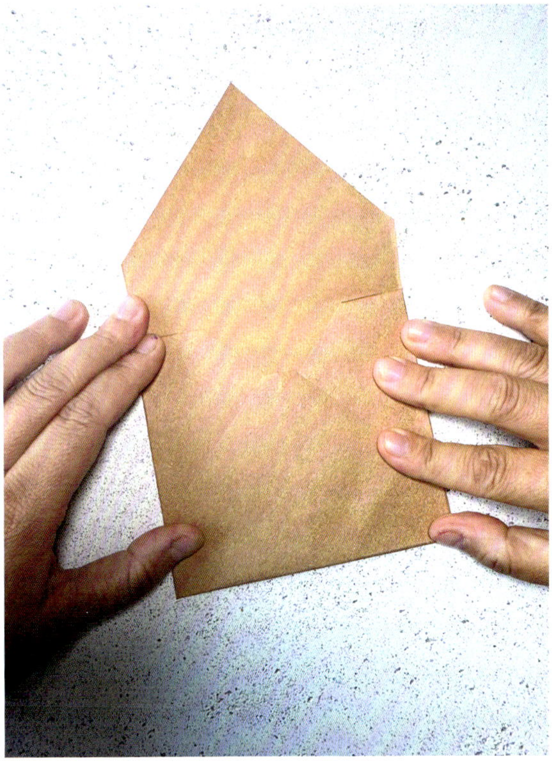

Step 10

Slide your card inside to check the fit.

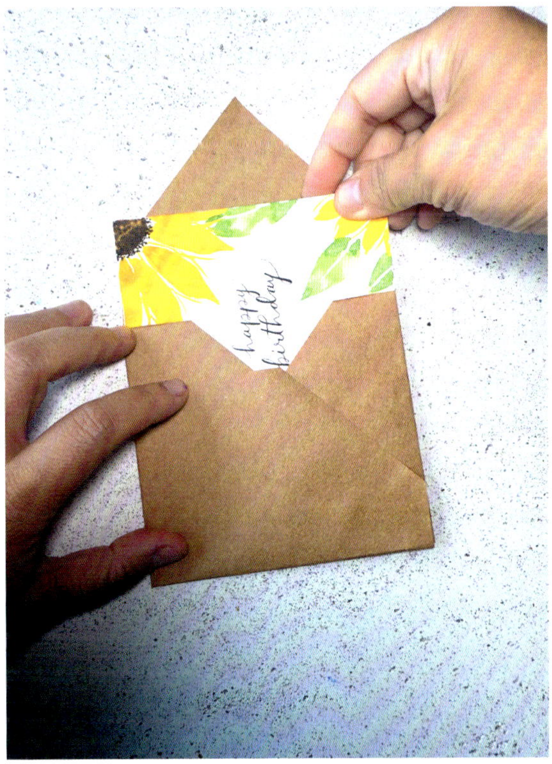

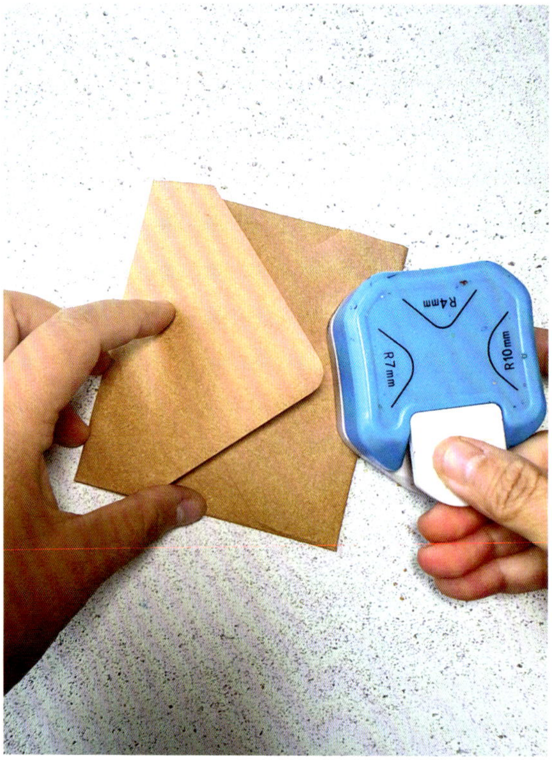

Step 11

Optional: Round the corners of the top flap if you'd like a softer look.

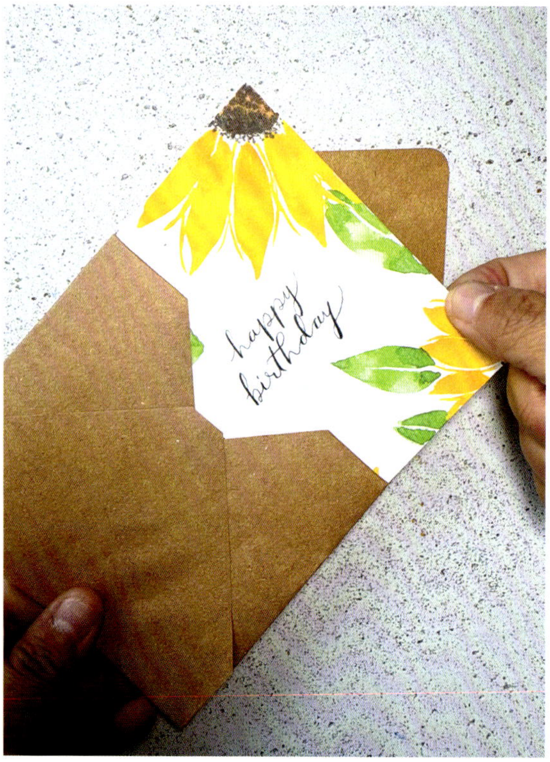

Step 12

Your envelope is ready to use.

Final Thoughts

Thank you for painting along with me.

I hope this book reminded you that watercolor does not need to be perfect to be beautiful. Sometimes all it takes is a brush, a little water, and a few quiet minutes to create something meaningful. Whether you followed every step or simply used the ideas as inspiration, I hope you found joy in the process and confidence in your own style.

I'm also grateful to the wonderful team at Rocky Nook, especially my editor Kelly Reed. Thank you to my husband, Alex, for reviewing the pages with me along the way. I'm thankful for my family, friends, and the amazing Instagram, Facebook, and Tiktok community that paints along with me. Your encouragement inspires me every day.

You can find more projects, behind-the-scenes peeks, and new ideas at mamapandapainter.com. You can also connect with me on Instagram, Facebook, and Tiktok as @mamapandapainter. I would love to see what you create!

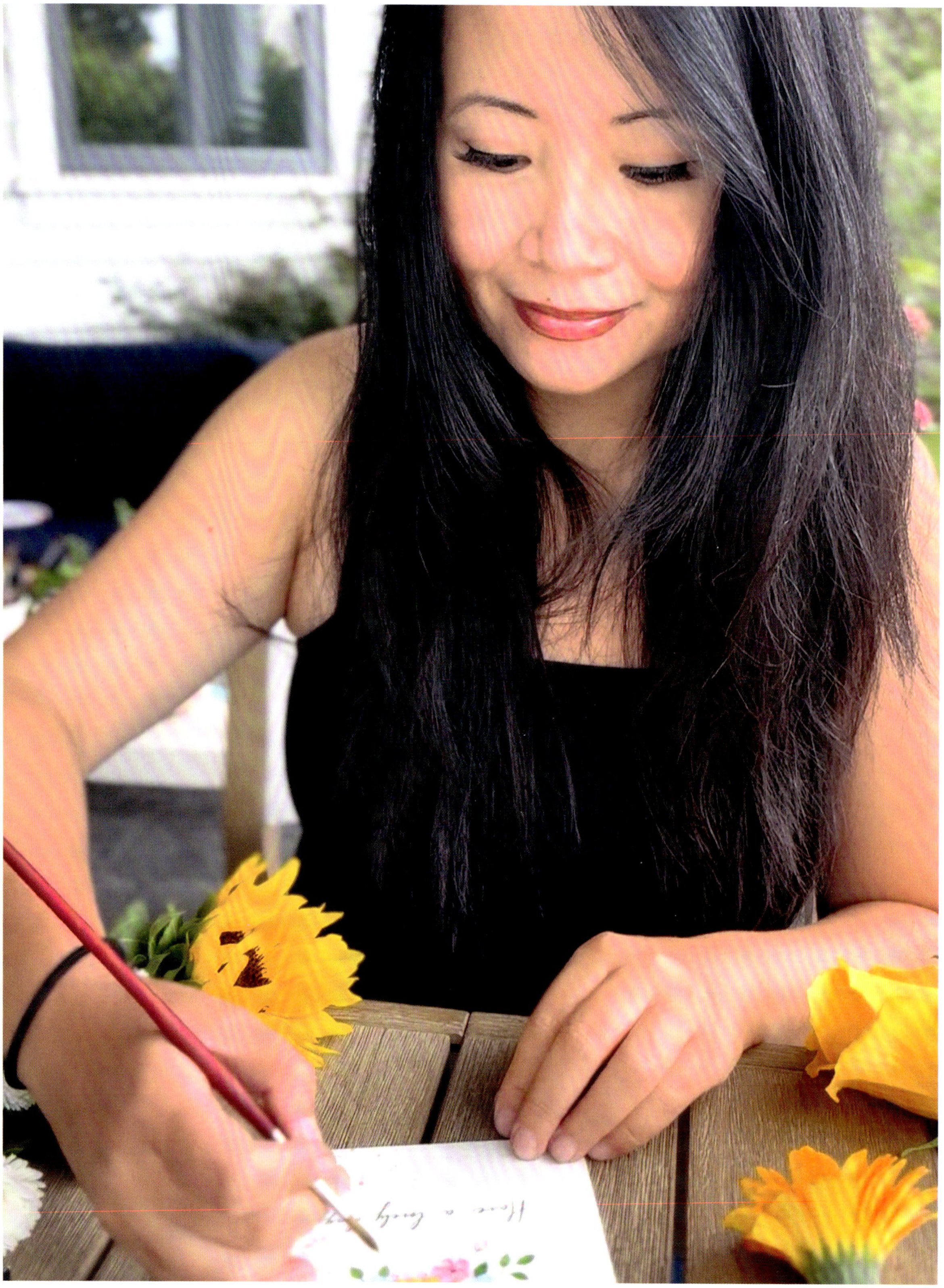